Radical Friendship

Radical Friendship

The Politics of Communal Discernment

Ryan Andrew Newson

Fortress Press
Minneapolis

RADICAL FRIENDSHIP

The Politics of Communal Discernment

Copyright © 2017 Fortress Press. All rights reserved. Except for brief quotations in critical articles or reviews, no part of this book may be reproduced in any manner without prior written permission from the publisher. Email copyright@fortresspress.com or write to Permissions, Fortress Press, PO Box 1209, Minneapolis, MN 55440-1209.

Cover image: Thinkstock; Surovtseva / Night rainy background

Cover design: Alisha Lofgren

Print ISBN: 978-1-5064-2031-8

eBook ISBN: 978-1-5064-2032-5

This book was produced using Pressbooks.com, and PDF rendering was done by PrinceXML.

Contents

	Acknowledgments	vii
	Introduction	xi
1.	Incompetence, Liberalism, and Democracy	1
2.	Outline of the Promise of a Practice	41
3.	Power, Discernment, and the Politics of Binding and Loosing	81
4.	Practical Matters	119
5.	Radical Friendship	161
	Bibliography	199
	Index	211

Acknowledgments

At first blush, one might think there is a certain irony in spending many hours by oneself in order to think and read and write about moral discernment as it takes place in communities of people: "Read this book about the communal nature of knowledge. I wrote it all by myself." And yet, I have found just the opposite to be the case. While it is certainly true that in order to write I spent a lot of time in quiet rooms alone, I was given that time because other people allowed it, enabled it, tolerated it, gave me the space to withdraw. Moreover, the ideas and insights contained in these pages—whatever they may be—were born of ongoing conversations with friends who nurtured my inchoate thoughts into actual, verbalized arguments. Perhaps the arguments do not work, but that they are *arguments* is due to their having gone through the fire of discerning conversations with friends. Finally, without a community to sustain me with joy and laughter, none of this work would have been worth pursuing. It is no exaggeration to say that without friends, there is no way that you would be reading these words now. As such, I dedicate this work to the friends who helped me through this process, in ways they both know and will never know.

Nancey Murphy guided this work in ways that go far beyond what is evident in the footnotes and bibliography; I am indebted to her not simply for what, but *how* I think—which is the greatest compliment and heaviest burden I can place on another. Tommy Givens's keen insight, book recommendations, and embarrassing generosity guided me in ways that are incalculable. I could put a footnote citing conversations with Tommy under nearly every sentence that follows, as there is no way that I would have seen many of the paths to be taken without him; nor still would I have had the courage to amble down them. My conversations with my late advisor Glen Stassen were also critical to the formation of this book; he was especially encouraging of the idea right from the beginning. Although I have little doubt that we would have had much to argue about in the pages that follow, I am also sure that Glen's influence stands behind my work in ways that I myself cannot fully see. It saddens me that we did not get a chance to argue about these concepts further. Erin Dufault-Hunter thought with me about several intellectual difficulties (or temptations) that arose as I formed these arguments—only some of which she knew were connected to my research. Finally, Stanley Hauerwas provided invaluable feedback that colors much of what follows, and I am grateful for his generosity and wisdom.

Certain teachers from my past stayed in touch during this time, helping me clarify my thoughts and providing a sympathetic ear as I struggled with institutional decisions that were far beyond my control. In particular, I will be forever grateful for the kindness and wisdom of Diane Lipsett (Salem College), Jeffrey Pugh (Elon University), and Kevin Jung (Wake Forest University).

I am also grateful to the friends I gained in the process of writing this book: Barbod and Molly Salimi, Samantha Curley, Jacob Blackstock, Ryan and Leslie Little, and Abigail Cook. I am humbled by the generosity shown to me and my family by First Baptist Glendale. Ongoing (and likely annoying) correspondence with Scott Looney, Matthew Spainhour, and Kyle Caudle was particularly helpful, as was the advice, reading, and editing provided by my colleagues, Amy Chilton Thompson, Brian Lee, Brian Robinson, Eric Schnitger, and Becky Shenton. Foremost among these friends, however, is Jake Cook, who read and discussed my ideas in a way that always made them better—sometimes while brewing beer; and Andrew Wright, whose

ACKNOWLEDGMENTS

kindness, willingness to talk, and keen intellect make me want to be a better theologian and a better man.

To my parents, I will always cherish the memory of our year at home. It is a happy thing when parents and children become friends, and I can only hope a similar transition happens for me and mine. To my children, I love you from the gut, and am humbled that I get to watch you grow up.

And finally, to Rebecca: all of this is possible because of you. You sustain me, and I cannot thank you enough for all that you do. Ours is a friendship that I do not deserve, and that I am not quite sure how I stumbled into, but am grateful that I did, by whatever grace.

Introduction

As the Donald Trump phenomenon took off in the beginning of the summer of 2015, one of the most interesting features of his campaign was the way political commentators at first dismissed his candidacy, then underestimated his chances, and then scrambled to account for his continued success. Some pointed to his willingness to say what you're not "supposed to say,"[1] others made connections between Trump supporters and those disposed toward authoritarianism,[2] and still others looked at socio-economic and racial correlations. Regardless, many agreed that Trump said something about our current cultural moment that needed to be addressed; he said something about our present and, perhaps ominously, our future.

Other commentators saw in Trump something of historical significance. David Brooks, for instance, saw Trump's success as the culmination of trends from the last thirty years that consistently deprecated the realm of "politics," with its attendant compromises and willingness to work with persons with whom one disagrees, and which thus paved the way for some form of dictatorship.[3] More striking in this vein was Andrew Sullivan's argument that Trump's rise was an "extinction-level event," the logical consequence of a political culture that valued too much difference and in which inequality was so rare

---

1. Rand Richards Cooper, "The Appeal of Trump," *dotCommonweal*, August 31, 2015, accessed June 1, 2016, https://www.commonwealmagazine.org/blog/appeal-trump.
2. Amanda Taub, "The rise of American authoritarianism," *Vox*, March 1, 2016, accessed May 27, 2016, http://www.vox.com/2016/3/1/11127424/trump-authoritarianism.
3. David Brooks, "The Governing Cancer of Our Time," *New York Times*, February 26, 2016.

as to be considered intolerable. Meditating on a passage from Plato's *Republic*, Sullivan argued that democracies end when they are "too democratic" precisely because such unchecked democratic sensibilities leave systems inherently unstable.[4] In referring to ours as "hyperdemocratic times" that ironically threaten democracy, Sullivan echoed the voice of the Trilateral Commission, which famously argued that the United States was weakened by the people's overactive participation; we were suffering from "an excess of democracy."[5] Thus for Sullivan Trump stood as a threat born of our recent past, and a death knell for the future of democracy.

The inclination to look to the past seems right to me; Trump could not have emerged *ex nihilo* or from within an otherwise healthy society. But I wonder if Trump reveals something different about that past than the dangers of a democratic society now becoming too democratic. Rather than a new threat built on the insidious spread of hyperdemocracy, what if Trump is the latest iteration of, and response to, conditions that have affected political and moral sensibilities for far longer than the last thirty years, unique simply in the force with which he made us look ourselves in the mirror and recognize that we may not be as democratic as we thought? Whatever the case may be, that Trump said what he said is much less troubling than the fact that he succeeded by saying it, and should generate reevaluations of the soil that could produce such strange fruit.

In my view, this soil is made up of a series of political, philosophical, and theological elements that mark a kind of dis-ease found both in those who loathe Trump and in those who support him. For those opposed to Trumpism, a sense of futility grew regarding protests to his presidency, precisely because nothing one said seemed to deter his followers. Even if one recognized the reasons for this—Trump's success was driven by factors bigger than Trump himself—it was no less discouraging. For supporters, a great many of whom are poor,

---

4. Andrew Sullivan, "America Has Never Been So Ripe for Tyranny," *New York*, May 2, 2016.
5. Michel J. Crozier, Samuel P. Huntington, Joji Watanuki, *The Crisis of Democracy: Report on the Governability of Democracies to the Trilateral Commission* (New York: New York University Press, 1975).

INTRODUCTION

white, and disaffected, Trump is compelling because they too felt powerless to address issues—real and imagined—that threatened their economic stability, family life, and security. Regardless of the fact that Trump only exacerbates these issues, it seems clear that the engine of his popularity rests in this disaffection.

Theologically speaking, these concerns are compounded by the fact that Trump enjoyed wide-scale support from Christians, not least (white) evangelicals, who saw in his candidacy an articulation of their convictions about society and its ills. To be sure, Christians have severely misdiagnosed threats throughout history—that is nothing new. But in such moments as well as today, what this represents even if only in retrospect is a failure of discernment—failure of the capacities of individual Christians and Christian communities to hear and articulate what to do, or who to be, in the face of moral threat. In the United States today, it is painfully apparent that Christians as a whole are lacking in these capacities; we embody the incompetence that stands behind Trumpism along with everyone else.

My goal in this book is to begin to address this incompetence at its roots (i.e., radically). As we seem to suffer from a diminishment in our modes of moral discernment, I seek to bolster this lack using resources from my own Christian tradition, and that may enable Christians and others alike to faithfully, competently "go on" in our current context without legitimating the way things have been. All Christians have a stake in this task, insofar as it connects to our calling to foster clear-eyed hope in the possibilities that emerge from the gospel unveiled in human history—from a God who does not give up on bringing a good creation to completion. Thus at bottom this is a work of theology for Christians who are seeking discernment through the incompetence that we too inherit. My aim is to describe our current political moment well, but in service to the larger goal of aiding Christians struggling to remain faithful within it without either acquiescing to the feeling of incompetence (bringing with it a faithless realism or despair), or else yearning for a time before such incompetence was prominent, perhaps flocking to the voice that most loudly promises to protect us from our woes. Instead, in the following pages I articulate a path to Christian moral competence without acquiescence or retreat. While it is written from and for my particular convictional community, if it is successful I believe much of it will be of interest to people of other traditions who share a similar desire to foster flourishing in a world that can seem bent against that end.

As such, this work sits at the intersection of ecclesiology, political theology, and radical democratic engagement, though its implications extend well past the boundaries normally assumed by these divisions. My thesis is that the practice of communal discernment constitutes a unique and under-appreciated path to moral competence in the current context, both within congregations and as disciples work with others in radical democratic movements, and which is well described using the metaphor of friendship.

1 Terms and Conditions

Unpacking this thesis is the task of the project as a whole, but a few words of explanation are in order about each term employed before moving forward. To begin, I must speak to my use of "political theology." This phrase originated with German philosopher and Nazi sympathizer Carl Schmitt, and while a thing's origin does not determine its subsequent meaning, it is at least relevant that Schmitt sought to resist a certain kind of circumscription imposed on theology by political liberalism, albeit from a profoundly autocratic perspective. As I use the phrase, political theology evokes theology's refusal to stay "where liberalism would prefer to put it. Theology is politically important, and those who engage in either theology or politics ignore this fact at a certain peril." It functions as a family term that deals with discourse about God that is relevant to "politics" in the broadest sense: "the self-governance of communities and individuals." Together, political theology involves "analysis and criticism of political arrangements (including cultural-psychological, social, and economic aspects) from the perspective of differing interpretations of God's ways with the world."[6] Two things are clear from this description: first, there is no neutral place from which to engage questions in this arena. The particular community through which one understands who God is and how God acts in the world inescapably colors how one will read, challenge, critique, and conceptualize the sorts of politics that lead to human flourishing, and arrangements that are detrimental to this goal. There is no "political theology" in general. Thus to take just one example, as a Christian I cannot approach questions about authority while bracketing my conviction that Jesus's peaceful, graceful, and direct way of leadership is the picture of what true authority looks like. Any answer to such questions assumes *some* theological conviction; the real question is whether one will be aware of these convictions or not.

Second, I use political theology a bit more loosely than some might prefer. I have in mind the delineation between "political theology" and "theological politics" articulated by Arne Rasmusson.[7] I recognize Rasmusson's reasons for making this distinction: "political theology" tends to operate with an understanding of the political that is limited to the imaginative realm of the nation-state, whereas "theological politics" expands this vision to include the organization of social relations embodied in and by the church, and which therefore goes beyond what folks typically mean by "politics." I simply do not think much hinges on strictly avoiding the phrase "political theology." The more pressing issue is whether or not one's use of the phrase reinforces the picture of the world that Rasmusson rightly works to resist. So while I employ these phrases by and large interchangeably, my use consistently reflects my desire to go beyond the limits of politics-as-statecraft, and to articulate a politics that is faithful to Christians' central convictions. In this process, I aim to show that this desire is consonant with many of the aims articulated and defended by political philosophers known as "radical democrats."

Now, it should be clear at this point that the problem I hope to address is one of "moral incompetence." This phrase is drawn from

---

6. William T. Cavanaugh and Peter Scott, "Introduction," in *The Blackwell Companion to Political Theology*, ed. Peter Scott and William T. Cavanaugh (Malden, MA: Blackwell, 2004), 1.

7. Arne Rasmusson, *The Church as Polis: From Political Theology to Theological Politics as Exemplified by Jürgen Moltmann and Stanley Hauerwas* (Notre Dame: University of Notre Dame Press, 1986).

theological ethicist Willis Jenkins, which he coins in order to describe climate change and the depth of the challenges it will create for humans in the coming centuries. For Jenkins, moral incompetence names an inability to conceive how one might address such a pervasive, overwhelming threat, or even say anything that is adequate to the challenge at hand. Incompetence is the result of realizing a moral tradition's categories, language, and narratives are ill-equipped to speak to threats that it has, to this point in its history, had no reason to address.[8] In chapter one, I argue that Jenkins's description of incompetence in reference to climate change can also be applied to understanding the sense of political, civic apathy that is widely recognized to be occurring in the contemporary United States. In particular, I connect this political incompetence with some of the more pernicious consequences that have resulted from the rise of political liberalism. By "liberal," I do not mean "progressive" or "Democratic" (nor the theological liberalism associated with Friedrich Schleiermacher), but rather the constellation of governmental, economic, philosophical, and theological forces that have come together to organize human life in particular ways. These moves have been driven in particular by a picture of the world in which no robust, explicitly theological conception of the common good is permitted in "political" matters, unless they are translated into a "public," neutral language. Instead, political liberalism promotes the free exchange of ideas among individuals and the free exchange of commerce between like-minded nation-states, without interference—a promotion that globalization continues with gusto. Thus, perhaps counterintuitively, Ronald Reagan and Margaret Thatcher are quintessential liberals in this sense of the term, given that the perfection of neoliberal political-economic policies came about in the 1980s, heavily promoted by the United States and Great Britain.[9]

---

8. Willis Jenkins, "Atmospheric Powers, Global Injustice, and Moral Incompetence: Challenges to Doing Social Ethics from Below," *Journal of the Society of Christian Ethics* 34, no. 1 (2014); and *The Future of Ethics: Sustainability, Social Justice, and Religious Creativity* (Washington, DC: Georgetown University Press, 2013).
9. Rebecca Todd Peters, *Solidarity Ethics: Transformation in a Globalized World* (Minneapolis: Fortress

INTRODUCTION

In connecting the sense of incompetence felt in the contemporary United States with political liberalism, I will rely heavily on the work of political philosophers that are known as "radical democrats." This phrase in particular requires preliminary explanation, given that it is not commonly used. Briefly, radical democracy refers to a movement among political philosophers and social activists that differentiates liberalism in the sense just specified from democracy (against their usual conflation, as in the phrase "liberal democracy"). These activists and philosophers argue that liberalism in actual practice is inimical to rule by a competent, active people (democracy). For philosopher Sheldon Wolin, conflation of the two leads to a distinctively modern form of politics in which state power is wed to neoliberal global corporations, and purposely undermines the sort of thriving, informed, civically engaged citizenry necessary to democracy properly so-called.[10] Against this, radical democracy refers to the kinds of participatory and local political movements that emerged during the civil rights era of the 1950s and 1960s, a politics generated "outside of, and often in opposition to, established political institutions.... It was, in large measure, a politics of *improvisation*, of bricolage."[11] Thus the qualifier "radical" serves a rhetorical purpose, differentiating "democracy" from liberalism. "If 'democracy' were not so persistently deployed as a rhetorical weapon to advance so many anti-democratic institutions and practices, we could simply say 'democrat.' 'Radical democrat' is a rhetorical effort to distance ourselves from the erosion of the term 'democrat' that results from this deployment."[12] This is what I mean by radical democratic engagement, then: engagement in society that is not beholden to—and attempts to subvert—the rules of the game as specified by political liberalism, without pretending one can get completely outside of liberalism as such.

Press, 2014), 4. These policies, it goes without saying, have been pursued by Democrats as well. On this, the two parties are united.

10. Sheldon S. Wolin, *Politics and Vision: Continuity and Innovation in Western Political Thought*, exp. ed. (Princeton: Princeton University Press, [1960] 2004), 559, 564–65.
11. Ibid., 522.
12. Stanley Hauerwas and Romand Coles, *Christianity, Democracy, and the Radical Ordinary* (Eugene, OR: Cascade, 2008), 3n4.

My goal is to enter into this struggle as a Christian, and specifically as a baptist. The term "baptist" is drawn from theologian James McClendon, and refers to a recurring type of Christian community that reads scripture as though the injunctions and narratives therein were addressed to them. Rather than positing a chasmic distance between the contemporary community and the world discussed by the various authors of the Bible, such congregations read with the conviction that the words "then" are relevant—directly if not simplistically—to "now"; that the problems we face today ("this") are not completely dissimilar to the problems faced by Jesus and his followers ("that"). This hermeneutical strategy is labeled "baptist" because of its employment by many of the sixteenth-century Christians often called "Anabaptist"; McClendon simply prefers to omit the prefix *ana-*, as these radical Christians did not believe they were being baptized "again," but rather were being baptized for the first time legitimately. However, McClendon recognizes that communities who have worked in this way are not limited to those in the Anabaptist stream, but recur throughout history and across confessional boundaries: Catholics and Lutherans have sometimes operated in this way, while Anabaptists and Baptists have sometimes neglected the wisdom of this approach to scripture and world. As such, baptists are marked by a considerable degree of variety, even while there are practical limits to what the term can be used to happily describe (it is not a cipher, to be filled by whatever one prefers).[13]

In my stated thesis, the central focus rests on the promise inherent to a practice that is regularly, if imperfectly, utilized by this loose group of Christians: the practice of communal discernment. I articulate what I mean and do not mean by this practice at length in the following pages, as is appropriate given the central role it plays in my argument. Briefly, by communal discernment, I mean the practice performed by Christians whereby one gathers with one's fellow disciples and attempts to figure out what God wants an individual or a congregation

---

13. James Wm. McClendon Jr., *Ethics: Systematic Theology, Volume 1*, rev. ed. (Nashville: Abingdon, [1986] 2002), ch. 1. Others use "believers' church" and "free church" to designate this phenomenon.

to do in a particular circumstance. "Discernment" refers to the struggle to suss out what is good, right, and true in a situation, which will adjust as the situations themselves evolve over time. As such, discernment is closely related to what Aristotle called *phronesis* or prudence (practical wisdom) with a crucial difference. As theologian Luke Bretherton writes, discernment "better emphasizes how faithful political judgments are *responses* to the prior and ongoing creative action of God in the midst of the world."[14] On the other hand, "communal" refers to the typically baptist conviction that this process is best done within a corporate, congregational setting marked by reading scripture together, praying together, arguing together. Through these practices and others besides, one begins to see the blind spots of which one would remain unaware if he or she tried to discern alone, as well as begins to gain an ear for the dynamic God whom one hopes to follow. The passage of scripture that paradigmatically describes communal discernment is Acts 15, in which early church leaders are divided over the question of what is required of the many non-Jews who are joining the budding Jesus movement. Not quite sure what to do in light of this unprecedented (messianic) moment, Christians gather together, listen to testimonies from relevant parties, including Peter's experience with Cornelius, and then issue a firm yet contextually open decision on what God requires (cf. Acts 15:23–29).

It is communal discernment thus understood that I claim is particularly helpful for articulating a faithful contribution to radical democratic engagement; put differently, the political theology it assumes is helpful for Christians as they go about engaging in grassroots political movements, as well as helpful to those movements as such. So while I intend to describe communal discernment accurately, my larger aim is to develop the promise I believe it carries for directly responding to the sort of incompetence I mentioned above. Of course, one cannot name such promises without also naming its dangers and liabilities: its potential to overemphasize "decisions," or

---

14. Luke Bretherton, *Christianity and Contemporary Politics: The Conditions and Possibilities of Faithful Witness* (Chichester, UK: Wiley-Blackwell, 2010), 30n75.

else reinforce communal boundaries such that the discerning congregation is insulated from the world; its tendency to get used only in matters of little consequence (carpet color) rather than the deeper issues a congregation may face ("Why are we here?" "Who is God for us, and for our neighborhood, today?"); its use as a tool for power-consolidation within the congregation itself; and on and on. I do my best to name these dangers as I go along; still, I remain convinced that communal discernment's potential for generating dynamic, competent, humble action in its adherents is real, and has yet to be fully appreciated.

Finally, I suggest that the fruit of communal discernment is helpfully described in terms of "friendship," particularly when viewed as a practice of political theology. By friendship, I do not mean a light-hearted relationship based around mutual pleasure and recreation; indeed, to refer to the "relationship" I have with people I interact with through Facebook and Twitter as "radical friendship" would make little sense. Rather, by friendship I mean something closer to the robust sort of relationship described by Aristotle—the deep, long-lasting relationships that bolster virtuous behavior in one another, and which can emerge from deliberative action together. For Aristotle, friendship was the glue that held well-functioning societies together—a view that is nearly incomprehensible to contemporary ears. On the widespread contemporary use of "friend," friendship and politics would have little to do with one another, except perhaps in terms of the former making the latter more tolerable. As will become clear, a robust sense of friendship is a helpful metaphor for the kind of social relationship that forms Christians for faithful engagement in radical democratic movements, and which Christians can look for in the world as people from a variety of convictional communities work together for a common purpose.

2 Brief Outline

Much of the work I am about to undertake has already been introduced through this brief explanation of the major terms to be utilized.

Nonetheless, it is important to provide a roadmap of the path that lies ahead, for those who wish to know where they are headed. In chapter one, I set out to describe the specific form of political incompetence that is endemic to life in the United States, following in large part the work of political philosopher Sheldon Wolin.[15] One of the ablest defenders of the need to differentiate liberalism from democracy, Wolin is especially helpful in tracing the contemporary trends and challenges in the United States back to arguments that occurred at the nation's beginnings among its founding leaders. Through Wolin, one gets a clear sense of how and why an active, engaged citizenry was resisted by key figures in the country's founding, and how this same resistance is manifest today. By beginning in this way, chapter one subverts the notion that ethicists should only respond to problems as they are posed, and instead takes up the task of constructing and interpreting the problem itself—a task that is at least as important as providing answers to such problems (because rightly describing a threat allows one to avoid the many false steps that come from not knowing the full extent of the problem one hopes to address). As Jenkins writes, "Ethics cannot be a disciplinary operation performed by specialists after some problem is posed; it must be a capacity of practical reasoning cultivated within interdisciplinary research struggling to interpret and frame emerging problems."[16] I conclude the chapter by assessing three representative theological responses to contemporary incompetence that I find inadequate, not so much in their recommended solutions as in their understanding of the problem, and begin to articulate the ways in which a response born of baptist theological resources might be worth considering—resources that are well fitted for fostering a politics "from below," to use Jenkins's phrase.

In chapter two, I provide a robust, contextualized description of communal discernment, which I argue has the potential to form the sort of competency that is needed to engage in truly democratic practices well. After situating the practice's reclamation by sixteenth-

---

15. Throughout the book, my focus is on the United States, although many of the diagnoses and prescriptions are relevant to any context where liberalism is present.
16. Jenkins, *Future of Ethics*, 9.

century Anabaptists in its historical, socio-political context, I describe how communal discernment carries promise for radical democratic engagement, specifically noting the way it prepares adherents to trust the dynamic, ongoing work of a God that moves ever before us, rather than hoping for an idolatrous (and chimerical) form of certainty.

Chapter three shifts to address an important question in political theology: how and when certain voices might be excluded from the sort of pluralistic, discerning, ongoing conversation advocated in the previous chapter. In radical democratic organizations and communities of discernment alike, decisions need to be made, the necessity of which raises the question as to who gets final say in such situations, and what sort of power ought to be operative in discerning churches engaged in such matters. I address this question through an investigation of binding and loosing (drawn from Matthew 18), or what is colloquially called "the ban," the controversial practice of "loosing" certain members from the discerning body that is intimately related to communal discernment as such. Through this investigation, binding and loosing reveals itself to be a vital piece of any realistic community's discernment processes, and understood well, has interesting lessons to teach democratically engaged citizens.

In chapter four, I shift to describe one way that communal discernment functions to empower baptists to engage in radical democratic work: as a practice that counters many of the deleterious ends to which the forces identified by Wolin and others seek to direct our behavior, and enables people to move discerningly among the various practices constituting both social life and individual identity. After outlining the importance of recognizing society's multifaceted, "practical" nature, I name three ways that communal discernment enables resistance to the kind of politics that dominates the contemporary landscape: it creates an ability and willingness to listen patiently to others; it trains its adherents to value structural change through local attention; and it fosters the importance of being confrontational in working for peace and justice. Each of these attributes are valued by proponents of radical democracy, in their own ways and using their own terminology.

A few years ago, my argument may have ended here, affirming communal discernment as constituting a unique politics of the church, and against the assumptions and limitations embedded within nation-state politics. While this remains important, I have become convinced that Christians who focus on practices (as I do) must be more explicit in their affirmation of *how* these kinds of practices relate to the good work going on outside the *ekklesia*. This is all the more important for me to specify, given that many seem to conceptualize the alternatives to be either insulation within church walls, or else participation in nation-state politics wholesale and on its own terms. Thus in chapter five I articulate the form of politics that communal discernment builds to and is consonant with, which I describe in terms of "radical friendship." My argument is not only that communal discernment itself helps produce relationships that foster this kind of politics; it is also that communal discernment enables Christians to see and welcome certain types of political deliberation that occur in radical democratic engagement as seeds of the Reign of God that ought to be tended, watered, and celebrated. Put differently, communal discernment gives one eyes to see certain instantiations of the Beloved Community as they occur in the world, and the ability to incorporate these surprising discoveries into the ongoing life of the church.

My hope is that as a whole this argument represents a compelling and coherent articulation of a practice through which the beginnings of a baptist political theology is specified—and which additionally is suited to equip Christians to boldly and receptively engage in democratic struggles for competency against the forces that undermine those very capacities. In this process, I also hope to defend and stretch baptist ecclesiology itself using resources gained from radical democratic philosophers. Through this gift exchange, perhaps a faithful witness will be provided to the crucified Lord whose peaceable life, sacrificial death, and vindicating resurrection remains the light and hope of a weary, beautiful, grace-soaked world.

1

Incompetence, Liberalism, and Democracy

Few would argue that political discourse in the contemporary United States is in a state of disarray. The average person is aware of challenges as important as they are numerous, and many of which seem insoluble, at least by any of our efforts. Thus many are left with a pervasive feeling of being overwhelmed by forces beyond our control, even as we listen to those in power say, "All is well" (cf. Jer 6:14). Meanwhile the "developed countries of the West spend most of their time bickering among themselves, and cynically use that bickering to distract their citizenry from the real problems of the present and foreseeable future, and all those citizens, like the narcotized masses of Aldous Huxley's *Brave New World*, sleepwalk through life on an endless diet of inanities and trivialities."[1] Left speechless in the face of daunting moral challenges, the only thing we seem able to do is heed George W. Bush's advice following the attacks on September 11, 2001—go shopping. Given this attitude, lobbying one's representative (who likely will make one feel "heard" before going about his or her business) and voting on occasion become the extent of political agency.

---

1. Charles Mathewes, *The Republic of Grace: Augustinian Thoughts for Dark Times* (Grand Rapids: Eerdmans, 2010), 14.

And as these avenues show themselves to be less and less effective, apathy creeps into the populace.

Simply put, my aim in this chapter is to map the contours of what I will call political incompetence, which many recognize requires urgent address. I begin by clarifying what I mean by incompetence, and how political philosopher Sheldon Wolin narrates the depths to which this incompetence has infected our political imaginations. Next, I move to describe how this precise type of incompetence arose, largely following the work of Wolin, though also utilizing such figures as Romand Coles and Alasdair MacIntyre. My goal is to utilize Wolin's argument that the theory of political liberalism and the practice of democracy need to be distinguished from one another, and thus to show that it is precisely the dominance of liberalism that has caused the sort of incompetence that worries so many. Crucially, Wolin makes this claim not in the name of some antiquated traditionalism but as a defender of "democracy" (carefully defined) who sees political liberalism as deficient in fostering open, pluriform engagement across convictional lines. In short, it is insufficiently radical. I conclude by examining representative Christian responses to this incompetence that serve to elucidate contours of the argument that may otherwise go unnoticed, and tempting paths that ultimately show themselves to be deficient in providing a way to go on in the milieu described by Wolin and company. I will gesture toward an emerging type of response that is more capable of inhabiting the world Wolin describes, and to ways the practice of discerning the dynamic will of God in community *may* be uniquely able to provide a democratically robust, free church path to political competence.

1 Moral Incompetence

It may seem odd to begin this task by exploring something called "moral incompetence" from an ethicist writing about climate change and sustainability. And yet it is precisely because Willis Jenkins wishes to speak to a set of issues that *so* overwhelm our moral sensibilities, and that have only recently emerged in human history, that he makes for such a helpful dialogue partner in political theology. For, as will become clear, humanity faces powerful, relatively recent political phenomena that similarly overwhelm our abilities to find a place from which to speak or think about them intelligently, as Christians or otherwise.

Jenkins's aim is to show that there is no "fixing" climate change, especially if that is meant to imply that mere tweaks to life as we currently experience it will be adequate to address our ecological crisis. Rather, given the irreversible damage to the earth's climate that has already been done, and that would continue to negatively impact life on this planet for centuries to come even if humans stopped pumping carbon into the air tomorrow, the proper perspective on climate change is that it is the new reality humans unavoidably inherit.[2] There is no magic fix to climate change, despite some who hope for just this through science and technology;[3] it now indelibly marks our existence. What is more, Jenkins notes that the very real threats associated with climate change do not admit of a single person or group to blame, either now or in the past. While it is certainly true that particular groups, countries, cities, corporations, and even individuals shoulder more of the responsibility for excessive carbon emission than others, the real rub is that climate change is an inheritance to which *everyone* has contributed.[4] In the inimitable words of Pogo, "We have met the enemy and he is us."

For the average twenty-first-century inhabitant, this recognition tends to breed a profound sense of being ethically overwhelmed. Adequate responses to climate change seem to elude us, "in part because atmospheric powers outstrip the capacities of our inherited traditions for interpreting them. Insofar as the problem requires moral competencies that we lack, climatic change reveals humanity as ill adapted to the conditions of life that its powers are making."[5] That is,

---

2. Willis Jenkins, *The Future of Ethics: Sustainability, Social Justice, and Religious Creativity* (Washington, DC: Georgetown University Press, 2013), 20.
3. Ibid., 32.
4. Ibid., 22.
5. Ibid., 17.

a problem of humanity's own creation now exceeds the capacity of our moral imaginations and undermines our ability to take responsibility for it. Jenkins's name for this condition is *moral incompetence*. The image goes beyond moral agents and traditions, including religious traditions, not knowing what to say in a particular instance, and more elicits an inability to even think or speak morally about a given subject—a sense of moral frozenness. This is not the same as the problem of moral failure, hypocrisy, or *akrasia*;[6] it is instead a problem of wanting to do good but not knowing how, feeling incapacitated from doing the good that one wants to do, or being unable to even identify quite what "the good" is. If social practices housed within traditions typically provide the means to this sort of competence, moral incompetence is the realization that entire moral traditions find their categories, language, and stories inadequate to address a particular problem due to its fast-growing and overwhelming nature. Again, Jenkins is careful to differentiate incompetence from impotence. In certain situations, a form of political impotence may hold in which moral agents have no felt power to enact immediate change in an unjust system, but may at least have a sense of how to proceed, even if tentatively, even if proceeding looks like martyrdom.[7] Incompetence is no insult, but describes why agents may feel overwhelmed by an issue, which if left unaddressed leads to apathy.

My claim is that moral incompetence also helps clarify the contemporary Western political context. Moral traditions have been similarly outstripped in their ability to respond to political and economic forces that have come to dominate and then undermine human agency. No less our own creation than climate change, liberalism (and what has spawned from it) now seems to have a life of its own, subtly delimiting what is considered "realistic" by political philosophers and theologians, and creating new threats to human life to which moral traditions struggle to respond. The kind of issues I have in mind are typically listed toward the beginning of most books

---

6. Willis Jenkins, "Atmospheric Powers, Global Injustice, and Moral Incompetence: Challenges to Doing Social Ethics from Below," *Journal of the Society of Christian Ethics* 34, no. 1 (2014): 68.
7. Ibid., 70.

on political theology. For instance, it has become a near prerequisite for political theologians to note that the variety of intermediate associations that for so long sustained life in the United States are in a process of erosion, weakened by a number of complex, interlocking factors. *Habits of the Heart* is perhaps the best-known of these analyses, presenting as it does a clarion call to take heed and resist the sort of civic disintegration that already in 1985 required urgent address, especially of and among religious communities.[8] This argument has been repeated over the intervening decades, including by Robert Putnam, Jeffrey Stout, and Cornel West, among others.[9] In fact, Stout's work provides a salient analysis of this widely recognized context for political theology, seeing as he does real possibilities for on-the-ground democratic action as it has been practiced (as opposed to theorized about), but nonetheless recognizes that his preferred sort of civic involvement is under threat, such that the plight of the poor is ignored, real social engagement neglected as people retreat into lifestyle enclaves, and militarism and nationalism abound.[10] And this is just one example. An array of moral theologians have in different terms noticed the same phenomenon, to the point that William Cavanaugh can observe, "Although potential solutions to the problem are hotly contested, the empirical fact of the decline of intermediate associations is not. The Council on Civil Society, for example, which includes such diverse figures as Francis Fukuyama and Cornel West, William Galston and Mary Ann Glendon, is able to treat the disintegration of 'civil society' as a given."[11] The common concern amidst obviously diverse responses is that this attenuation leaves average citizens ill-equipped to lead lives of flourishing, subject to the whims of various forces; in Jenkins's terms, incompetence abounds.

---

8. Robert N. Bellah et al., *Habits of the Heart: Individualism and Commitment in American Life* (Berkeley: University of California Press, [1985] 2007).
9. Robert D. Putnam, *Bowling Alone: The Collapse and Revival of American Community* (New York: Simon & Schuster, 2000); Jeffrey Stout, *Democracy and Tradition* (Princeton: Princeton University Press, 2004); Cornel West, *Democracy Matters: Winning the Fight Against Imperialism* (New York: Penguin, 2004), ch. 1.
10. Stout, *Democracy and Tradition*, 24.
11. William T. Cavanaugh, *Migrations of the Holy: God, State, and the Political Meaning of the Church* (Grand Rapids: Eerdmans, 2011), 29.

For political philosopher Sheldon Wolin, this emergence of political incompetence is not accidental, but is endemic to our late-modern political context dominated by diffuse, neocapitalist corporations and huge "megastates," which largely serve the former, to the point that Wolin provocatively argues that the Western political world is marked not merely by incompetence, but "inverted totalitarianism." By inverted totalitarianism, Wolin means the unique form of social control enabled and exercised by the family of governing powers that find unique expression in the United States. If traditional versions of totalitarianism seek to consolidate power by *suppressing* liberal political practices, which "had sunk only shallow cultural roots," inverted totalitarianism *draws from* and *saps* the energies that were traditionally squashed; it is "Nazism turned upside-down."[12] If traditional totalitarianism seeks a constantly mobilized, controllable populace, inverted totalitarianism sees that it is far easier to have a *"politically* demobilized society that hardly votes at all."[13] Wolin is obviously speaking in types here, and is not suggesting that the United States is like traditional forms of totalitarianism, despite protests to the contrary.[14] While perhaps overdrawn, Wolin's point is that the forces that have caused the shift in the demos from citizens to occasional voters carry with them certain tendencies, logics, and aspirations that move *toward* totalizing power.[15] It is not to suggest that this is the same as traditional totalitarianism: indeed, inverted totalitarianism marks a much more diffuse phenomenon enabled by the wedding of globalizing capital, state power, and corporate power, and is all the more pernicious for its limited gains and hiddenness. As

---

12. Sheldon S. Wolin, *Politics and Vision: Continuity and Innovation in Western Political Thought*, exp. ed. (Princeton: Princeton University Press, [1960] 2004), 591; cf. his *Democracy Incorporated: Managed Democracy and the Specter of Inverted Totalitarianism* (Princeton: Princeton University Press, 2008), esp. 51–60.
13. Wolin, *Politics and Vision*, 592.
14. Eric Gregory, for instance, quotes Hans Joas who says that "whoever calls Western democracies a more subtle form of totalitarianism, does not know what totalitarianism is." Cf. *Politics and the Order of Love: An Augustinian Ethic of Democratic Citizenship* (Chicago: University of Chicago Press, 2008), 128n96. Luke Bretherton thinks it's "too negative" and "precludes any possibility of constructive politics"; cf. *Christianity and Contemporary Politics: The Conditions and Possibilities of Faithful Witness* (Chichester, UK: Wiley-Blackwell, 2010), 118n118. Wolin is aware of the visceral reaction this phrase will cause; Wolin, *Democracy Incorporated*, 42–43.
15. Wolin, *Politics and Vision*, xvi.

such, this is the inherited logic in which we all gambol, and leads by design to a frozen and manipulable "citizenry" unable to intelligibly communicate, let alone cooperate, with one another across differences.

Understanding how the United States got to this point is both complicated and necessary if we want to accurately assess "what's going on," let alone attempt any sort of response that avoids unwittingly reinscribing the very problems that got us here in the first place. To this end, I will provide an assessment of how this incompetence emerged below, following and unpacking Wolin's analysis. The point here is to acknowledge where my investigation begins: with the felt recognition of big, slippery, structural issues that undermine our capacity even to imagine life without them, let alone think about them with clarity. And as Wolin will argue, this challenge is compounded by the fact that these elements are entrenched in US history.[16] The question will be whether a response can be found that disarms and unmasks the powers causing political incompetence (cf. Col 2:13–15), thus enabling ways of inhabiting the world that are both "realistic" and that refuse to grant that "the way things are" is the same as "the way things should be." After all, some ways of imagining the world, particularly those that breed injustice, domination, and impoverishment, ought to go away; "Some aspects of our world *should* collapse."[17]

2 The Political Landscape: Paths to Incompetence

To discern how best to proceed in this milieu, one must provide an account of how our precise form of incompetence arose. In my view, Wolin provides one of the more nuanced descriptions of this history available. Wolin not only maps the history of political philosophy in the West, but uses this map to better understand the contemporary American context and to rule out certain antidotes to incompetence as not getting to the root of the issue—in some cases showing themselves

---

16. Ibid., 551–56.
17. Jenkins, *Future of Ethics*, 19.

to be continued manifestations of what got us here in the first place. In the original sense of the word, they are insufficiently radical. Thus it is to Wolin's description that I now turn.

2.1 Mapping the Origins of Liberalism

Wolin's central thesis is that political liberalism and democracy are antithetical to one another, despite commonly being treated as interchangeable. For Wolin, it is precisely the gradual victory of liberalism over democracy that has led to the form of incompetence we now "enjoy." It took Wolin time to begin this "journey from liberalism to democracy."[18] Driven in part by his philosophical labors, but also, as Romand Coles reminds us, by his involvement in the activist struggles of the 1960s,[19] Wolin became convinced that the primary locus of and impetus for the "political" was not the state, as he had previously thought, but the grounded, "fugitive" forces of democratic change that governmental powers had clearly worked against. At this stage, my aim is to outline Wolin's mature description of how liberalism emerged as the predominant political mode in the United States, and the subtle implications this shift has for people struggling for moral competence in such a setting.

In Wolin's account of liberalism, the shift leading to the kind of malaise that now marks the contemporary United States is the gradual dominance of economics as the paradigm by which we conceptualize politics. Wolin is clear that our understanding of "the political" changes over time, and notes that increasingly, "the political" is spoken of in exclusively economic (or else sociological) terms. Wolin illustrates this shift by imagining reactions to Thomas Hobbes, noting that the average contemporary reader is apt to too-easily dismiss his work for paying insufficient attention to how political and socio-economic factors interrelate. Crucially, Wolin's point is not to deny

---

18. Wolin, *Politics and Vision*, xv.
19. Romand Coles, "Democracy and the Radical Ordinary: Wolin and the Epical Emergence of Democratic Theory," in Stanley Hauerwas and Romand Coles, *Christianity, Democracy, and the Radical Ordinary: Conversations between a Radical Democrat and a Christian* (Eugene, OR: Cascade, 2008), 113–73.

the importance of economics or sociology, but to show that such a criticism is now inherently plausible and to ask why such criticisms seem fair—even "obvious." His answer is that we have been trained to reduce everything, including matters political, to economic causes (*perhaps* colored by cultural influences), based on the assumption that socio-economic factors lie behind all other phenomena, driving the rest.[20] This assumption finds its way into the subtleties of our speech: as Luke Bretherton shows, using language like "social capital" to describe the "glue" that holds civil society together may seem innocent, but it actually betrays the degree to which economic metaphors now color our political imaginations.[21] While it may feel purely descriptive, it in fact rests upon "an evaluation which remains concealed because its historical origins are not well understood."[22]

The problem for Wolin is that this shift erodes the ability to even *speak* politically, let alone foster anything like goods in common that lead to mutual flourishing. Far from an academic observation, Wolin suspects a deep connection exists between the predominance of the purportedly value-neutral social sciences and "the groping failure of Western societies to sustain a belief in the importance of political activity except by appealing to a confused mixture of diluted religious ideas spiced with a dash of market-place virtues."[23] And indeed, Wolin notes that few would argue that "Western societies exhibit little in the way of a widespread political consciousness among its members and fewer still would doubt that political things are mostly held in disrepute by the members of these societies."[24] This certainly holds true for the contemporary United States. As Charles Mathewes writes, "The problem is not simply apathy, but also positive repugnance: . . . Americans *hate* politics."[25]

For Wolin, liberalism names the theoretical and practical supports designed to aid this economic turn, and thus is unavoidably colored

---

20. Wolin, *Politics and Vision*, 257–58.
21. Bretherton, *Christianity*, 39–40; cf. Putnam, *Bowling Alone*, 18–26.
22. Wolin, *Politics and Vision*, 258.
23. Ibid., 259.
24. Ibid., 260.
25. Charles T. Mathewes, *A Theology of Public Life* (Cambridge: Cambridge University Press, 2007), 147.

by what Coles calls the logic of "currency."²⁶ This turn happened gradually, growing from a genuine belief that economic behavior was free from all "traditional" imposition, and thus provided a path to the uncoerced ordering of human relationships, "relating them in time and space and integrating them into a rhythmic pattern without relying upon compulsion."²⁷ "Politics," on this conception, was restricted to the coercion needed to create the space in which these "uncoerced" social-economic interactions could occur. Wolin patiently traces how this liberal conception emerged from Locke's writings, classical economists, French liberals, and English Utilitarians. Contrary to popular misconceptions, liberalism was profoundly aware of human irrationality and the limits of reason, and is thus a philosophy "born in fear, nourished in disenchantment, and prone to believe that the human condition was and was likely to remain one of pain and anxiety."²⁸

For Wolin, one cannot understand why liberalism took this form without understanding three connections it has with Enlightenment patterns of thought. First, Wolin points out that liberalism's success paralleled the ascendancy of sociology as the "queen of the sciences" (as Auguste Comte proclaimed), and social scientists as the self-appointed "new intellectual elite." Warrants for such claims were mostly pragmatic: as opposed to political philosophers and certainly theologians, social scientists were exclusively fitted to help determine public policy because they traded in social *facts*; and while everyone may err, they at least committed better mistakes.²⁹ Thus liberalism's emergence was initially built on a picture of the world that

---

26. Romand Coles, *Beyond Gated Politics: Reflections for the Possibility of Democracy* (Minneapolis: University of Minnesota Press, 2005), 43–46. As Coles writes, this logic gives rise to the belief that the only path for political action is the "fungibility" of moral concepts, such that the latter must be translated into a "common currency" before being of public value.
27. Wolin, *Politics and Vision*, 261.
28. Ibid., 263. H. Richard Niebuhr similarly connects liberal democracy with a lack of optimism about human nature; cf. Timothy A. Beach-Verhey, *Robust Liberalism: H. Richard Niebuhr and the Ethics of American Public Life* (Waco, TX: Baylor University Press, 2011), 162. Cf. Coles, *Beyond Gated Politics*, ch. 1, esp. 7–11.
29. Wolin, *Politics and Vision*, 262.

distinguished "value" from isolatable facts which social science, or some other discipline, could observe and manipulate.[30]

The fact-value distinction is largely taken for granted by contemporary citizens of liberal orders. However, in the seventeenth and eighteenth centuries Enlightenment thinkers had to argue for the notion that a gap existed between a thing's appearance and its reality—a gap that empiricists traversed by way of pure experience ("sense-data"), and natural scientists through careful adherence to their methodology.[31] Champions of this distinction included Descartes, who was searching for a way to resolve the "value-laden" religious conflicts of his day, and David Hume, who decimated those who simplistically moved from "is" to "ought" without warrant.[32] Indeed, it was this very turn to "the facts" stripped of unnecessary additions that inspired the self-given "Enlightened" moniker. In place of the Aristotelian view that an action is explicable in terms of the ends one aims for and that humans ought to aim for what is good for humans as such (thus no strong distinction between fact and value), Enlightenment thinkers viewed human behavior as manifestations of underlying and sufficient conditions with no necessary place for an agent's intentions or beliefs. "Fact" on this new understanding excluded a priori what humans considered valuable, and as a result human behavior was considered predictable and manipulable.[33]

The problem, as MacIntyre shows, is that the notion of a fact as a value-free "collectible" was more eighteenth-century prophecy than discovery—but despite never finding "facts" of this sort, the prophecy itself had very real, pernicious consequences. For MacIntyre, the fact-value distinction never really fit the sciences, particularly the social sciences, whose genuine strength is their willingness to countenance

---

30. Of course, not all liberals accept the fact-value distinction (Richard Rorty comes to mind); I am highlighting liberalism's historical ties with the fact-value distinction, and suggesting ways liberalism is still colored by this origin; Coles, *Beyond Gated Politics*, 44–45.
31. Alasdair MacIntyre, *After Virtue: A Study in Moral Theory*, 2nd ed. (Notre Dame: University of Notre Dame Press, [1981] 1984), 80.
32. Alasdair MacIntyre, *A Short History of Ethics*, 2nd ed. (Notre Dame: University of Notre Dame Press, [1966] 1998), 171–72. MacIntyre shows that Hume's arguments do not entail that one may *never* move from "is" to "ought," but that the move needs to be made with care; ibid., 173–74.
33. MacIntyre, *After Virtue*, 82–84.

the systematic unpredictability of the human condition, providing guidelines that cannot be reduced to perfectly predictive, law-like maxims.[34] Unfortunately, many social scientists were quite willing to present their work in such "universal" terms, as this allowed their services to be seen as useful to corporate and governmental agencies seeking control over such facts[35]—that is, the combined forces of liberal organization, which I will explore shortly. Liberalism, on this read, emerged as a political mode seeking to organize, streamline, and manipulate these "facts."

The second way Wolin sees liberalism connected to Enlightenment thought-patterns is in the distrust or outright rejection of past thought, paradigmatically represented by Francis Bacon. While political theorists always tended to see their own time as superior to those prior, this reached new heights in the sixteenth century, as they contrasted their own "renaissance" in human individuality with the "Dark Ages" allegedly left behind, marked by unquestionable authority and unsettleable debates.[36] For a better society to emerge, Bacon "dismissed the utility of retaining some usable past, arguing that the rejection of past philosophies and scientific methods was a necessary preliminary in laying an entirely new 'foundation' for society. . . . Bacon introduced a different standard by which to condemn ancient philosophy in general and Aristotle's in particular, not as wrong but as impotent."[37] By this rejection Bacon hoped to endow humanity with new discoveries and powers which *could not come* without rejecting what had come before. And while Stout and Stephen Toulmin helpfully remind us that this outright rejection of tradition was not the only

---

34. Ibid., 90–92, 96–97, 105–6. A different critique of this distinction is to note that the only possible candidates for "pure" facts—one's sense of the color "green," or two plus two equaling four—have a limited range of relevance. Even *if* one granted these as self-interpreting, what robust claim follows? Cf. Nancey Murphy, *Anglo-American Postmodernity: Philosophical Perspectives on Science, Religion, and Ethics* (Boulder, CO: Westview, 1997), 26.
35. Ibid., 88–89, 85. See also "Social Science Methodology as the Ideology of Bureaucratic Authority," in *The MacIntyre Reader*, ed. Kelvin Knight (Notre Dame: University of Notre Dame Press, 1998), 53–68.
36. Wolin, *Politics and Vision*, 395–96; cf. Stephen Toulmin, *Cosmopolis: The Hidden Agenda of Modernity* (Chicago: University of Chicago Press, 1990).
37. Wolin, *Politics and Vision*, 396.

narrative underway during modernity, it certainly was the dominant one.

In any case, Wolin shows that most hedged on this rejection, happily praising pre-Christian sources. This is understandable, given that the Enlightenment struggle was to overcome mistakes inherited from Ptolemaic astronomy and Christian theology in particular. And as philosophers like Hobbes saw the advancements in astronomy that resulted from rejecting these modes of thought, he too sought to make similar strides in the realm of politics by purging the discipline of any hint of Christian cosmology.[38] Basically, Hobbes wanted to create an analogous "science of politics" by making similar moves, combining *total* rejection of Aristotle and Christian theology with an embrace of the fact-value distinction.

Finally, an important warrant for liberalism's rejection of the immediate past was the perception that irrational and value-laden religious beliefs had caused the brutal Thirty Years' War. "Public" religion clearly fostered superstition and violence; those past mistakes could be eliminated by privatizing religion's influence, which (so the story goes) was a huge accomplishment of liberalism. This narrative is ubiquitous, and is assumed by philosophers from Rorty to Rawls. For instance, Rawls's reply to those who challenge his liberal conception of justice is, in essence, "Do you have an alternative that will prevent the religious wars of the seventeenth century?" The implication is that his is the only or the best means to avoid repeating this catastrophe.[39] The only problem with this narrative, as William Cavanaugh shows, is that it is not true. The so-called "wars of religion" did not result from "religious beliefs" provoking innocent nation-states into unsought wars, but were themselves the birth pangs of the nation-state, which itself was in the process of becoming sacralized.[40] In any case, the story

---

38. Ibid., 219–20.
39. John Rawls, *Collected Papers*, ed. Samuel Freeman (Cambridge, MA: Harvard University Press, 1999), 620. Cf. John Rawls, *Political Liberalism* (New York: Columbia University Press, [1993] 1996), xxi–xxvii. As Coles observes, Rawls less argues for and more *conjures* this narrative, deploying "the phantom of an easy slide toward a tragic abyss in order to reassure the choir and deflect the critics"; Coles, *Beyond Gated Politics*, 8–9.
40. Cf. William T. Cavanaugh, *Theopolitical Imagination* (London: T&T Clark, 2002), ch. 1; William T. Cavanaugh, *The Myth of Religious Violence* (New York: Oxford University Press, 2009), 130–41,

liberalism told itself was the emergence of a value-neutral politics that could rescue humanity from a slide into chaos, and which therefore had the inalienable right to govern. Regardless of its accuracy, this story had far-reaching implications, for as the Thomas theorem states, "What is perceived as real is real in its consequences."

2.2 The Politics of Tending and Intending

In the United States, this liberal story was prominent from the beginning, and featured in a very important disagreement that took place over the political vision the emerging nation should follow. This disagreement was woven into the fabric of the republic, and understanding its contours helps to clarify the threat Wolin thinks liberalism poses to political competence, as well as introduce his preferred democratic alternative.

As politicians, lawyers, and generals gathered to discuss the form of government the newly independent United States should take, Wolin notes that two contrasting visions were present. On the one hand, the liberal desire for a government run by a science of politics was represented by Alexander Hamilton—the father of federalism—who fought to craft a system of centralized power. In Hamilton's words, "Government is only another word for POLITICAL POWER AND SUPREMACY."[41] Wolin calls attention to Hamilton's preoccupation with efficiency and bureaucratic management, which was already "partially hidden in the language of constitutionalism" and could also be called "the discourse of organizationism."[42] Wolin names this persistent mode of thinking about and practicing politics the *politics of intending*, which he sees as inherent to liberalism. Wolin calls this politics "intending" because of the sense of intentionality associated with its preferred mode of action, as well as its inherent propensity for

---

151–60, 183–94. Of course, Christian convictions were deeply implicated in these wars; the point is that the role they played was not instigators of violence between otherwise innocent secular rulers, as the standard myth suggests. Cavanaugh clarifies this in "A Response to Ephraim Radner's *A Brutal Unity*," *Syndicate* 1, no. 1 (May/June 2014): 2–10.

41. Quoted in Sheldon S. Wolin, *The Presence of the Past: Essays on the State and the Constitution* (Baltimore: Johns Hopkins University Press, 1989), 84.

42. Ibid., 92.

spreading itself—the root definition of "intending" carries a sense of "to stretch forth." In Wolin's words, the politics of intending implies

> a straining toward the future, an effort that requires power, and hence the agent intensifies, focuses, his or her powers. There is an expansionist ideology implicit in the idea of intending that is evident in a letter of 1803 by Gouverneur Morris, one of the important members of the Philadelphia Convention: "I knew as well then as I do now that all North America must at length be annexed by us. Happy, indeed, if the lust of dominion stops there."[43]

The politics of intending is best understood in contrast to its opposite—the *politics of tending*; rather than a "constitution of government," its first concern is in fostering a "political culture" within the messiness of the civic realm.[44] On this view, political life *is* the local give-and-take that takes place at the "associational" level; citizens' and governments' task is to care for this activity. "Tending" thus evokes the image of caring for a garden or a loved one, and is marked by a thick attention to the detailed history of the people and places where one participates; it does not seek to *use* local skills for some greater end, but requires a "feeling of concern for objects whose nature requires that they be treated as historical and biographical beings. . . . [P]roper tendance requires attentiveness to differences," and implies "respect that is discriminating but not discriminatory."[45] In George Mason's words in defense of the House of Representatives, "It ought to know & sympathise with every part of the community; and ought therefore to be taken not only from the different parts of the republic, but also from different districts of the larger members of it, which had . . . different interests and views arising from difference of produce, habits, etc."[46] Wolin points to Alexis de Tocqueville's *Democracy in America* as a wonderful exposition of a politics of tending, especially given Tocqueville's focus on the local practices in the United

---

43. Ibid., 90.
44. Ibid., 84.
45. Ibid., 89.
46. Quoted in ibid., 88.

States that engender "habits of competence or skill that are routinely required if things are to be taken care of."[47] Indeed, Tocqueville thought that the United States' project was succeeding precisely because of the *mores* (or "habits of the heart") that were fostered by active political life in local communities. It was this "political culture," necessarily fostered at the local (now-endangered) "associational" level in church meetings and town halls, that made America "work"—not its drive to centralization.[48]

Wolin sees the 1787 ratification of the United States Constitution at the Philadelphia Convention as the turning point for these two visions. Both were represented, and while each compromised in order to mutually support the new system, in the course of the arguments their contrasts were put on stark display. "Intenders" emphasized centralized power and *future* effectiveness,[49] while "tenders" fought for a pluralistic localism. "Antifederalists" appealed to the need to instill civic skills in an informed citizenry, while "federalists" showed a disdain for difference as *weak*, since it signified "exception, anomaly, local peculiarities, and a thousand other departures from the uniformity that a certain kind of power prefers."[50] And most fundamentally, advocates of the politics of intending expressed a desire to allow the citizenry "only a limited influence while extracting from them the raw materials of power in the form of taxes, military skills, enthusiasm, and opinion," as it states in *The Federalist Papers*; for advocates of the politics of tending, this was but a thinly veiled disguise for a new aristocratic government.[51]

In Philadelphia, with the ratification of the Constitution the politics of intending emerged victorious over the politics of tending. And even as it took another half-century for the victory to take hold, "the tending conception was so deeply wounded by the encounter that its viability remained in doubt for most of the two centuries that

---

47. Ibid., 89. Cf. Alexis de Tocqueville, *Democracy in America*, ed. Harvey C. Mansfield and Delba Winthrop (Chicago: University of Chicago Press, 2000).
48. Of course, Tocqueville doubted this was sustainable; cf. Wolin, *Politics and Vision*, 596.
49. Wolin, *Presence of the Past*, 90.
50. Ibid., 92–93.
51. Ibid., 85, 88.

followed."[52] The intenders' strategy at Philadelphia was revolutionary, proposing a constitution "without a political culture distinctive to it," and because of this required the superimposition of its form of politics

> on top of political life forms that at the time did not represent local politics because there was virtually no national politics to which they could be compared. Ratification of the new constitution necessarily signified the subjugation of other forms of politics.[53]

This victory had several markers, none more significant than Hamilton's vision of a "science of politics" (following in the path of Hobbes) that could justify and empower a new state "with magnitudes of power previously thought to be dangerous."[54] Although James Madison's concerns with centralized power were accommodated by the concept of the balance of powers, this concept proved insufficient to resist Hamilton's bent toward centralization, as it paradoxically moved the rationale for state power to an "extra-constitutional plane" where state rationality—and hence state power—could operate relatively independently. That is, the balance of powers turned out to be easily incorporable into a politics of intending, *especially* as it too was taken with reductionist rationality and a science of politics based on "impersonal laws" and "objective knowledge." The only difference was that while Hamilton used this "science" for the advancement of power, Madison used it for restraint or negation.[55] Hamilton and Madison fed off one another, representing the *two key moments* in the victory of liberalism in *The Federalist Papers*: Hamilton deliberately criticizing Montesquieu's claim that a large-scale republic (like the one Hamilton envisioned) was a "contradiction in terms," and Madison arguing that "democracy is a practical impossibility as well as undesirable and that an 'extensive Republic' is to be preferred."[56] Do not let that slip past: democracy was described as impossible and undesirable.

52. Ibid., 82.
53. Ibid., 87.
54. Ibid., 114.
55. Ibid., 115–18.
56. Ibid., 94.

Nonetheless, the politics of tending did not disappear, and continued to exist as a rival, if unequal, tradition in the United States. In this, both Stout and Toulmin are right to point out that liberalism marked by Enlightenment assumptions was not the only stream of thought that endured through the nineteenth century, Stout pointing to poets like Emerson and Whitman, Toulmin to the Romantics and adherents of the Renaissance.[57] But they are also misleading given that, while the narrative of modernity was not monolithic, one storyline definitely became predominant—and it was undoubtedly "of Hamilton." Indeed, the actual trajectories of American liberalism, including its reinvention as neoliberalism, "were far different from the prescriptions of Rawlsian justice."[58] It did not follow the path of social welfare, but ballooned such that it remained "state-centered, but its state was now imperial, its reflexes conditioned by anti-communism and Cold War exigencies, its political outlook accommodative to elitism and its politics to technocratic conceptions of policy and expertise"[59]—the total victory of the politics of intending. Thus Wolin narrates how the stage was set for a particular kind of bureaucratic power to grow in the United States, and led to the average inhabitant being viewed more as consumer than citizen, politically "active" only by occasionally voting—quite occasionally, as it turns out. Of course, as intending grows more and more dominant, its final victory becomes our forgetting that a debate over the form of US politics ever took place, even as theorists use a variety of terms to try to resist the effects of intending's victory.[60]

2.3 Modern Power, Postmodern Power, and the Eclipse of the State

Even with all this stated, the real value of Wolin's analysis lies in his

---

57. Stout, *Democracy and Tradition*; Toulmin, *Cosmopolis*, ch. 5.
58. Wolin, *Politics and Vision*, 551. For a critique of Rawls's *Political Liberalism*, see Troy Dostert, *Beyond Political Liberalism: Toward a Post-Secular Ethics of Public Life* (Notre Dame: University of Notre Dame Press, 2006).
59. Wolin, *Politics and Vision*, 551.
60. Cf. Wolin, *Presence of the Past*, 82–83, 87.

INCOMPETENCE, LIBERALISM, AND DEMOCRACY

showing the extent to which the consequences of this story as they have played out in the United States have been devastating to political competence. If someone is tempted to think that liberalism has been neutral or even beneficial to civic engagement, Wolin provides a rude awakening from such dogmatic slumbers, showing that the logic articulated at liberalism's theoretical founding and woven into American intending politics saps democratic energies.

Wolin shows that liberalism was infatuated with what he calls "modern power," which carried negative consequences for competent political, democratic engagement. The aforementioned economic turn, especially when combined with the notion of the fact-value distinction as both true and relevant to human behavior, created an imaginative horizon in which preventing political conflict seemed possible. This is because as soon as one conceives of the existence of value-free "facts" that are in principle manipulable, and designates a class of experts able to read such facts as a psychic would tea leaves, the temptation is to find a way to efficiently organize political life such that it would run more smoothly. On Wolin's reading, the nation-state emerged as the combination of forces cooperating to attempt just this, utilizing technology, administration, and organizational prowess to keep "the economic sphere" uninterrupted.[61] Keeping that space free from impediment or unnecessary civil conflict *is* the task of political liberalism.

Of course, as Wolin observes, the prospect of this task is daunting, and naturally leads to a preoccupation with "bigness"—big ideas, big power, big government[62]—as the only hope of achieving this degree of organizational efficiency. Thus did a new class of people emerge who were allegedly able to achieve such efficiency through their command of the facts: social scientists, pollsters, and their kin. For Wolin, this bureaucratic class formed a "new aristocracy" without whom the "scientific, economic, and political revolutions" of the Enlightenment and post-Enlightenment era could not have occurred.[63] MacIntyre

---

61. Wolin, *Politics and Vision*, 261.
62. Ibid., 399.
63. Ibid., 401.

agrees, to such an extent that he names the "bureaucratic manager" as a "central character of the modern social drama" who claims the right to govern due to his purported ability to efficiently manipulate the sorts of "facts" that everyone should be able to affirm, given that they are value-free.[64] By definition, then, to refuse their authority would be "unreasonable," as their attempts at control—either by way of sustained managerialism or overt violence if and when control stubbornly eludes the would-be manager's grasp—are justified.

The resulting form of modern power, which was clearly championed by Hamilton and other "intenders" at the United States' founding, was devastating to the competence of the populace, despite protests to the contrary. For Wolin, the result is the erosion of any concept of goods shared in common, leaving instead only appeals to private (mostly economic) interests; the organization and control of political space is left mainly in the hands of organizations, corporations, and those with the necessary "organizational" expertise.[65] As these shifts are increasingly accepted as normative rather than disputable, a level of indifference comes to mark the average citizen; ironically, the political energies of liberal democratic citizens have transferred to other outlets even as "democracy" is spread throughout the world.[66] Rapid industrialization, mobilization, and technologization has created "uprooted populations with a deep sense of loneliness and bewilderment," longing for community in an organizational age that works against it.[67] Indeed, community emerges as a hoped-for antidote to bureaucratization, even as the forms this hope takes tend toward utopianism, in Wolin's assessment. Even in 1960, Wolin saw that order had "won out" over these bare appeals to community, leaving the populace with a sense of *anomie*, in Durkheim's parlance.[68] As this

---

64. MacIntyre, *After Virtue*, 76–77.
65. Wolin, *Politics and Vision*, 315–22. Put differently, liberalism's creation of "safe space" is the desolation of *truly* common space, for to be "common" space must be contested, if constructively so. Liberal political theory as a family of associated assumptions and projects has as its goal the avoidance of "seriously contentious, hence socially straining, public dispute"; see Mathewes, *Theology of Public Life*, 153.
66. Wolin, *Politics and Vision*, 315–16.
67. Ibid., 319.
68. Ibid., 357.

victory continues to be made manifest, Wolin argues that we are shaped to become not citizens but "subjects of power," or better, consumers of a kind of "political" good. Whether intentional or not, the consequence is that the *demos* is further depoliticized.[69] And while the theoretical goal of liberalism may have been to enable people with different "comprehensive moral doctrines" to coexist, it actually led (as Marx saw) to a social contractarianism in which citizens give their power to a representative to the point that they (like workers) lose civic skills of self-government, while the state itself (like capital) becomes the "custodian of alienated power."[70]

If this was the full scope of the challenge, it would be bad enough. But the real trick is that this form of modern power did not remain stagnant; rather, in the last few decades it has transmuted into more subtle and more diffuse modes of control, what Wolin calls "postmodern power." Far from moving us beyond the problem of incompetence, postmodern power is a higher distillation of the same logic contained within liberalism, and thus earns from Wolin the moniker "inverted totalitarianism."

Wolin, to his great credit, recognizes as clearly as anyone the emergence of new, late-twentieth-century political forms that do not fit traditional molds, and focuses particularly on "Superpower" as one such hybridization. While the phenomenon is given a variety of names (post-industrial, postmodern, "post-political"), the essence of Wolin's description is that distinctively modern political forms have been superseded, marked most significantly by the eclipse of the sovereign state. For Wolin, the emergence of global corporations, "the 'internationalization' of culture," organizations like the World Bank, and the proliferation of non-governmental organizations that are no respecters of national borders all challenge the notion that the state is the primary locus of political activity today.[71]

Understanding this shift is complicated, but the crucial move that Wolin allows one to see is that these "globalizing" and subsuming

---

69. Ibid., 273, 401.
70. Ibid., 430.
71. Ibid., 559.

trends utilize the same logic that birthed the liberal nation-state in the first place. If the "intending" vision of the state, which had increasingly claimed the hearts and minds of the populace, aimed to control and efficiently manage through centralized power, the "postmodern" reality was the extension of that model; it sprang from the soil of intention. If economic logic was a primary marker of modern liberalism, that logic claims total victory in the new era—both dominant and internalized in all manner of thinking and speaking; if the central image of modern power was the factory, for postmodern power it is electronic communication; and if the modern mode of social control was "big," heavy, and settled, the postmodern mode is *internalized* and fleeting, accomplished not by imposition but apathy and acquiescence. Put simply, the aforementioned commitment to power that *stretches out* undergoes serious transformation with globalization, but is nonetheless retained.[72] As Cavanaugh observes, although many speak of globalization as a shift away from the nation-state and modern modes of power, these moves are "in fact the *hyperextension* of the nation-state's project of subsuming the local under the universal."[73] If liberalism and the politics of intending sought to place particular bodies and alliances under the direct purview of the state, the state is now just one more particular in the equations of international trade—important, but relativized. For their part, nation-states have willingly genuflected to this trend, subsuming *themselves* under the power of the World Trade Organization, for instance—an act of self-sacrifice that is incomprehensible unless one sees, with Wolin, that this move is not the end of the state project, but its generalization across space and time. As the nation-state freed markets from the "interventions" of local custom, so does globalization free commerce from the nation-state, "which, as it turns out, is now seen as one more localization impeding the universal flow of capital."[74]

While some argue that this interpretation is too-narrowly "economic,"[75] Wolin argues that while postmodern power *is*

---

72. Ibid., 562–64.
73. Cavanaugh, *Theopolitical*, 99.
74. Ibid., 103–5.

multifaceted and complex, it is nonetheless marked through and through by the final dominance of economic logic as the "real" basis of society. What began as a relationship between political economy and a system of power ended with the former rivaling, then prompting, then mastering the latter.[76] In the meantime, "democracy" has been confined to "procedural guarantees"—such as equal rights to vote or speak—that are masterfully managed by a cadre of interpreters, pollsters, and think-tanks who strive to make the political realm predictable and manageable. The citizen is "shrunk to the voter: periodically courted, warned, and confused but otherwise kept at a distance from actual decision-making and allowed to emerge only ephemerally in a cameo appearance according to a script composed by the opinion takers/makers."[77]

Such is the fruit of liberalism's vine, of corporate and governmental forces coalescing, of the politics of intending: *incompetence*. If Wolin is correct, liberalism and political competence (let alone civic engagement) are inversely related in actual practice, despite textbook theories that claim otherwise. Hamilton's aristocratic vision has come to fruition, and the result is the presence of a kind of determinism deeper than Marx could have imagined, as most of us have accepted "economy" as properly basic to human existence, to the point that no one—politician, civic group, or individual—thinks to alter its structure.[78]

2.4 Size Matters: Radical Democracy as a (Fugitive) Alternative

Thus far, I have followed Wolin's account of how the West, particularly the United States, has reached the level of political incompetence and associational deterioration that most recognize as problematic. If one accepts Wolin's diagnosis about liberalism's growth, dominance, and

---

75. Max Stackhouse, *God and Globalization, Volume 4: Globalization and Grace* (New York: Continuum, 2007), 8.
76. Wolin, *Politics and Vision*, 405.
77. Ibid., 564–65. This cameo appearance of the "average voter" was on display in 2008 when Sarah Palin continually appealed to "Joe Six-Pack," as well as Barack Obama and John McCain appealing to "Joe the Plumber."
78. Ibid., 578.

deleterious effects, the next question must be: What alternative can we hope for? Certainly, one finds in Wolin no forlorn atavism, although he recognizes that some may mistakenly read him this way.[79] Further, Wolin is clear that no alternative has any hope of success that neglects the aforementioned roots of the problem. To this end, Wolin's hope is in the possibilities of a *radical democracy* that is distinguishable from liberalism, although he's clear that this possibility is necessarily chastened in the shadow of Superpower. By "democracy," Wolin does not mean the "Superpower Democracy" that is conflated with liberalism and does nothing for an actively engaged citizenry. Rather, Wolin means the kind of participatory, egalitarian, and necessarily local politics that flared up in the United States during the 1950s and 1960s (in a manner unprecedented since the controversy over the ratification of the Constitution), an improvisational politics largely generated "outside of, and often in opposition to, established political institutions."[80]

For Wolin, democracy is not really a concrete form of governance, but "a project concerned with the political potentialities of ordinary citizens: that is, with their possibilities for becoming political beings through the self-discovery of common concerns and of modes of action for realizing them."[81] Radical democracy, Wolin states, is perpetually at odds with forms of political "management" and "organization" that would direct it to other ends (as Wolin points out, "intenders" sought to give democracy a carefully circumscribed "place," rather than suppress it altogether). A transgressive phenomenon, democracy resists such incorporation, and is lost as soon as that kind of appropriation occurs. Political philosophers throughout history have recognized this democratic "wildness," which has led to its being feared, delimited, and outright denigrated, including by the authors of *The Federalist Papers*.[82] Thus the qualifier "radical" serves a rhetorical

---

79. Wolin, *Presence of the Past*, 119.
80. Wolin, *Politics and Vision*, 522.
81. Sheldon S. Wolin, "Fugitive Democracy," in *Democracy and Difference: Contesting the Boundaries of the Political*, ed. Seyla Benhabib (Princeton: Princeton University Press, 1996), 31.
82. Ibid., 36-37. Cf. David Graeber, *The Democracy Project: A History, A Crisis, A Movement* (New York: Spiegel & Grau, 2013), ch. 3.

purpose, differentiating "democracy" from its conflation with liberalism, the latter of which is ironically deployed to advance "so many anti-democratic institutions and practices."[83]

For Wolin, democracy *of this sort* provides a precarious means of resisting the postmodern apathy that concerns so many precisely because it is not inherently connected to liberal institutionalism, but provides a heterogeneous path to the political understood as public deliberations over the exercise of collective power used to promote some collectivity's flourishing.[84] Even so, Wolin's democratic alternative is tentative and leans toward suggestiveness. This is for two reasons: First, Wolin's democracy is local in character. Radical democracy is in many ways the advocacy of a politics of tending, especially in its commitment to serving and caring for a local place and people. While particular skills are needed for democratic tending to be done well, equally important is that one cares for things close at hand, as we saw above, including the differences discovered through such careful attention. Indeed, such politics must be local, as they are born from the kinds of practices and "habits of competence" that so impressed Tocqueville, and "practices" necessarily limit one's scope to body-to-body interaction and participatory games that form the sorts of skills required for successful democratic "politicking." Size matters in democratic practice, for "small scale is the only scale commensurate with the kind and amount of power that democracy is capable of mobilizing, given the political limitations imposed by prevailing modes of economic organization."[85] Its power is diffuse, pluriform, and improvisational in a manner that is "anathema to centralization" (whether of the state or corporation): it is anti-totality politics, relying on local modes of politics, which because of its scale enables ordinary people to invent temporary forms to flourish.[86] And even while federalists attempted to corral this power (through a science of politics marked by checks and balances, an independent judiciary,

---

83. Hauerwas and Coles, *Christianity*, 3n4.
84. Wolin, "Fugitive Democracy," 31.
85. Wolin, *Politics and Vision*, 603.
86. Ibid.

representative government), they acknowledged that "republic" was a virtual synonym for participatory democracy in which citizens had a stake in common affairs, and that "the larger the republic, the less democratic."[87]

This local focus actually leads Wolin to curb his enthusiasm for radical democracy, precisely because liberalism's politics of size and concentrated power prevailed, the two natural enemies of democracy. For Wolin, the possibility of local politics is a chastened one in our time; its attractiveness was intentionally devalued by Hamilton and company, who wanted the populace to eschew commitments to family and neighborhood for national commitments[88]—and we largely have, as evidenced by our contrasting levels of interest in local and presidential elections. Further, Wolin knows that "locality" per se is no silver bullet, for the agent who lacks the time, skills, and competence to engage at the national level will not automatically gain these once they move to the local level. Thus Wolin sees democracy as fugitive, meaning on the run, "illicit," and for that reason hard to pin down. In the late modern world, Wolin says that democracy *cannot* be a complete political system, given the "awesome potentialities of modern forms of power and what they exact of the social and natural world." Rather, democracy must be reconceived as "a mode of being conditioned by bitter experience, doomed to succeed only temporarily, but . . . a recurrent possibility as long as the memory of the political survives."[89]

Because of this inherent occasionalism, Wolin is tentative in his advocacy of democracy as an alternative: it is "fugitive" not only in the sense of illicit but also *fleeting*. Democracy is a "political moment" for Wolin, an "engine" of the political that is recurrent but continually lost. Democratic gains from one generation do not necessarily carry to the next, get co-opted such that they "slip" in meaning, or "attenuated so as to serve other ends," the most fundamental end usually being "the establishment and development of the modernizing state."[90]

---

87. Wolin, *Presence of the Past*, 96.
88. Ibid., 98.
89. Wolin, "Fugitive Democracy," 42–43.
90. Ibid., 42.

Democracy is not a thing, for Wolin, but a *process* that takes a variety of forms: at base a "creation of those who must work, who cannot hire proxies to promote their interests, and for whom participation, as distinguished from voting, is necessarily a sacrifice."[91] Inherently opposed to the dominant institutions of our society even at the local level, its movements will be episodic, circumstantial, ad hoc, in the ebb and flow of the everyday.[92] And yet, when it is practiced, it addresses incompetence in a way that few things can.

I have provided thus far a sketch of "radical democracy," less an opposing theory to liberalism than an alternative set of practices. In my view, Wolin's commitment to fugitivity in the sense of illicit is dead-on, while his dedication to its fleetingness overdrawn. Nonetheless, Wolin is right to recognize "the futility of seeking democratic renewal by relying on the powers of the modern state," looking instead to the fact that "ordinary individuals are capable of creating new cultural patterns of commonality at any moment."[93] The key to Wolin's brilliance is his refusal to provide an alternative theory to liberalism, seeing instead that what's at stake is the question of who dominates politics and who has responsibility for the care of civic life—whether this is a common task, or not. In any case, Wolin suggests a way to transformatively inhabit our current milieu without eulogizing bowling leagues.[94]

3 Contemporary Christian Responses

In many ways, the rest of this book is an exploration of what a baptist theological politics might look like given this context. Before proceeding, I will spend the remainder of this chapter briefly assessing three contemporary political theologians' responses to our current situation utilizing the previous description of what's going on: Timothy Beach-Verhey, Eric Gregory, and Max Stackhouse. Each theologian has strengths, and each recognizes something like the threat I have

---

91. Wolin, *Politics and Vision*, 602.
92. Ibid., 604.
93. Wolin, "Fugitive Democracy," 43.
94. Wolin, *Politics and Vision*, 605.

described, but each also neglects the *root* of our incompetence (connected, as Wolin shows, with liberalism), such that I must move beyond them. Note that my goal is not to provide a comprehensive summary of every current position, but to respond to paradigmatic positions such that I can point out tendencies that ought to be avoided in political theology. In the concluding section, I will point to a growing consensus among certain theologians who reclaim something like Wolin's democratic practices.

3.1 A Robust Liberalism?

The most obvious response to my argument thus far is that its assessment of liberalism is overly negative. This response predominantly takes one of two forms. The first is represented by Timothy Beach-Verhey's *Robust Liberalism*, which is a distillation of a popular strain of political theology and thus starkly embodies that strain's strengths and inadequacies. For Beach-Verhey, the primary challenge in the United States today is to develop *public* modes of political discourse and solidarity that avoid paternalistic liberalism that is hostile to religious arguments being used in public *and* a religious parochialism that leads to isolationism, or even "wars of religion."[95] The representatives of these errors, and Beach-Verhey's primary adversaries, are Rawls and Hauerwas. For Beach-Verhey, both erroneously refuse the "perennial" Christian struggle of reconciling the "particular" and the "universal." Regarding Rawls, the problem is not his liberalism—Beach-Verhey advocates a version of liberalism from Christian warrants—but his strict delimitation of religion in public discourse (however much he nuanced this prohibition) and his constricting limits on what *counts* as "public reason."[96] In short, in promoting "justice" in liberal societies Rawls overemphasizes "the universal." Regarding Hauerwas, the problem is his purported overcorrection of Rawls toward "the particular," which creates a

---

95. Beach-Verhey, *Robust Liberalism*, 2–3. Beach-Verhey follows the standard "wars of religion" narrative, criticized above; cf. ibid., 4, 41, 161.
96. Ibid., 30–31.

closed circle around the church that has little interest in working for justice in the shared political world, since moral discourse with those of other traditions is supposedly *impossible*.[97]

For Beach-Verhey, both approaches present a zero-sum choice: either social contract liberalism or public Christian faithfulness.[98] His central argument is that resources found in H. Richard Niebuhr allow one to avoid this false dichotomy, successfully reconciling the "particular" and the "universal" where others with similar aims fail. Beach-Verhey is mostly taken by Niebuhr's concept of "radical monotheism," the God who is above all and relativizes all human endeavors—political, ecclesial, or otherwise.[99] This concept allows Niebuhr a universal, objective reality independent of all interpretation that does not neglect the particular through which the universal is mediated, and thus provides the means to shore up inadequacies in liberalism that is replacing the "republican" paradigm for "very good reasons."[100] Niebuhr thus argues for a "robust liberalism" on Christian grounds, growing especially from a theory of original sin that requires Madison's "balance of powers," and a covenant theology that promotes mutual interactivity under a higher power.[101]

Leaving aside whether this is the only possible interpretation of Niebuhr, one can now imagine Beach-Verhey's response to my assessment of liberalism: it applies to Rawlsian liberalism, but it ignores the robust, covenantal version that "actually" took root in the United States and is ably represented by Niebuhr; and that this robust liberalism relates "the particular" to "the universal" better than does Wolin's work (which would be too "particular"), such that it is the best political option available for Christians who wish to be publicly faithful without veering into sectarianism.

Beach-Verhey's goal of finding a path to charitable political

---

97. Ibid., 13, 52–59. I set aside Beach-Verhey's inaccurate presentation of Hauerwas's position, mostly because I am convinced that his inability to understand Hauerwas is caused by the philosophical bewitchments I specify below.
98. Ibid., 18.
99. H. Richard Niebuhr, *Radical Monotheism and Western Culture* (Louisville: Westminster John Knox, [1943] 1960).
100. Beach-Verhey, *Robust Liberalism*, 25. Beach-Verhey means "republican" in the Jeffersonian sense.
101. Ibid., ch. 5.

discourse in the midst of disagreements, as well as alleviating Christian political ennui, is admirable. Unfortunately, his habit of addressing these problems in such abstract terms blinds him to some flaws in his argument, the most prominent of which is his insistence on separating something called "the particular" from "the universal." Of course, Beach-Verhey does work hard to bring the two into dialectical relation; my concern is less with whether he successfully relates them or not, but that he works with these broad abstractions that allow him to conceive of them as separable in the first place. The operative picture is that of a universal, neutral, uninterpreted reality sitting "out there" with which humans "dialogue"; the threat is collapsing reality into perception or boxing out "reality."[102] These concerns are hardly unique to Beach-Verhey, and in his work one can see why they are deficient: as high-level abstractions, the language itself *creates* the problem of how to relate "reality" and "particularity." Following Wittgenstein, reality is always already interpreted by ourselves and others.[103] This is not to deny a version of "critical realism": it is only to deny that reality and interpretation, "universal" and "particular," "language" and "world," can be divorced.[104]

This deficiency is not of mere abstract interest, but something that infects this strand's politics. For one thing, the separation tends to lead to the universal becoming *the thing* politically, despite Beach-Verhey's attempt to value both. That is, the relationship takes on a level of instrumentality such that the church ought to be *directed toward* the universal, or that the particular "drives" us to the universal.[105] Even Jesus is subordinated to his more universal message, a bit of Christological confusion. While I do not want a "closed circle" church (a *communio incurvatus in se*), Beach-Verhey is mistaken to think that

---

102. Ibid., 58.
103. Unsurprisingly, this view is accompanied by a deficient view of language as "mediating" reality; ibid., 63–65. Unsurprising, for as Toulmin writes, the entire thrust of Wittgenstein's supposedly "linguistic" work in *Philosophical Investigations* is "directed at a 'theory-centered' style of philosophizing—i.e., one that poses problems, and seeks solutions, stated in timeless, universal terms"; Toulmin, *Cosmopolis*, 11.
104. For a full treatment of these themes, cf. Brad J. Kallenberg, *Ethics as Grammar: Changing the Postmodern Subject* (Notre Dame: University of Notre Dame Press, 2001), esp. 162–64.
105. Cf. Beach-Verhey, *Robust Liberalism*, ch. 4, 137.

the only way to be open is through affirming a neutral reality. Further, while Beach-Verhey recognizes the deleterious effect market and state have had on citizen engagement,[106] because his main concern is to reconcile "universal" and "particular," and because he analyzes liberalism only in terms of these abstractions, he is silent about any possible distinction between "liberalism" and "democracy," let alone the ways liberalism has *caused* the state-market threat to citizen competence that rightly troubles him. Thus even while pointing to an emerging group of writers who affirm pluralistic dialogue, Beach-Verhey tellingly adds that this group seeks to "participate in the discursive possibilities *presented by the current system*."[107] After Wolin, assuming that these possibilities are presented by the system is at the very least questionable. Finally, Beach-Verhey's advocacy of covenant as a helpful mode of governance avoiding both hyper-individualism and formless community, while perhaps desirable, leads him to describe the contemporary United States in terms that appear idealistic. Beach-Verhey doesn't mention that the United States has in practice followed nothing like a covenantal vision; indeed, it is no small irony that Beach-Verhey cites Niebuhr's appreciation for Madison and Hamilton's federalism as deeply Christian given the negative effects their politics of intending had on "pluralistic democratic dialogue." Beach-Verhey thus exemplifies the theologian who ignores arguments calling his categories into question, and thus is unaware that these categories may serve to reinscribe the very threats he rightly seeks to address.

3.2 Augustinian Liberalism and Ambivalent Affirmation

The argument that my assessment of liberalism is overly negative can take a second form, one that avoids some of the mistakes of the first group while affirming many of the same points. The claim here is that whether or not liberalism is *best* is less important than the fact that it is a reality with which we must deal, now and for the foreseeable future.

---

106. Ibid., 154.
107. Ibid., 112. Emphasis added.

The faithfully Augustinian task is to carefully participate in liberalism rather than criticize it wholesale or seek to escape its influence. This chastened version of liberalism is well represented by Eric Gregory's *Politics and the Order of Love*.

Gregory's overview of Augustinian liberalism nuances the debate as normally conducted, showing that there are in fact multiple "Augustinianisms" despite the fact that many associate the whole of the tradition with the "Augustinian realism" of Reinhold Niebuhr, with its pessimistic view of politics and competitive conception of justice and love. Gregory's goal is to elucidate and promote "Augustinian civic liberalism," which he claims has the strengths of Augustinian realism and Rawlsianism while avoiding their weaknesses. Gregory does not want to deny Augustinian affirmations of sin, limited government, or the importance of community that extends *beyond* the state, but to *also* advocate a positive Augustinian liberalism that enables "critical appreciation" of society, even liberal society.[108] This Augustinianism is drawn not from Book 19 of *City of God* (as is typical), but from Book 10 where one finds "the heart of Augustine's account of the true worship of the crucified God and the charitable service of neighbor in *collective caritas*."[109] By focusing on Augustine's moral psychology, Gregory attempts a theory of liberal citizenship rather than statecraft, and argues that a truly Augustinian liberalism connects God-love and neighbor-love rather than puts them in competition.[110]

Gregory's Augustinian civic liberalism, following exemplars like Martin Luther King Jr. (purportedly) and Jean Bethke Elshtain, places heavy emphasis on ambivalently affirming the political order, both because of the futility of escape and because the duty of neighbor-love requires it. Indeed, ambivalent affirmation, issuing a yes and no to society, is a common Augustinian trope: transformative participation is taken to be the Christian's calling, while retreat a sign of bad faith.[111] Thus the response of this group to my analysis of liberalism would

---

108. Gregory, *Politics*, 79, 107.
109. Ibid., 379.
110. Ibid., 319–20, ch. 6.
111. Cf. Beach-Verhey, *Robust Liberalism*, 63, 112.

be that it is not easily avoidable, and that the harder, transformative calling is to move within liberalism, finding the means to say a no *and a yes*. While indeed hopeful about the possibilities of civic participation, the tone is also measured: This is the form of politics that we have, and we had better not indulge the luxury of total criticism, or liberalism will be completely left to its own devices. Besides, while not unequivocally good, neither is liberalism totally evil: it is morally ambivalent—and in any case, no structural alternative is currently imaginable.[112]

Gregory's arguments against political escapism, against a "love" that would dominate and possess the beloved, and for "ambivalent affirmation" are illuminating in their own right. Nonetheless, problems remain for this version of liberalism that lead me down other avenues. After reading Gregory's account of ambivalent affirmation, I am left asking, "What now?" Granted that we should eschew escapism and love our "thickly described" neighbor through civic involvement, what does that entail? Gregory expresses concerns with overly pessimistic evaluations of liberal democratic orders,[113] but from here does not really specify how Christians can foster a truly ambivalent affirmation of these orders that avoids underwriting liberalism's dominance. Simply put, how does Gregory's "yes and no" avoid collapsing into a "yes" only? It seems to me that this strand has an unequivocally positive view of "participation," but is not as clear in specifying participation *in what*.

Further, I think Wolin is simply correct to differentiate liberalism from democracy—a distinction that Gregory, like Beach-Verhey, does not make, though for Gregory it might clarify some points of concern. For instance, while Gregory's description of Hauerwas's project is much more accurate than Beach-Verhey's, he remains confused by the purported ambivalence in Hauerwas's rhetoric, noting that Hauerwas sometimes seems to affirm something like Gregory's view, but at other times is hostile toward liberalism.[114] After Wolin, this ambivalence is

---

112. Gregory, *Politics*, 370.
113. Ibid., 383–84.
114. Ibid., 116.

perhaps more understandable: Hauerwas has been struggling to articulate a stance against the hegemonic, "neutral" moves represented by Rawlsian liberalism, not least for the way these underwrite bureaucratic capitalist power, without conceding that this implies a withdrawal from anything. Thus Wolin, Coles, and Stout helped Hauerwas clarify what he had been arguing for some time: that there's a difference between radically democratic "participation" and liberal "democratic" theory. Democracy is still not Hauerwas's goal, but Wolin articulates a "non-Constantinian" (or non-dominating, as Gregory would have it) democratic politics that Hauerwas can faithfully participate within. Indeed, without this distinction, Gregory's "participation" may end up looking sanguine, and leads me to wonder when or if a prophetic "no" would be discernible. And finally, if Wolin is right about the pernicious effects of liberalism on the politics of tending, I doubt that "ambivalence" will be strong enough to resist its lures.

Ultimately, Gregory too works at a level of abstraction ("universal" and "particular," "sin" versus "love") that makes any structural alternative unimaginable. There may not be any such alternative, but perhaps what we should be searching for is not liberalism's equal and opposite, as sweeping and extensive as its enemy, but alternative practices akin to Coles's hopeful, differentiated, local-yet-networked communities of discourse. Certainly, we need more than new theoretical grounding for a project that has shown itself to be inimical to democratic practice. Thus while I too want to avoid quietism and triumphalism, to foster "civic friendship," and to avoid being paralyzed by the limits of politics,[115] I must do so by other paths, and on a different scale, than Gregory.

3.3 Globalization as Salvific

A third prominent response to my assessment of liberalism, tempting but deficient, is that it is helpful as far as it goes, but that I have not

---

115. Ibid., 38, 124, 350–62.

taken the reality of globalization seriously enough. This response is well represented by Max Stackhouse, for whom the relativization of the nation-state in the face of emerging, global realities marks

> a potential civilizational shift that involves the growth of a worldwide infrastructure that bears the prospect of a new form of civil society, one that may well comprehend all previous national, ethnic, political, economic or cultural contexts. It portends a cosmopolitan possibility that modernity promised but could not deliver, and thus can be considered as the most profound postmodernism.[116]

Stackhouse speaks effusively of the possibilities and the dangers of these developments, and denigrates those who would refuse the challenge or who would affirm a kind of "localism" that is borderline offensive in the new, "global society." Globalization is more than just an economic reality for Stackhouse, and what it desperately requires is a public theology capable of guiding it toward justice. Christians should guide or attempt to guide every aspect of society,[117] and globalization provides but a new iteration of this calling.

In my view, this is a tempting avenue to take, as it sounds nice to affirm "globalism," and who can deny that the world is "shrinking"? However, I am convinced by Cavanaugh that globalization is in fact the hyperextension of liberalism, and thus is in many ways the expression of its project *par excellence*, rather than a "postmodernism" of any sort. If it extends the parts of modernity that Stackhouse admires (on his view: democracy, human rights, science, international law, mass media),[118] it also carries the incompetence that so marks modern societies, even "internationalizing" that incompetence. As Coles argues, globalism does not move us past the paternalistic stance industrialized nation-states took toward the rest of the world, but reinscribes it for a new era; though officially eschewing colonialism for "justice for all," it does not renounce "the colonizing posture that would govern the terms of a reformed order. . . . In this way,

---

116. Stackhouse, *Globalization*, 2.
117. "Introduction," in *Public Theology for a Global Society: Essays in Honor of Max L. Stackhouse*, ed. Deirdre King Hainsworth and Scott R. Paeth (Grand Rapids: Eerdmans, 2010), xiii–xiv.
118. Stackhouse, *Globalization*, 2.

liberalism's 'gift' of a common currency of shared principles participates hand in hand (and in spite of itself) with unfettered economic markets as a part of the latest form of neocolonialism, globalization."[119] Thus in response to Stackhouse's oft-repeated insistence that globalization is a partial result of Christian theology,[120] one might wonder whether that is an indictment of the strands of Christianity so responsible. Finally, following Wolin does not automatically lead to a parochial fetishization of the "local"; it simply disavows a false move to "the global" on liberalism's own terms, and wants the moves "up" not to be at the expense of on-the-ground, politically engaged communities, but more like the image of networks of discerning communities suggested by Coles.[121]

4 An Interruption: Alternative Practices and Communal Discernment as Site

Amidst differences, a commonality among the previous three positions is their shared desire to "move up" with liberalism, either because liberalism is good, unavoidable, or at the least a context in need of guidance. Each recognizes the problematic developments of associational atrophy, political apathy, citizen incompetence, but do not see them as inherent to liberalism, and thus seek paths to live faithfully within liberalism, eschewing Wolin's analysis as either unnecessary or reactionary. Helpfully, theological ethicist Rebecca Todd Peters has delineated two broad-stroke responses to this context (marked by globalization, as she sees it): "working within" it as best as possible (which she names the *neoliberal* and *developmental* responses), and "resisting" globalism's negative consequences more readily seen in the forgotten corners of the world (named *postcolonialist* and *earthist*).[122] The Christian responses so far examined are of the former group.

---

119. Coles, *Beyond Gated Politics*, 44.
120. Stackhouse, *Globalization*, 35–36.
121. Cf. Romand Coles, "Of Tensions and Tricksters: Grassroots Democracy between Theory and Practice," in *Christianity*, 283.
122. Rebecca Todd Peters, *In Search of the Good Life: The Ethics of Globalization* (New York: Continuum, 2004).

INCOMPETENCE, LIBERALISM, AND DEMOCRACY

But there is another path to moral competence that does not dismiss Wolin's analysis out-of-hand, and that avoids the "sectarian" withdrawal from politics that so worries defenders of liberalism. For a diverse group of Christian political theologians, liberalism *is* problematic in the ways that Wolin helps us see, and while its effects may, strictly speaking, be unavoidable given the pervasiveness of its reach, subversive resistance to its lures is called for, not by "going up" with it, but by on-the-ground practices. For instance, Willis Jenkins argues that the best response to moral incompetence comes not by creating concepts from scratch to guide people through unprecedented quandaries, or by providing new and better concepts, metaphors, or theories that help us "reinterpret" the world,[123] as if the problem of incompetence were one of bad mental imagery or the lack of just the right moral concept; Jenkins's hope is in the generous traditioned creativity that works with concepts in the Christian tradition, and those one finds elsewhere, and thus through new practices one may "learn how to make our concepts do new things."[124] If we find ourselves incompetent to love our neighbors, do justice, or worship God, then Christians must be pressured to "invent ways for central practices of their tradition to begin to answer for the world in which they live," but Jenkins then immediately adds: "Religious ethics makes an interesting difference, I think, only insofar as it demonstrates possibilities of agency that overcome features of the problem that defeat moral response."[125] In light of Wolin's description, this means discovering practices that subvert and recolor the day-to-day relations that reproduce the liberal imaginary. It is crucial to note that practices do not automatically make a difference, for Jenkins, but must be purposely moved in that way. As Traci West (a powerful proponent of dialogical practices' ability to disrupt injustice and incompetence in a violent, sexist world) notes, Christian practices do have that potential,

---

123. Jenkins calls this the "strategy of moral cosmology," and names William Schweiker, Niebuhr, and Stackhouse as adherents; Jenkins, *Future of Ethics*, 75–81.
124. Ibid., 43. He calls this "the strategy of theocentric pragmatism," and sees that it too has precursors in Niebuhr's work; ibid., 81.
125. Ibid., 46.

but they can also reinforce cultural patterns that undermine any good the practice may be capable of.[126] Thus this emphasis does not say that local practices are automatically salvific; it's that they *can* generate moral-political agency; indeed, if inverted totalitarianism is squarely faced, it can "generate practical inventiveness that begins to make moral cultures more competent to meet their challenges."[127]

Jenkins and West are not alone. Luke Bretherton emphasizes the hopelessness of fostering a Christian politics in today's world that neglects practices of inhabitation and resistance; besides responses that place the church under the state's patronage, or reinforce identity politics, or view Christian alternatives as more consumer goods, Bretherton is taken by Christian responses that foster generous, democratic practices that are not beholden to the state (as represented by Saul Alinsky and the Industrial Areas Foundation, or IAF), while maintaining as an Augustinian a desire for subversive inhabitation at the national and global levels as well. Mathewes, another Augustinian, sees the same problems with liberalism as does Wolin, and advocates a practiced, Christian reclamation of civic republicanism (a "politics of tending") that goes far beyond voting to practiced civic participation through cultivation of certain virtues—not least hope.[128] Stout's *Democracy and Tradition* is a benchmark of this approach, focusing as he does on a robust set of local, democratic practices that have sustained democracy in the United States thus far, and need to be maintained if the threats to its practice are not to overwhelm them completely. And recently, Hauerwas and Coles have written a book together that explores the many surprising points of connection between radical democracy and radical Christianity, exemplifying the kind of dialogical patience that both see as vital moving forward.

Obviously this group is far from uniform, and I do not mean to minimize their differences. But amidst their disagreements, they

---

126. Traci C. West, *Disruptive Christian Ethics: When Racism and Women's Lives Matter* (Louisville: Westminster John Knox, 2006), 112-13. Cf. James Wm. McClendon Jr., *Doctrine: Systematic Theology, Volume 2* (Nashville: Abingdon, 1994), 33.
127. Jenkins, *Future of Ethics*, 18.
128. Mathewes's advocacy of republicanism is not unequivocal; he fears civic republicanism veers toward "immanentism" and an "apocalyptic" fanaticism; Mathewes, *Theology of Public Life*, 172-80.

represent a broad type of response—or better, an argument—that I will enter into using baptist resources and categories. If Coles is correct that it is "primarily practices of dialogue that cultivate the orientations, disorientations, virtues, and knowledges that are necessary not only for identifying and resisting the worst but also for struggling with others toward visions of what might be better,"[129] then we must be specific, *naming the practices* suited for such a task, along with the ends, virtues, narratives, and (Coles would interject) "ateleological" sensibilities.

Thus the remainder of my argument fleshes out what a baptist theological politics looks like that happily participates in radically democratic "politics of tending" while resisting as far as possible the manifestations of liberalism that threaten it. I do this through close attention to the specific practice of communal discernment, which I will show fosters the "orientations, disorientations, virtues, and knowledges" needed to sustain discerning, pluralistic, and faithful civic engagement in the face of political incompetence. Communal discernment alone is not sufficient, of course: Coles is right that we need a "tensional ecology of practices that gradually work beyond the limits of the present toward a more generous and receptive justice."[130] And yet communal discernment is an intriguing and oft-neglected piece of that puzzle for Christians, especially in light of the types of practices that Coles lists as vital to a robust democratic politics with any chance of resisting liberal forces: not only deliberation, but a patient listening to those different from oneself, movement to neglected parts of society, and hope in unforeseen, ecstatic possibilities that come in surprising forms—possibilities Christians would list as gifts of the Spirit.[131] Nonetheless, even as the current cultural moment is reframing many of the assumptions that had made it difficult for baptist theopolitical contributions to be heard, our task is still to provide a faithful witness to the arrived and now arriving Kingdom of God, in this as in all contexts.

129. Coles, *Beyond Gated Politics*, 39.
130. Ibid., xxx.
131. Ibid., xxviii–xxx.

2

Outline of the Promise of a Practice

Not finitude, but the denial of finitude, is the marker of tragedy.[1]
—Stanley Cavell

Those who lay claim, to whatever extent, to the heritage of the radical reformation in all its diversity have often found themselves marginalized from arguments in political theology, hastily labeled sectarians for failing to offer a morality that is of "public" import. Whether this marginalization is intentional or not, the sentiment is that such radicals may provide helpful explorations of character formation or gospel faithfulness, but their relevance ends at the borders of the church. I am uninterested in rehashing rebuttals to this charge, which successfully expose assumptions embedded within the accusation itself.[2] Rather, my interest is the sense in which this exclusion seems predicated on a picture of the political landscape that Sheldon Wolin and company have called into question—from a decidedly non-confessional stance. If it is true that the context itself as

---

1. Stanley Cavell, *The Claim of Reason: Wittgenstein, Skepticism, Morality, and Tragedy* (Oxford: Clarendon, 1979), 455.
2. Cf. Stanley Hauerwas, "Why the 'Sectarian Temptation' Is a Misrepresentation: A Response to James Gustafson," in *The Hauerwas Reader*, ed. John Berkman and Michael Cartwright (Durham, NC: Duke University Press, 2001), 90–110.

described by radical democrats calls for a reconsideration of criticisms that had given the sectarian charge its plausibility, then perhaps a way is opened for renewed interest in what those labeled "Anabaptist" have to contribute to the field of political theology, besides a decontextualized commitment to pacifism. In any case, I wish to go beyond mere throat clearing, and toward a description of what faithfulness looks like in the context described by Wolin.

At the end of the previous chapter, I noted Romand Coles's remark that in struggling for radical democracy against the acids of liberalism with which it is intermixed, a central task must be naming the practices that might equip communities and individuals for that struggle. This is a task that previously disregarded Anabaptist theologians are now in a unique position to undertake, for if they have anything to teach the wider church, it is how to move discerningly within and among amorphous, hostile political forces. Indeed, Anabaptists have long specified certain practices that have proved helpful in this task. Searching for practices of this sort need not entail quietism; as ethicist Traci West writes, practices carry the potential for disrupting patterns of injustice, as well as stand in need of being continually "disrupted" from potentially reinscribing injustice.[3] Nor ought it entail isolationism: despite fears that a focus on practices in general and communal discernment in particular creates a deafness to others and a barrier to friendship, my goal is to show that when practiced well communal discernment helps achieve both openness to others and true friendship—both inside and outside the *ekklesia*.

To that stated end, my task in this chapter is to outline communal discernment as an important member of the "tensional ecology of practices that gradually work beyond the limits of the present toward a more generous and receptive justice"[4]—both its possibilities and liabilities as a practice that marks a distinctively "baptist" way of inhabiting the world. I begin with some orienting reflections on

---

3. Traci C. West, *Disruptive Christian Ethics: When Racism and Women's Lives Matter* (Louisville: Westminster John Knox, 2006), ch. 4.
4. Romand Coles, *Beyond Gated Politics: Reflections for the Possibility of Democracy* (Minneapolis: University of Minnesota Press, 2005), xxx.

discernment, which introduce my approach to the descriptive task of this chapter. Next, I describe communal discernment itself as thickly as I can, including the socio-political context in which it was reclaimed by certain sixteenth-century Anabaptists. I conclude by correlating this description of discernment to the political context described in the previous chapter by Wolin and company. Because I will continue to do this in the chapters that follow, at this stage I limit my focus to an exploration of how communal discernment cultivates competence to name and resist some of liberalism's acidic tendencies without sacrificing a respect for the finite, "relative" nature of this competence. This is an important reason communal discernment carries such promise for political theology: it fosters a way forward that is neither withdrawn nor acquiescent, neither formless nor rigid—and which values ongoing trust in a God on the move over certainty.

1 Communal Discernment as Promise

Of course, the task of moral discernment has been a perennial struggle for Christians. Whenever a community or any conscientious person faces a morally weighted situation, the skill of discernment will be exercised, however poorly. Classically, Aristotle devoted large portions of the *Nicomachean Ethics* to the virtue of *phronesis* or "prudence," in which he describes the practical wisdom acquired in the midst of ordinary life. For Aristotle, *phronesis* is not only directed to "normative" questions, but is deeply relevant to who an agent is going to be; when mastered, in other words, *phronesis* is internalized, exercised "intuitively" and without deliberation, even in situations rife with ambiguity. Thus in political climates that breed moral incompetence, one may say that discernment is the first casualty, precisely because "inverted totalitarianism" does not simply control the behavior of a populace, but erodes its ability to even see that this is happening.

Over time, several approaches to moral discernment emerged among Christians to supplement this task: one ought to rationally follow certain rules, or exercise one's "graced imagination," or obey church tradition, and adequate discernment will thus occur.[5] As Christian theologians became increasingly indebted to Enlightenment patterns of thought, the question of discernment faded as the moral focus narrowed on the bare "moment of decision" faced by the autonomous individual. Ethics tended to be reduced to a kind of "decisionism" that ignored the character, community, and background narratives that made this hypothetical decider who he or she was,[6] and thus manifested a "modern generic individualism" whereby individuals were considered identical for "all relevant political and ethical purposes."[7]

Fortunately, the inadequacy of such approaches was exposed by a diverse group of theological ethicists, some of whom were rediscovering virtue ethics and many of whom found ways to describe *phronesis* (discernment, prudence, practical wisdom) in new, helpful ways. James Gustafson, for instance, characterized discernment as analogous to the skill utilized in a variety of aesthetic arenas: with music, art, or even fine food, we naturally speak of people with "discerning" tastes, "who seem to be more perceptive, wiser, more discriminating than others are in judging, whether the object judged is a performance of a symphony, a person and his behavior, a political situation, or a novel."[8] In particular, Gustafson compared discernment to aesthetic vision, in the sense that both skills are honed in their continued employment: as one judges art over time, for instance, "one's own perceptions of the text or the painting are altered."[9] Gustafson is drawing attention to the lack of any checklist that one could formulaically apply in order to achieve moral discernment. While such checklists may help the beginner avoid obvious error, they

---

5. James M. Gustafson, "Moral Discernment in the Christian Life," in *Moral Discernment in the Christian Life: Essays in Theological Ethics*, ed. Theo A. Boer and Paul E. Capetz (Louisville: Westminster John Knox, 2007), 25.
6. James Wm. McClendon Jr., *Biography as Theology: How Life Stories Can Remake Today's Theology*, rev. ed. (Philadelphia: Trinity Press International, [1974] 1990), ch. 1. Cf. James M. Gustafson, "Context versus Principles: A Misplaced Debate in Christian Ethics," in *Moral Discernment*, 1–24.
7. Nancey Murphy and James Wm. McClendon Jr., "Distinguishing Modern and Postmodern Theologies," in *The Collected Works of James Wm. McClendon, Jr., Volume 2*, ed. Ryan Andrew Newson and Andrew C. Wright (Waco, TX: Baylor University Press, 2014), 46–48.
8. Gustafson, "Moral Discernment," 27.
9. Ibid., 27, 35.

remain "external" to both observer and situation observed. "They do not in themselves have or require the qualities of empathy, appreciation, imagination, and sensitivity that seem to be involved in discerning perception and judgment."[10] A host of theological ethicists have followed Gustafson in emphasizing the "fluid" nature of discernment, using conversation partners from Aristotle to Wittgenstein.[11] The point emphasized repeatedly is both that the goods of moral discernment are most clearly seen in its exercise, and that once mastered it leads to a moral *virtuosity* in which the discerning person can assess varying situations and tell a "fitting" response to what is going on: a skill that involves, at minimum, "a reading of the case at hand, an expression of what constitutes the character and perspective of the person, some appeals to reason and principles both to help one discern and to defend what one discerns. Excellence in moral discernment involves various combinations of these."[12]

For Christians, discernment is vital as we attempt to live faithfully in the world without letting our particular witness become subsumed into obscurity, *and* as we go about the hard work of transforming the world ("by the renewing of [our] minds"; Rom 12:1-2). This "yes and no" quality is central to the Augustinian tradition, but it is not peculiar to it—it is a struggle for all Christians the moment there is a community that is distinctive in any way, to any degree, from the rest of society. Indeed, as Luke Timothy Johnson observes, the key element in decision making, viewed "as an articulation of the church's faith in the Living God," is discernment, which

> enables humans to perceive their characteristically ambiguous experience as revelatory and to articulate such experiences in a narrative of faith. Discernment enables communities to listen to such gathering narratives for the word of God that they might express. Discernment enables communities, finally, to decide for God.[13]

---

10. Ibid., 28.
11. Cf. Brad J. Kallenberg, *Ethics as Grammar: Changing the Postmodern Subject* (Notre Dame: University of Notre Dame Press, 2001), 1–2, 162–63.
12. Gustafson, "Moral Discernment," 30–32.
13. Luke Timothy Johnson, *Scripture and Discernment: Decision Making in the Church* (Nashville: Abingdon, 1996), 109.

Johnson unpacks several New Testament phrases used in relation to discernment ("judging," "testing," and "discerning the spirits"), and argues that the use to which these terms are put suggests "the capacity of judging, testing, or discerning to be a gift of the Holy Spirit that works in and through human intelligence. Like prophecy itself, it is a gift that uses the mind. We would not go far wrong, then, if we were to regard discernment as similar to the virtue of prudence (*phronesis*)."[14] In other words, for Christians, discernment describes a habit of faith by which disciples are disposed to hear and respond to God amidst the hurly-burly of life.

Helpful though these resources are, my focus in this chapter is slightly different. Gustafson, for instance, rightly argues that being a Christian does not make one non- or super-human, but that Christian capacities for discernment will be of the same kind as in all people: "The human processes of discernment are no different among Christians than they are among other men."[15] However, in putting an essentially anthropological point in this way, Gustafson leans toward eliding the difference between Christian *processes* of discernment and those of other peoples, despite protests to the contrary; put differently, the Church and the Spirit are notably absent from Gustafson's observations on discernment.[16] More deeply, Gustafson's account of moral discernment seems colored by an individualism that I want to temper. Gustafson's reading of Romans 12:1–2, for instance, ignores the fact that Paul is invoking the second-person plural in that passage, and while he rightly highlights the "virtuoso" quality of discernment that is more than assent to a list of propositions,[17] his process of Christian discernment seems to involve the group mostly as a collection of individuals, some of whom are virtuosos, others "flat-footed." The specter of modern generic individualism lingers.[18]

---

14. Ibid., 109–10.
15. Gustafson, "Moral Discernment," 33.
16. Gustafson's ecclesiological reflections are contained in *Treasure in Earthen Vessels: The Church as a Human Community* (Louisville: Westminster John Knox, [1961] 2008).
17. Gustafson, "Moral Discernment," 34.
18. Cf. Gayle Gerber Koontz, "Meeting in the Power of the Spirit: Ecclesiology, Ethics, and the Practice of Discernment," in *The Wisdom of the Cross: Essays in Honor of John Howard Yoder*, ed. Stanley Hauerwas et al. (Grand Rapids: Eerdmans, 1999), 343.

In contrast, my attention is on a robustly communal picture of discernment, a kind of "communal *phronesis*" that is recurrent in the New Testament witness. By communal discernment, I mean the practice indicated by passages like Matthew 18:15–22, 1 Corinthians 5, and Acts 15, an adaptable set of activities by which communities of faith patiently listen for how God would have them move in some particular circumstance. Through gathering and engaging in prayer, scriptural interpretation, honest argumentation, and patient listening, the hope is that the community will apprehend—even if imperfectly and not always—contextually specific guidance from God. As McClendon clarifies, communal discernment

> is no mere ballot-box democracy, far less is it a mere opinion poll of the church membership. Discernment is rather a communal *practice*, deliberately undertaken, in which issues of moment for the ongoing life of God's people are addressed in meeting, brought under mutual study in the light of all the Scripture and all experience, committed to ultimate authority in earnest prayer, and at last brought to the judgment of those rightly concerned.[19]

My interest is in the potentialities of communal discernment for the political context described in chapter one. My thesis is that this practice carries enormous potential for fostering a faithful approach to radical democratic engagement. More important to me than the conclusions to which it has led (important though these are) is the form of reasoning—indeed, the form of ecclesiology—that it embodies. In short, my interest in communal discernment is not based on an infatuation with decisions, unavoidable though decisions are; nor is my goal to foster a communal decisionism. My interest is in a process that, when practiced well, creates communities and individuals well suited for faithful, democratic involvement.

Finally, before moving to a thicker description of communal discernment, I must clarify my approach to the forthcoming descriptive task. In looking at historical and contemporary Anabaptist

---

19. James Wm. McClendon Jr., "The Concept of Authority: A Baptist View," in *Collected Works, Volume 2*, 125.

theology, I am not arguing that Anabaptists always and everywhere have practiced communal discernment perfectly, or even consistently seen it as crucial to their witness. While I do think there are Anabaptist streams that are more faithful and worthier of emulation than others, the tradition is far too diverse to speak in such simplistic terms.[20] Thus my approach goes beyond "mere" description, and is closer to the task of critical theory as described by Iris Young: "a mode of discourse which projects normative possibilities unrealized but felt in a particular given social reality."[21] That is: my focus is on a significant aspect of the ongoing Anabaptist argument that I think *should* be fostered; if giving and receiving counsel has fallen out of favor in contemporary churches—even if for understandable reasons—this ought not remain the case, as we are living in a time when analogous practices are being sought by political theorists.[22] Thus while communal discernment is a possibility that persistently haunts Anabaptists, I am recommending the practice from out of a complex historical landscape.

Put differently, I am looking for embodiments of communal discernment, not as the only part of Anabaptist history, but as the marker of a *type* of Christianity that has been manifest through time—in McClendon's terms, "a recurrent historical phenomenon, arising in different settings in various periods of history, but repeatedly displaying common features," as well as "considerable variety."[23] Over the course of this investigation, certain images will

---

20. Cf. James M. Stayer, Werner O. Packull, and Klaus Depperman, "Monogenesis versus Polygenesis: The Historical Discussion of Anabaptist Origins," *Mennonite Quarterly Review* 49, no. 2 (April 1975): 83–121.
21. Iris Marion Young, *Justice and the Politics of Difference* (Princeton: Princeton University Press, [1990] 2011), 6.
22. This constitutes a partial response to John Roth: "Even if one assumed that an Anabaptist consensus on hermeneutical principles persisted despite this diversity in theological orientation, a second closely-related question still needs to be asked: namely, how—or if—these principles were ever actually implemented in the life of the congregations and communities they served." John D. Roth, "Community as Conversation: A New Model of Anabaptist Hermeneutics," in *Essays in Anabaptist Theology*, ed. H. Wayne Pipkin (Elkhart, IN: Institute of Mennonite Studies, 1994), 40. My focus is on the *how* of implementation, and my short answer is: in fits and starts.
23. James Wm. McClendon Jr., "Balthasar Hubmaier, Catholic Anabaptist," in *The Collected Works of James Wm. McClendon, Jr., Volume 1*, ed. Ryan Andrew Newson and Andrew C. Wright (Waco, TX: Baylor University Press, 2014), 270.

emerge that might show the contemporary church a path to discernment, and provide material for the ongoing development of a baptist political theology. I turn now to describing communal discernment as a *promise* and *possibility* for the church today, much more than an achievement.[24]

2 Moral Improvisation: Communal Discernment in Outline

When someone says "Anabaptist," different things may come to mind: an emphasis on discipleship, the practice of nonviolence, the courage of martyrs in the face of nasty persecution. Important as these are, my focus is on another, less flashy facet of the Anabaptist witness that is of equal weight: a communal, contextual practice of moral discernment utilized throughout its history. This practice constitutes an important gift Anabaptists have to offer a Western church that continues to emerge from the throes of Christendom, and to Christian political theologians who are working out, perhaps for the first time, what it looks like to provide a faithful Christian witness without the explicit or tacit support of governing authorities. Before we can fully appreciate the ways this practice is suited for a radically democratic politics, we must first get a grasp on the practice itself.

2.1 Anabaptists in Socio-Political Context

Too often, recommendations of Anabaptist practices pay little attention to the political milieu in which they arose, at best minimizing how these elements "might have been shaped by the particular social, political or economic context of its readers."[25] While reducing Anabaptist theology to such factors is a mistake,[26] understanding communal discernment and its contemporary implications does depend in part on understanding this backdrop. Thus I begin by

---

24. Cf. John Howard Yoder, *Revolutionary Christianity: The 1966 South American Lectures*, ed. Paul Martens et al. (Eugene, OR: Cascade, 2011), 16.
25. Roth, "Community," 42.
26. Gerald Biesecker-Mast, *Separation and the Sword in Anabaptist Persuasion: Radical Confessional Rhetoric from Schleitheim to Dordrecht* (Telford, PA: Cascadia, 2006), 59–67.

recounting the socio-political soil in which Anabaptism, and the often-utilized practice of communal discernment, took root. Making these connections must be done carefully, especially since Anabaptists traditionally sought to distance themselves from the violent sixteenth-century insurrections with which they were wrongly associated wholesale. Further, as Arnold Snyder writes, Anabaptists have typically found the detached social histories of the early Reformation, while important, unable to attend to the pastoral and ecclesiological concerns of contemporary congregations and their leaders trying to engender faithful discipleship.[27] Thus attention to this socio-political context must be done with an eye toward this latter end, without reductionism or the pretensions to scholarly neutrality that have sometimes marked such investigations.

In the early sixteenth century, a climate of discontent permeated Europe, in no small part because "the gap between the church's truth claims and the actions of many Christians was in general apparent and sometimes enormous."[28] Indeed, part of Martin Luther's immense popularity is explained by this climate, which predated him and which he harnessed against the political and economic power of the Catholic Church.[29] While in the centuries before Luther many had called for reform, these calls typically remained "within the fold," focusing on the gap between the hierarchy's behavior and claims—as with Desiderius Erasmus, who lambasted Catholic hypocrisy but did not see this as warrant for defection. Whether because of Erasmus's neoplatonism, which assumed there was always a gap between something's appearance and its reality,[30] or simply because the church, even when faulty, remained the institution that taught true doctrine and was entrusted with the sacraments,[31] large-scale revolt was not forthcoming.

---

27. Arnold Snyder, "Beyond Polygenesis: Recovering the Unity and Diversity of Anabaptist Theology," in *Essays in Anabaptist Theology*, 6–8.
28. Brad S. Gregory, *The Unintended Reformation: How a Religious Revolution Secularized Society* (Cambridge, MA: Belknap and Harvard University Press, 2012), 139–40.
29. Michael G. Baylor, *The German Reformation and the Peasants' War: A Brief History with Documents* (Boston: Bedford/St. Martin's, 2012), x, 6–7.
30. Biesecker-Mast, *Separation*, 90.
31. Gregory, *Unintended Reformation*, 85–86.

OUTLINE OF THE PROMISE OF A PRACTICE

While the influence of Reformation preaching and Christian humanism on Anabaptists is widely recognized, seismic shifts in the economic and political mores of the time were also being felt—in the same territories that Anabaptism would spread.[32] These shifts paint the "broader context of social and political upheaval constituted by the commoners' response to the Lutheran Reformation and its rhetoric," and provide "a more thorough picture of the exigencies to which early Anabaptist rhetoric was a response, than does a narrow focus on the conflicts in Zürich."[33] Thus does Michael Baylor speak of "dual rebellions" or "twin upheavals" in the Holy Roman Empire: the one revolving around Luther; the other emerging from longstanding animosity toward feudalism, intensifying after the Reformation began, and leading to the German Peasants' War (1524–1526), "the greatest popular rebellion in European history prior to the French Revolution."[34] Both upheavals occurred during a period of deteriorating economic conditions in which commoners were being stripped of economic autonomy briefly gained during a period of late-medieval prosperity.[35] Further, many princes had grown their "administrative apparatuses" in order to override local customs and impose legal uniformity over what had been, in late-medieval Europe, only loosely unified; such developments were funded through taxes that commoners greatly resented.[36] For Baylor, these changes provide the best explanation for "the mood of malaise and discontent that hung over the cultural life of the empire in the late fifteenth and early sixteenth centuries. Many people shared a growing feeling that the times were out of joint and that a profound societal disturbance was impending"—a mood that was made all the more acute by the

---

32. See the map detailing the spread of the German Peasants' War in James M. Stayer, *The German Peasants' War and Anabaptist Community of Goods* (Montreal: McGill-Queen's University Press, 1991), xi.
33. Biesecker-Mast, *Separation*, 70. This contextualizes the events at Zürich; it does not ignore them.
34. Baylor, *German*, 1.
35. Ibid., 4–5. Gregory, *Unintended Reformation*, 263–64, 367. As Gregory puts it, the view of those in power seemed to be: "Alms for the poor were an imperative; enough alms to alleviate poverty were a perversion"; ibid., 255.
36. Baylor, *German*, 6. For an example of the kind of popular grievances cited against those in power, see the articles of *The "Poor Conrad" Movement in Württemberg 1514*, in Baylor, *German*, 40–42.

awareness of an external danger to the Holy Roman Empire lurking just over the border: the Turks.[37] The psychological impact of this awareness was profound—put in terms from chapter one, sixteenth-century Europe was marked by incompetence; moral categories themselves were in flux, and seemed ill-suited to deal with the possibility that "the entire political and social structure of the Holy Roman Empire—as well as its traditional religio-ecclesiastical system—might be overturned."[38]

The threat represented by these shifts was surely heightened given that at that time, Europe was "enchanted," in Charles Taylor's terms: Western society had yet to move away from a "naive supernaturalism" in which "it was virtually impossible not to believe in God."[39] Relatedly, humans were not viewed as sharply bounded, "buffered" selves with an impermeable line separating an "inner" self from the "outer" world, but "porous" and susceptible to being affected by various forces in the universe.[40] Communities (whether towns, states, or empires) were similarly conceptualized as vulnerable to outside spiritual forces that could manifest themselves concretely—such as the Turks—and *as a whole* had to employ "good magic" to protect against such dangers. "Heresy," then, was no personal matter; it threatened the efficacy of a community's defenses: "The deviancy of some would call down punishment on all."[41] Thus each religio-political shift potentially threatened society's very existence; to live amidst such changes was to live in precarious times—and made statements like the following particularly subversive: "Therefore it is not wholly out of place to consider whether it would now be desirable for the Turks to be lords over us, in the hope that they would allow the gospel to be preached to us freely and without hindrance."[42]

As this sense of discontent increased in the wake of the "economic,

---

37. Baylor, *German*, 6–7.
38. Ibid., 3.
39. Charles Taylor, *A Secular Age* (Cambridge, MA: Belknap and Harvard University Press, 2007), 3.
40. Ibid., 33–39.
41. Ibid., 42.
42. *To the Assembly of the Common Peasantry* May 1525, in Michael G. Baylor, ed., *The Radical Reformation* (Cambridge: Cambridge University Press, 1991), 119–20.

social, political, and religious" transitions of early sixteenth-century Europe, including the move from craft to capitalistic modes of production,[43] several social revolts bubbled up, especially in territories near Switzerland—site of a successful rebellion against the Habsburgs and the earliest Anabaptist congregations.[44] From 1502 to 1517, these groups joined forces under the name *Bundschuh* (bound shoe), a common symbol of the peasantry, and expressed deep misgivings with serfdom and proto-capitalism, articulating a communal, egalitarian vision that prompted landlords to defend the legitimacy of their lordship.[45] By 1521, Luther had developed his doctrine of *sola fide*, had been excommunicated, and had appeared before the assembled estates at the Diet of Worms. As Biesecker-Mast puts it, Luther opened up new "discursive possibilities" among commoners, which led to more explicit and increasingly violent calls for political reform at least among some of his readers,[46] and which horrified Luther. Luther wanted to limit his reforms to the "religious" hierarchy, delineated from the political, but others refused this distinction.[47] From 1521 to 1525, "localized revivalist movements outran the ability of Luther or anyone else to control or restrain them," extending and radicalizing the rejection of clerics, authority, and the papacy such that mud was thrown at priests, sermons interrupted, and churches raided to destroy sacred images.[48] Zwingli argued that the gospel indeed had political implications, but that such revolutionary changes needed to be performed through the "proper agency," meaning the governing authority of the province (so in Zürich, the city council), except as an absolute last resort.[49] Thomas Müntzer went the other way, supporting violent rebellion against unjust rulers. And as we shall see, the Swiss Anabaptists disagreed with them all: against Luther, the gospel was

---

43. Biesecker-Mast, *Separation*, 71. Cf. Gregory, *Unintended Reformation*, ch. 5.
44. Baylor, *German*, 8.
45. Biesecker-Mast, *Separation*, 72.
46. Ibid., 81.
47. Those who refused this delineation were by no means unified in what its refusal *meant*, as is illustrated by the fact that both Zwingli and the revolutionary Müntzer refused it. For an excerpt of Zwingli's views, see Huldrych Zwingli, *The Sixty-Seven Articles* 1523, in Baylor, *German*, 61–65.
48. Baylor, *German*, 10–11.
49. Ibid., 13; cf. Zwingli, *Sixty-Seven Articles*, 61–65.

politically weighty; against Müntzer, they eschewed violence; and against Zwingli, governing agencies had no final say in matters of Christian faithfulness.[50]

Eventually, this unrest coalesced into the Peasants' War, which did not exclusively involve peasants, was not concerned with a national Germany, and did not constitute much of a war, given that it was not meant as an act of war by those who started it and given that it was more a one-sided slaughter.[51] The Peasants' War has no precise beginning, but evolved from a series of defiant acts from workers who refused to do agricultural work for meager pay; refused to pay labor dues and tithes (on one occasion burning the tithes in fields rather than paying them); and listed their grievances from spring to the fall of 1524.[52] In September 1524 in Mühlhausen a violent rebellion emerged that attempted to oust the city council in favor of a government that would rule in accordance with divine justice (meaning that it would treat peasants equitably), and which was spurred on in part by Müntzer's preaching, who had no issues with violence for a just cause: "Beloved ones, do not offer us any stale posturing about how the power of God should do it without your application of the sword. Otherwise, may the sword rust away in its scabbard on you."[53] As it progressed, the rebelling peasants merged "old sociopolitical tensions with new Reformation ideals,"[54] forming a deeply "religious" movement both in their demands and their responses to critics like Luther. The demands found in the "Twelve Articles of the Upper Swabian Peasants," for instance, "would have restructured landlord-tenant relations, eliminated all the disabilities of serfdom, and radically shifted the balance of political power and ecclesiastical control away from the lords and prelates in favor of the local community."[55] And the anonymous "To the Assembly of the Common Peasantry," unique only in its eloquence, responded to Luther's "Admonition to Peace" and

---

50. Biesecker-Mast, *Separation*, 88–89.
51. Stayer, *German Peasants' War*, 20; Baylor, *German*, 28.
52. Baylor, *German*, 15.
53. Thomas Müntzer, *Sermon to the Princes 1524*, in Baylor, *German*, 72.
54. Baylor, *German*, 16.
55. Ibid., 22.

precipitated his vitriolic "Against the Murdering and Robbing Hordes of Peasants," stating:

> May God, in his justice, not tolerate the terrible Babylonian captivity in which we poor people are driven to mow the lords' meadows, to make hay, to cultivate the fields, to sow flax in them, to cut it, comb it, heat it, wash it, pound it, spin it—yes, even to sew their underpants on their arses. . . . They tax and tear out the marrow of the poor people's bones, and we have to pay interest on that![56]

Many were sympathetic with the cause, but after the turn to violence those uneasy with that strategy were marginalized from the struggle. Best described as a protest movement that was prepared to fight,[57] fight they did, and it spread rapidly from 1524 into 1525, with regional factions that remained in encouraging communication with one another. Even as late as March 1525, the revolt was basically a series of demonstrations voicing grievances and destroying property.[58] Once imperial forces finally mobilized to engage the military peasant-bands, full-scale fighting commenced, and they were easily squashed.

My goal in recounting this history is to examine the context from which Anabaptism or proto-Anabaptism emerged, and in which communal discernment was recommended with gusto. These events forced choices on all involved. Luther was appalled at the application of his ideas, became entrenched in his "two kingdom" political theology, and gloated over the peasants' defeat and harsh repression.[59] For Luther, rebels flouted all authority in violation of Romans 13, and killing them was akin to killing a mad dog.[60] The governing authorities grew more vigilant, leading to a "protracted period of more conservative, orderly, and hierarchically directed Reformation," in which it was imperative to deploy "the power of the state to go after religious dissidents and deviants,"[61] lest another revolt occur. Only

---

56. *To the Assembly*, 108.
57. Stayer, *German Peasants' War*, 21.
58. Baylor, *German*, 18–20.
59. Martin Luther, *An Open Letter on the Harsh Book against the Peasants*, in Baylor, *German*, 137–40.
60. Martin Luther, *Against the Murdering and Robbing Hordes of Peasants*, in Baylor, *German*, 131. Conversely, the peasants claimed they were shown "*less* pity than a mad dog"; *To the Assembly*, 109.
61. Baylor, *German*, 30.

carefully controlled reform would be allowed: reform that challenged Rome but allowed other princes to retain unquestioned power.[62]

Anabaptists had been broadly sympathetic with the cause, agreeing that reform was needed of all social hierarchies, not just the magisterium,[63] and while some Anabaptists took up arms in the peasants' fight, these instances were rare. In any case, in the wake of the revolt's failure, Anabaptists continued to resist ecclesiastical *and* imperial rule in their own, quieter ways. Baylor goes so far as to argue that Anabaptists constituted "a dissenting minority [that] sought to continue the communal and popular ideals of the early Reformation and the Peasants' War," symbolized by their rejection of established churches and the subversive act of adult baptism.[64] Anabaptists were never homogenous, and some would condone violence again (during the Münster rebellion, for instance, or in the writings of Balthasar Hubmaier), but these remained outliers. Mostly, Anabaptists supported neither violence nor quietism, but a resistance from below, utilizing communal discernment as a way to know what to do next in muddied waters while remaining open to God's guidance. Put differently, the Protestant Reformation, Renaissance humanism, and popular unrest provided the "discursive horizon encountered by Anabaptists."[65] My focus now turns to a promising way that Anabaptists faced this horizon.

2.2 Communalism

"Master Huldrych! You have no authority to place the decision in Milords' hands, for the decision is already made: the Spirit of God decides. If therefore Milords were to discern and decide anything that is contrary to God's decision, I will ask Christ for his Spirit and will

---

62. Biesecker-Mast, *Separation*, 71.
63. Ibid., 259n8.
64. Baylor, *German*, 30. Stayer provides substantial evidence that "the same persons were participants in the Peasants' War and Anabaptists," and thus that the Anabaptists constituted "the logical continuation of the social Gospel of the Reformation . . . , a very radical, albeit non-violent, expression of the commoners' Reformation during and after the suppression of the Peasants' War"; Stayer, *German Peasants' War*, 7. Cf. ibid., ch. 3.
65. Biesecker-Mast, *Separation*, 81.

teach and act against it."⁶⁶ Simon Stumpf's bold rejoinder to Zwingli in a disputation before the Zürich City Council in October 1523 represents one of the earliest articulations of an Anabaptist moral vision that from then on would find recurrent expression, if in fits and starts. Whether or not it marks the precise origin of Anabaptism, the exchange encapsulates a deep difference between two pictures emerging within the aforementioned discursive horizon. While Luther, Zwingli, and Anabaptists all echoed the Reformation slogan of *sola scriptura* as the basis for Christian morality, each used this language in different ways. Luther, for example, emphasized scripture's power to free the individual conscience for dutiful servanthood to all. Zwingli, and Heinrich Bullinger after him, emphasized scripture's role in forming the holy commonwealth on earth, which included all citizens in a given region. Anabaptists were unique in their radically Christocentric interpretation of scripture whose meaning was to be discerned in the context of the local community, distinct from the auspices of governing authorities.⁶⁷ To organize my examination of this approach, I will follow the Zürich disputation closely (though not exclusively) —not as the origin or only expression of Anabaptism, but as a clear exemplification of the "images" I wish to highlight for contemporary consideration. These images, which will organize the rest of this section, are *communalism, humility*, and *contextualism*.

So to begin, the dispute between Stumpf and Zwingli reflected a difference in prioritization at a very basic level: the Swiss Brethren believed that a decision reached by the local community of disciples trumped any other authority, including that of the Zürich city council. To be sure, Stumpf's claim that Zwingli had "no authority to place the decision in Milords' hands" because "the Spirit of God decides" could be challenged by asking, "And how do you know that the Spirit of God

---

66. "The Second Zürich Disputation," in *The Sources of Swiss Anabaptism*, ed. Leland Harder (Scottdale, PA: Herald, 1985), 242. Portions of what follows are significantly revised from Ryan Andrew Newson, "Ethics as Improvisation: Anabaptist Communal Discernment as Method," *Mennonite Quarterly Review* 87 (April 2013): 187–205.
67. Thus Gregory's list of the many supporters of *sola scriptura* obscures more than it illuminates, because the phrase was used in such different ways; cf. Gregory, *Unintended*, 87–88. Cf. John Howard Yoder, "The Hermeneutics of the Anabaptists," *Mennonite Quarterly Review* 41 (October 1967): 291–308.

has so decided?" The answer would neither come from an immediate, idiosyncratic revelation of the Holy Spirit, nor from an isolated appeal to scripture by the solitary individual, though everyone at the disputation agreed that scripture was the final authority. Although the debate did center on what scripture taught, the issue between Stumpf and Zwingli was not scripture per se.[68] Rather, the debate was about how one discerned the Word (or Spirit) of God, the proper pace of reform, and who got the final say in making this decision.

Although the 1523 exchange unfolded just before a colorful variety of Anabaptist congregations began to spring up in Switzerland, southwest Germany, and Moravia in the wake of the Peasants' War, one feature that united these radical congregations was implicit in Stumpf's response: namely, their readiness to disobey the secular authorities when they conflicted with what the congregation understood to be taught in scripture. Indeed, this helps explain why both Conrad Grebel and Zwingli looked back on these Zürich disputations as revealing a much deeper rupture between the two groups, long before anyone had been "re-baptized" or made any pronouncements concerning the sword.[69]

Thus when these same Swiss radicals amid increasing political pressure from the Zürich council decided to write a letter to Thomas Müntzer less than a year later (around the start of the Peasants' War), it is not surprising to find it framed in the first-person plural. After listing ways Christians have neglected the witness of Jesus in the past, Grebel writes,

> *We* too have been in this total error.... But after *we* also took up Scripture and examined it on a great many issues, *we* became better informed, and *we* discovered the pastors' great and damaging deficiencies, and *ours* as well. *We* discovered that *we* do not ask God every day, seriously and with constant signs, to lead *us* from the destruction of every godly way and out of human abominations, and to the true faith and practices of God.[70]

---

68. This is the mistake of many scholars who argue that a literalist biblicism is the primary marker of Anabaptism: if nothing else, it amounts to a virtual denial of hermeneutics; cf. Roth, "Community," 41–42.
69. "Grebel to Vadian, Zürich, December 18, 1523," in *Sources*, 275–76; Harder, *Sources*, 475.
70. Conrad Grebel, *Letter to Thomas Müntzer*, in *Radical Reformation*, 37. Emphasis added.

OUTLINE OF THE PROMISE OF A PRACTICE

It is evident from this letter that these Christians took for granted a high view of scripture, and already prioritized the New Testament over the Old in correcting Müntzer's use of the sword.[71] But equally important is the practice that led to these convictions: taking up scripture together as a community of committed disciples. These men and women arrived at their convictions regarding baptism and the nature of Christian discipleship by meeting, praying, and studying scripture together in one another's homes; and they agreed that their conclusions could not be foisted upon the unknowing or unwilling.[72] It was a process of communal discernment that prompted the Swiss Brethren's decision to disobey the Zürich council's decree to baptize their children, and also provided the courage necessary to disobey such an order.[73] And two years later, a similar corporate gathering produced the articles recorded by Michael Sattler as the "Brotherly Union," better known as the Schleitheim Confession.

Communal discernment, expressed in different ways and with different emphases, continued to mark the Anabaptist movement as it sprang up in other contexts. Consider, for example, the writings of Pilgram Marpeck. Marpeck expressed great hesitancy about "the ban" (the practice of disciplining errant members of the congregation, inspired by Matthew 18:15-20 and which I consider in chapter three), emphasizing instead the unity that comes only through the Spirit of God. Still, Marpeck continued to assume that the Spirit of God is accessible to the individual primarily in the gathered community. "The true saints of God and children of Christ," he wrote, "are those whose ruler is the Holy Spirit in the Word of truth. *Where two or three are*

---

71. William Estep, *The Anabaptist Story: An Introduction to Sixteenth-Century Anabaptism*, 3rd ed. (Grand Rapids: Eerdmans, [1975] 1996), 41–42. This prioritization is common among Anabaptists; see ibid., 126, 193–96; Pilgram Marpeck, "The Admonition of 1542," in *The Writings of Pilgram Marpeck*, trans. and ed. William Klassen and Walter Klassen (Scottdale, PA: Herald, 1978), 225.
72. Estep, *Anabaptist*, 19. Such was Hubmaier's argument about baptism *and* the use of coercion in matters of faith; see Hubmaier, "On Heretics and Those Who Burn Them," in *Balthasar Hubmaier*, trans. and ed. H. Wayne Pipkin and John H. Yoder (Scottdale, PA: Herald, 1989), articles 16, 22.
73. Cf. "The First Believer's Baptism in Switzerland, Zürich, January 21, 1525," in Harder, *Sources*, 342. Note that these events transpired in the middle of the Peasants' War; indeed, baptism carried real political significance in this context. Because infant baptism had become a sign of belonging to Christendom, to "re-baptize" signified a refusal of this conflation, as well as the authority of the civil rulers in question.

gathered in His name, He is among them . . . . I pray God my heavenly Father that He will not allow me to be separated from such a gathering and fellowship of the Holy Spirit."[74] Marpeck assumed that discernment would be communal; his concern was simply that it be done in the right spirit—with patience, and without immediate threat of exclusion.[75]

Emphasizing the community as the locus of moral discernment has consistently recurred among Anabaptist theologians, such that it would seem to be a deep part of Anabaptist ecclesiology—a haunting possibility even when neglected—and so basic that it can go unnoticed. In a society marked by the emergence and glorification of the sovereign individual, who *is* because he thinks, an emphasis on community as the place where discernment is won will at best appear odd, if not downright dangerous.

2.3 Humility

Concomitant with this communalism is a recognition that every judgment by the gathered community should be held with a degree of humility. While Anabaptists have not hesitated to make moral pronouncements to each other and to the world, in the best of cases they have remembered that what has been communally discerned is always open to correction, and thus to cease communication with one another would be to cut off any means of correcting or being corrected by the sister or brother in Christ.

On the surface, it may appear that such epistemological humility was altogether lacking in the Stumpf and Zwingli dispute. After all, Stumpf was quite bold to say that the Spirit of God *had* decided over the matter of the Lord's Supper. And yet Stumpf and the rest of the Swiss Brethren were still there, arguing their case before the city council and before a man who was gradually becoming more enemy than friend. The fact that these soon-to-be-labeled Anabaptists continued to make their case in Zürich, even after they were banned from doing so,[76] suggests both

---

74. Pilgram Marpeck, "Judgment and Decision," in *Writings of Pilgram*, 331-32. Emphasis added.
75. See ibid., 333. For a comparison of Marpeck's method of moral discernment to that of Ignatius of Loyola and Jonathan Edwards, see Nancey Murphy, *Theology in the Age of Scientific Reasoning* (Ithaca, NY: Cornell University Press, 1990), 148-50.

OUTLINE OF THE PROMISE OF A PRACTICE

a strong missional zeal as well as a patient desire to continue the conversation, almost always framed with a desire for correction if it was based on scripture. Similarly, the proto-Anabaptists who wrote to Müntzer were not only exhorting him to adopt their position on liturgy and violence; they were also reaching out to a potential brother. To be sure, they did not mince words about what they had discerned, but they also clearly asked for correction if it could be shown that they were in error: "if we are not right about it, then teach us what is better."[77] They were not *simply* admonishing Müntzer: they were also seeking to "create a Christian community with the help of Christ and his rule."[78] It had seemed good to the Holy Spirit and to them (cf. Acts 15:28) that the sword was antithetical to Christian discipleship, even in service to a just cause like peasant mistreatment; if they were to be convinced otherwise, these young reformers knew that this would be discerned in the context of *continued* communal discernment.

This character of humble conviction cannot be equated with an easy trust in discussion itself, but arises specifically from the theological conviction that "'the Spirit would be granted to those who assembled in the name of Christ' (Matthew 18:20). The dialogue that [sixteenth-century Anabaptists] demanded was not called a discussion, but rather, a community."[79] Following the early Zwingli, these Anabaptists sincerely believed that the Spirit would lead them to unanimity in crucial matters of discernment, and that if such agreement had not been reached, it was because they had not yet "heard" one another. Thus if the will of God was to be discerned at all, it was crucial to continue talking, not because dialogue itself was salvific, but because it was by way of this practice that issues of moment for the ongoing life of God's people were addressed, "brought under mutual study in the light of all the scripture and all experience, committed to ultimate authority

---

76. "Council Decree Against the Anabaptists, Zürich, January 21, 1525," in Harder, *Sources,* 338. This letter betrays the interesting fact that the Swiss Brethren did not initially "separate themselves," but were separated *from:* the initial split was made not by the "sectarian" Anabaptists, but the magisterial reformers!
77. Grebel, *Letter to Thomas Müntzer,* 40.
78. Ibid., 42. This *contra* Estep, *Anabaptist,* 41.
79. John Howard Yoder, *Anabaptism and Reformation in Switzerland: An Historical and Theological Analysis of the Dialogues Between Anabaptists and Reformers* (Kitchener, ON: Pandora, 2004), 223.

in earnest prayer, and at last brought to the judgement of those rightly concerned."[80]

This combination of communal discernment and humility not only accounts for why early Anabaptists were so persistent in communicating with their leaders, their neighbors, and each other in ways that could not help but annoy the authorities—and one another—but it also helps explain the diversity that marked Anabaptism as it emerged outside of Switzerland. Anabaptists vehemently disagreed with each other on all manner of issues, especially as the movement emerged in new contexts. In the first forty years after 1525, for example, Anabaptists engaged in many debates concerning the use of coercive force. Most congregations were convinced that it was wrong to take up the sword at any time, a view that became the near-unanimous opinion of Anabaptists and one of their distinguishing features. But this was not the initial consensus. Balthasar Hubmaier advocated a position on the sword that resembled Zwingli's "real politic" position, according to which a Christian could legitimately serve in government, and in that capacity use coercive force.[81] Hans Hut, echoing Müntzer, argued that the sword could be used by the godly to help usher in the apocalypse, but only after this had been initiated *by God* through the invasion of the Turks.[82] In the Netherlands, Melchior Hoffman opposed Christian violence, but welcomed its use by the authorities, and crafted violent eschatological visions that made fertile ground for revolutionaries such as the followers of Jan van Leyden at Münster and the later Batenbergers.[83] And in 1568 the Waterlanders, who split off from the more conservative Mennonites, provided financial support for the war effort of the Prince of Orange.[84] Amidst these disagreements, one is hard-pressed to find an Anabaptist who says that these differences ought to

---

80. McClendon, "Concept of Authority," 125.
81. Hubmaier, "On Heretics," Article 22, and "On the Sword," in Pipkin and Yoder, *Balthasar*, 492–523. Hubmaier's position is truly unique among Anabaptists; James M. Stayer, *Anabaptists and the Sword*, rev. ed. (Lawrence, KS: Coronado, [1972] 1976), 336–37.
82. Estep, *Anabaptist*, 98, 118–19; Stayer, *Anabaptists and the Sword*, 190.
83. Estep, *Anabaptist*, 154–56; Stayer, *Anabaptists and the Sword*, 205.
84. Estep, *Anabaptist*, 176.

be forsaken for the sake of "unity." Rather, they seemed to intuitively sense that clarifying moral convictions came by way of inter- and intra-communal discernment, and in this process a diversity of opinion was necessarily "allowed" to persist as communities worked out the implications of the gospel over time.[85]

This makes sense if one regards traditions not as uniform monoliths, but rather ongoing arguments extended through time, with their own set of core convictions and authoritative texts that structure the argument.[86] Indeed, for Alasdair MacIntyre, any agreements within a community will necessarily be forged through conflict with those inside and outside the argument. Or as McClendon put it, "Theology is the very means by which those in one context encounter those of others for mutual witness and critical correction."[87] So especially for a tradition marked by communal discernment, some level of diversity is to be expected as core convictions are hammered out by each generation and within shifting cultural contexts. That the nonviolent position of Schleitheim was neither immediately articulated in 1525, nor accepted by all Anabaptists until around 1565, is but the consequence of a commitment to communal discernment.[88]

In light of this argument that communal discernment and epistemological humility are central characteristics of the Anabaptist movement, it might appear as if another persistent Anabaptist motif—an understanding of church discipline that can resort to the exclusion of individuals from fellowship—would be the very antithesis of these qualities. However, this is not necessarily the case, if "the ban" is considered within the preceding framework. First, despite its abuses, the practice of the ban is consistent with a humble posture of communal discernment in the fact that expressions of disagreement

---

85. Similarly, Snyder writes that understanding the diversity and unity of the Anabaptist movement requires recognizing that development "took place by means of much painful dialogue and disagreement, as well as consensus and schism, throughout the sixteenth century and beyond"; Snyder, "Beyond Polygenesis," 9.

86. Alasdair MacIntyre, *Whose Justice? Which Rationality?* (Notre Dame: University of Notre Dame Press, 1988), 12.

87. James Wm. McClendon Jr., *Ethics: Systematic Theology, Volume 1*, rev. ed. (Nashville: Abingdon, [1986] 2002), 35.

88. Stayer, *Anabaptists and the Sword*, 117.

never warrant a person's physical torture or death. While this may seem like a pretty low bar, authorities in sixteenth-century Europe (as Anabaptists knew well) were quite willing to torture and kill as a form of discipline. Indeed, any refusal of coercive forms of discipline implied that ultimate judgment belonged to God, who alone could sort the wheat from the tares—a position accepted by few sixteenth-century political or ecclesial authorities.[89] And second, the ban was supposed to have a redemptive intention to name and correct a divide that, descriptively speaking, had already occurred. That is, rightly understood, the ban was to be exercised only when a person or group was no longer willing to submit to the process of communal discernment. We all "may err," as Hubmaier confessed,[90] but if we cease "asking constantly for instruction" from a common authority—in this case, the community of disciples—at that point we have functionally separated from each another, and this should be named as such. None of this is to deny that the practice can be wildly misused, and it certainly needs careful explication if it is to be utilized, as I do in the following chapter. Nevertheless, even Anabaptists like Marpeck who warned against its potential misuse did not argue against "the ban" per se, but only its ungraceful abuse.[91]

2.4 Contextualism

Finally, communal discernment carries a recognition that moral knowledge is necessarily culturally apprehended and situated, and thus requires continual reassessment by a community that is, to some degree, separate from the world. Closely related to a conception of revelation as historical, this "Anabaptist contextualism" has been mostly implicit throughout its history, but is evident once one begins to look for it.

Since the beginnings of the movement, Anabaptists have had

---

89. See Hubmaier, "On Heretics," articles 9, 13.
90. Balthasar Hubmaier, "The Third Appeal to the Honorable Council of Schaffhausen," in *Balthasar Hubmaier*, 44.
91. For Marpeck's list of people, groups, and activities he would avoid, see Pilgram Marpeck, "Judgment and Decision," in *Writings of Pilgram*, 309–61.

strained relationships with the dominant culture, so much so that Stayer concluded, "if the Anabaptists were anything, they were illegitimate."[92] Indeed, while explicit in the fourth article of the Schleitheim Confession, some form of separation is as old as Anabaptism itself since it is implicit in the very act of "rebaptism." Undergoing that ritual not only marked oneself as distinct from society at large, but was a provocative judgment about the church and the civil authorities as constituted. Despite categorical claims about separation, however, in practice Anabaptists have as often sought cultural transformation as withdrawal. The meaning of their rhetoric becomes apparent by their actions, and although many Anabaptists drifted toward true sectarianism as time went by, many others qualified separation to the extent necessary to be formed into Christ-likeness and thus faithfully proclaim the gospel to the world.[93] And although it is understandable that such stark rhetoric would be misunderstood, the real goal—as Schleitheim proclaimed—was to avoid *fellowship* with evil.[94]

Instead, providing an answer to the question "To what extent should we be separate?" was itself a matter of communal discernment with the answer necessarily changing from generation to generation and culture to culture, depending on what the authorities were asking of their subjects. Thus, for example, Hans Denck argued that a Christian is not *automatically* precluded from serving in governmental leadership; at the same time, Denck's commitment to a form of Christian nonviolence led him to say that it was probably impossible to be simultaneously a faithful disciple and avoid being quickly removed from office.[95] In a context slightly different from that of Sattler, Denck showed that the answer to some moral questions could change without being a manifestation of incoherence.

---

92. Stayer, *Anabaptists and the Sword*, 337.
93. For an account of the shift toward "transformational" rhetoric, see Ervin R. Stutzman, *From Nonresistance to Justice: The Transformation of Mennonite Church Peace Rhetoric, 1908-2008* (Scottdale, PA: Herald, 2011).
94. "Schleitheim Confession," 37. My claim that "separation" is not synonymous with apolitical "withdrawal," but is a matter of sussing out the right kind of inhabitation, is drawn from Biesecker-Mast, *Separation*, 30.
95. Stayer, *Anabaptists and the Sword*, 149.

McClendon echoed this contextualism when he argued that Christian theology always issues from particular communities seeking to proclaim the gospel in some particular place and time; as such, there is a God-given and God-desired pluralism in moral discernment.[96] This, of course, is not to say that we should only speak to the world in hushed tones, or proclaim the gospel with a disclaimer. It is the harder work of *gospel* contextualism, of striving to be a faithful church without running away from the world. In order to do this work, Christian communities must be aware of the cultural concepts available to work with in order to say in each new context that "Jesus is Lord" without simply denouncing such concepts as wrong through and through.[97] Put differently, Christian communities should seek to express the "grammar" inherent within the confession, "Jesus is Lord," with whatever vocabulary is available.[98]

Anabaptists have a tradition of doing this culturally aware, transformative work, and have typically been unafraid to engage the debates of their day, pointing out where they saw disagreements that represented deeper fissures. Thus, for example, while the debate between Stumpf and Zwingli appeared to be over the Lord's Supper, Zwingli's unwillingness to disobey the city council in order to alter its observance "to conform to the Scriptures" revealed a deeper rift between the two. The young Anabaptists sensed that at that moment in time, the debate was about more than just the Lord's Supper. Similarly, advocacy for adult baptism—the conviction Anabaptists were most closely identified with—was a result of the distinctive Anabaptist ecclesiology that presupposed the church to be constituted by committed believers who consciously submitted to the rule of Christ, rather than all people born within a certain territory. In that time and place, to compromise on baptism was to compromise everything, a

---

96. James Wm. McClendon Jr., *Doctrine: Systematic Theology, Volume 2* (Nashville: Abingdon, 1994), 31, 42–44; McClendon, *Ethics*, 35.
97. Cf. John Howard Yoder, *Preface to Theology: Christology and Theological Method* (Grand Rapids: Brazos, 2002), 258; and John Howard Yoder, *The Priestly Kingdom: Social Ethics as Gospel* (Notre Dame: University of Notre Dame Press, 1984), 46–62.
98. McClendon, *Doctrine*, 108.

conviction that helps explain the viciousness with which Anabaptists were killed.

To summarize, in this section I have highlighted a practice that attempts to communally discern the will of God so that groups of disciples may know (sustainably and imperfectly) and proclaim (humbly) what "walking in the resurrection" entails. Once recognized, this practice provides a key to understanding some of the more well-known aspects of the Anabaptist movement, including separation from the world, adult baptism, the ban, and rejection of the sword. This unique combination of communalism, humility, contextualism, and boldness in proclamation is nicely summarized in the cover letter of the Schleitheim Confession: "Now that you have abundantly understood the will of God *as revealed through us at this time,* you *must* fulfill this will, now known, persistently and unswervingly."[99] Faithfully appropriating this tradition today does not entail adopting every position held by past Anabaptists—a move that would be impossible given the diversity of opinion among Anabaptists themselves on all manner of issues. Instead, it means employing a similar approach to moral reasoning in the variety of contexts in which we find ourselves. The approach assumes that the Jesus witnessed to in the Gospels is normative for all of life, and that the community of committed disciples has the final say in discerning the normativity of theological or ethical claims, regardless of what governing authorities or even cultural customs say otherwise. To faithfully inherit this tradition is to begin a process that cannot be completed by the exegete or the ethicist sitting alone in an office.

3 Competence without Certainty

With the haunting promise of communal discernment thus laid out, I will now begin to unpack how this practice holds potential for aiding in the articulation of a robust baptist political theology. The beginnings of this potential are best seen by correlating communal discernment (and

---

99. "Schleitheim Confession," 42–43. Emphasis added.

the socio-political context in which it was reclaimed) with the political context described in chapter one. There, in the face of widespread political incompetence, we saw that many radical democrats recognized the need for "practices of dialogue that cultivate the orientations, disorientations, virtues, and knowledges that are necessary not only for identifying and resisting the worst but also for struggling with others toward visions of what might be better."[100] Similarly, Catholic theologian William Cavanaugh argues both that practices like hospitality and the Eucharist constitute the church as a "distinctive public body," and that a significant response to neoliberalism by churches and others alike "would be creating spaces in which alternative stories about material goods are told, and alternative forms of economics are made possible."[101] Combining these concerns one reaches the question: What kind of "distinctive public body" does the practice of communal discernment help create? What about its right practice might engender "orientations necessary for struggling with others toward visions of what might be better"? And crucially, what dangers lurk within and behind its practice?

These questions are complex, and will occupy me for the remainder of this book. However, even at this stage of the argument it is important to assess how the "culture" created by communal discernment, and how the type of competence it engenders in communities and individuals alike, is precisely of the sort needed in our context. Communal discernment offers no guarantees of rectitude—indeed, this is a possible concern to raise about its use ("Don't we need more than *this*?")—but in my view, it is precisely this capacity to garner moral competence without pretensions to certainty that make it fit so well in a milieu marked inescapably by incompetence. Communal discernment does not try to get us above this fray or carve out a space free from this context, but instead fosters a means of going on faithfully within it. Put differently, in its

---

100. Coles, *Beyond*, 39.
101. William T. Cavanaugh, *Theopolitical Imagination* (London: T&T Clark, 2002), 90, 94.

communality, humility, and contextuality, communal discernment creates what Sheldon Wolin calls a politics of tending.

3.1 Incompetence and Overconfidence

Recall from chapter one a few of the factors that have coalesced into the forms of power that overwhelm our ability to formulate coherent response: The drive to efficiently "organize" basic societal elements (and, we could add, picturing society in terms of divisible "elements" in the first place); the erosion of the kind of "give and take" that typically happened at the local, "associational" level; and the ramification of these same forces into ephemeral, transnational entities concerned with the maximization of commerce through a less-complex, more manipulable populace. These factors form a dialectic wherein people vacillate between hope in individuals (or perhaps, slightly more broadly, the bonds of the "family unit") to resist the forces that impinge on every facet of our lives—"I am the master of my fate; I am the captain of my soul"—and acquiescence to the inevitability of these forces doing their organizational work on bodies, clandestinely manifest in cosmopolitan celebrations of these lines now being transnational in character. Communal discernment, as I see it, stands in fruitful tension with both tendencies.

On the one hand, the ebbing away of civic and specifically religious "associations" from public import has led to a degree of isolation from one another such that the locus for anything like political competence or "discernment" is atomized, privatized, and scattered. Put in terms popularized by Robert Bellah, the result has been an increased self-absorption and disaffiliation from communities, particularly religious communities. Bellah's famous example of this tendency is a woman named Sheila Larson who named her religion after herself ("Sheilaism").[102] Not only will such a hyper-individualized faith almost inevitably issue in a thin collection of aphorisms like "Love yourself" and "Take care of each other," and not only does it suggest "the logical

---

102. Robert N. Bellah et al., *Habits of the Heart: Individualism and Commitment in American Life* (Berkeley: University of California Press, [1985] 2007), 220–21.

possibility of over 220 million American religions, one for each of us,"[103] but from the perspective of moral discernment, it assumes that each person is individually competent to discern how best to "go on" in the face of forces that seek to direct one's will. The *individual* becomes the locus of discernment, rather than any community. From the perspective of the previous chapter, this sort of individualistic approach to discernment will not be nearly robust enough to foster the sorts of "orientations" needed to gain competence; in fact, the delimitation of discernment to such an individualized scope is likely but another, and perhaps the ultimate, expression of the aforementioned modern generic individualism that helped create the degree of incompetence it now hopes to combat.

On the other hand, recall that once citizens are isolated in this way, the goal of the "politics of intending" is to efficiently streamline, organize, and manage individual agencies such that our abilities to assemble and work toward goods shared in common are greatly diminished: "intenders" like Alexander Hamilton were wary of democracy. Because individuals were viewed as the same for all relevant purposes, a kind of monoculture was envisioned wherein attention to difference and diversity in a place was at best unimportant, if not downright denigrated, deemed inimical to more ultimate political goods. At this point in the argument, a tempting if hackneyed response is to say that we now live in an increasingly global, interconnected world that is not so tightly bound by the nation-state, and that therefore these concerns are no longer relevant. But the fact remains that a cosmopolitan picture of the world is in large part the extension, maturation, and perfection of tendencies learned from modern modes of power. The respect for difference so championed too often remains superficial at best, and at worst is the subtle imposition of a particular way of life—white, affluent, American—causing Coles, as we saw, to remark that globalization is but the "latest form of neocolonialism."[104] Interestingly, insofar as this habit of thought

---

103. Ibid., 221.
104. Coles, *Beyond*, 44.

inspires one to "pick and choose" one's identity from a variety of distilled "cultures," it actually cannot help but reinforce, even intensify, the same drive that lies behind Sheilaism.[105]

The desire for competence represented by these options is not wrong. In the face of tectonic shifts in the contemporary socio-political landscape, *some* way forward needs to be found—shifts, by the way, that echo those experienced in sixteenth-century Germany. In both, large groups of ordinary people struggle to find a sense of political agency and justice amidst emerging social structures; in both, people are spurred on by new philosophical and theological ideas; and in both, a sense of interconnectedness has come through technological advance. Even so, we must remain careful in two respects. First, in looking for political competence we must avoid recommendations that would ultimately reinforce tendencies that created the problem in the first place, or else stand as renewed expressions of that very incompetence. And second, we must be careful that in combatting incompetence we do not create the opposite problem: an *overconfidence* in which one is so completely at home in one's communal tradition that one grows deaf to those outside of it, or even denies the importance of remaining receptive to such voices at all.[106] This fear assumes that we need fully traditioned practices of various kinds in order to foster the politics of tending that Wolin so eloquently articulated—the competence that comes from knowing a place and knowing it well. It simply adds that too much "competence" may ironically reinscribe the very threat it sought to combat, where we are isolated from one another, not within traditions of our own making (Sheilaism), but within communities of overconfidence, certain that we have everything figured out. In the current political landscape, many Christians—with others—ache for competence; in seeking it out we must take care not to repeat or reinforce habits of thought that are worse than, or symptomatic of, the disease.

---

105. On this culturally consumerist anthropology and its relationship to globalization, see William T. Cavanaugh, "Migrant, Tourist, Pilgrim, Monk: Mobility and Identity in a Global Age," in *Migrations of the Holy: God, State, and the Political Meaning of the Church* (Grand Rapids: Eerdmans, 2011), 75–79.
106. Coles, *Beyond*, 99–107.

3.2 Toward Communal Discernment's (Relative) Competence

It is here that I see communal discernment as having the potential to create a broad culture of competence (not overconfidence) right in the midst of the political milieu such as it is, and of the sort that many radical democrats say is needed. It is a competence that remains comfortable with plurality and contingency in one's knowledge without falling into an affirmation of relativism or the belief that "anything goes"; put differently, it creates competence that is not rigid, and a fluidity that is not formless.

In contrast to the dual-temptations of Sheilaism and Cavanaugh's "tourism," at the heart of communal discernment is a commitment to listening to and obeying the dynamic will of God that is by definition contextual, and being so committed by remaining in receptive dialogue with one's fellow Christians, with one's neighbors, and even with those hostile to the cause. Recall the annoying persistence with which Anabaptists came to Zürich city council meetings. This did not leave Anabaptists unable to say anything robust or positive—indeed, they would often boldly proclaim what had been discerned. It only taught them to be open to correction, particularly when a matter remained unsettled, as communal discernment entailed a radical commitment to wait and seek unity through deliberation and patient listening rather than premature action. This practice creates competence to move faithfully in precarious circumstances according to its adherents, is communal where Sheilaism is not, and is derived from firmly held theological convictions—it does not advocate a way forward through convictionless irony.

Perhaps all this is true. However, there are some who wonder whether this is enough given the enormity of the threats we face, as did the Anabaptists' adversaries as soon as this was articulated. Indeed, some have suspected that this facet of the Anabaptist witness was at least partially responsible for the contemporary emotivist morass we now "enjoy," described so well by MacIntyre.[107] Historian Brad Gregory, for instance, argues that contemporary "hyperpluralism" originates from late-medieval theological shifts and the tipping point of the Protestant Reformation, which resulted in an infinite number of approaches to "the good" and the subordination of churches to nation-states—neither of which existed as problems during the height of Christendom. While Gregory's focus is the historical origins of this phenomenon,[108] it is sometimes hard to tell whether hyperpluralism is simply "the case," for Gregory, or if it represents a threat to be resisted.[109] Regardless, Gregory is concerned that "Christian" can now mean almost anything, and we lack the ability to determine which usage is correct.[110] For Gregory, this indeterminacy in meaning is in part the result of folks like Anabaptists, a "fissiparous lot,"[111] challenging the unity-in-diversity of the late medieval Catholic church. Thus on Gregory's reading, communal discernment will not achieve competence within an emotivist theopolitical swamp, but will likely only tolerate or exacerbate the moral incoherence that is our inheritance, liable as it is for getting us here in the first place.

Of course, from an Anabaptist perspective this "splintering" of medieval unity was providential, since that unity existed through the reinforcement provided by coercive violence. If challenging *that* led to "hyperpluralism," many would echo these words of Yoder: "From the Gospel perspective, modern pluralism is not a setback but a providential occasion for clarification. It may enable us to see something about the Gospel that was not visible before."[112] And because of this, Anabaptists would balk at Gregory's sentiment that because the medieval church lost control over the task of governance, which led to the states' attempts at control over churches, *therefore*

---

107. Alasdair MacIntyre, *After Virtue: A Study in Moral Theory*, 2nd ed. (Notre Dame: University of Notre Dame Press, [1981] 1984), ch. 2.
108. Gregory, *Unintended*, 75.
109. I remain unconvinced by Gregory's arguments concerning "relativism," which are not as nuanced as other strands of the book. Gregory mentions "hyperpluralism" and relativism throughout *Unintended*; see 18–19, 77–79. For a way to understand relativism without eschewing pluralism or accepting emotivism, see Brad J. Kallenberg, "The Gospel Truth of Relativism," *Scottish Journal of Theology* 53, no. 2 (2000): 177–211.
110. Gregory, *Unintended*, 75–76.
111. Ibid., 90.
112. John Howard Yoder, "Meaning after Babble: With Jeffrey Stout beyond Relativism," *Journal of Religious Ethics* 24, no. 1 (Spring 1996): 135.

"the pursuit of the kingdom of God as preached by Jesus" was made "almost impossible."[113] Anabaptists instead engaged in a struggle for faithful participation that was neither withdrawn nor conflated with the governing powers. For Anabaptists, far from rendering it impossible, eschewing control *began* the possibility for pursuit of the kingdom of God.

Rather than the secure unity of yesteryear or an acquiescence to "hyperpluralism," then, communal discernment fosters competence that constitutes a "politics of tending," and is indeed amenable to a form of plurality that fits radical democracy's aspirations—rather than the false plurality of political liberalism that masks hegemonic tendencies and is unhealthy for, even antithetical to, pluralistic cross-convictional dialogue and action.[114] A helpful image for the type of competent plurality that communal discernment creates is a river. According to Yoder, many people think of theology as a process of learning and systematizing a given set of propositions, valid once and for all, and then translating these propositions into the next generation or context with as little change as possible. The operative picture is of a series of boxes along a chain, which remain basically the same. Utilizing an image strikingly similar to one found in Wittgenstein,[115] Yoder argues that a better picture of the moral task is of a river into which the interpretive community enters. The community inevitably looks back at what has come before, and then speaks in ways that affect the stream's path down current. It is true, Yoder admits, that "it is more difficult to find security on this model"; but it also "is more representative of the experience of the church."[116]

What I like about this image in relation to communal discernment is its comfort with plurality and "fluidity" as given aspects of reality while retaining the conviction that for each situation, gospel mandates remain. The competence gained in this river analogy is real and

---

113. Gregory, *Unintended*, 147.
114. Coles, *Beyond*, ch. 1.
115. Ludwig Wittgenstein, *On Certainty*, trans. Denis Paul and G. E. M. Anscombe, in *Major Works: Selected Philosophical Writings* (New York: HarperCollins, 2009), §97.
116. Yoder, *Preface*, 382–83.

actual—but it is never "once and for all." Such competence is never final, but is knowledge of the next step in faithfulness; it goes through relativism rather than around it. Sussing out this way forward requires capacities within the discerning community similar to those identified above by Gustafson, it seems to me, not least capacities for empathy, appreciation, imagination, and sensitivity. Such capacities are central to a politics of tending, as we saw in the previous chapter: in particular, the competence won by "tending" to a particular place and its irreducible variety,[117] and which necessarily shifts as the context itself evolves over time (rather than issuing in moral injunctions purportedly *sub specie aeternitatis*, "from all temporal points of view").[118] In this way does communal discernment provide both sides of what I earlier quoted Coles as saying was needed for radical democracy: orientations and disorientations that keep us open to the continued guidance of the Spirit, without lapsing into "anything goes."

Of course, one may persist in wondering, "Given this 'fluid' nature of communal discernment, how does one know when an entire community has gone astray? Do not whole communities err in their understanding of God's will? And if so, what prevents this from leading to moral subjectivism?" In short, is communal discernment complicit in the creation of a society in which the only response we have to differing theological or moral practice is—as Gregory puts it—"whatever"?[119] Here, the river analogy does another kind of work. Of course we must baldly acknowledge the live possibility of error. As Christian history amply testifies, communities can "discern" their way into justifying all sorts of evil.[120] Indeed, Anabaptists have had a keen awareness that churches can go wrong, sometimes fantastically so—hence their critique of the failure of the medieval church, which they usually traced to the beginning of the reign of Constantine. In this sense, Reinhold Niebuhr is correct to acknowledge the penchant

---

117. Sheldon S. Wolin, *The Presence of the Past: Essays on the State and the Constitution* (Baltimore: Johns Hopkins University Press, 1989), 89.
118. John Rawls, *A Theory of Justice*, rev. ed. (Cambridge, MA: Belknap and Harvard University Press, [1971] 1999), 514.
119. Gregory, *Unintended*, 78.
120. Cf. Willard M. Swartley, *Slavery, Sabbath, War, and Women* (Scottdale, PA: Herald, 1983).

of groups for self-deception and the difficulty they have in acting morally.[121]

And yet he is only partially correct. Not all communities are equal, nor are they all abandoned to their own devices. Although communal discernment can go awry, it also has the resources to acknowledge and address this fact. Indeed, communal discernment presupposes the possibility of getting it wrong, but it also posits that this is a way Christian communities can "get it right," if we can get it right at all. Consider again the river analogy: if the community suddenly discerns something to be morally good that is not adequately connected to what has come before, it is at the least suspect. While the community does venture to say a new word in the present, if what is said has no connection to previous witnesses, the burden is on the new conclusion to show how it is a faithful interpretation of what has come before, rather than the beginning of a new tradition altogether. Thus discerning communities can be open to new revelation without deeming all development necessarily good.[122] The analogy is further helpful in demonstrating that moral reasoning probably does not go wrong all at once. Rather, under normal circumstances, the "river bed" erodes slowly and gradually by not attending to the sorts of practices that enable actual discernment in the first place: corporate prayer, binding and loosing, Bible study, and the willingness to be truthful with one another. So, for example, the error of Constantinianism was not first manifest with the historical events surrounding the man Constantine at the turn of the fourth century, but had been building for at least two centuries in the church, and allowed to grow, eventually blossoming in the church-state fusion that continues in various forms today.[123]

Another way of expressing the possibility of communities erring

---

121. Reinhold Niebuhr, *Moral Man, Immoral Society: A Study in Ethics and Politics* (Louisville: Westminster John Knox, [1932] 2001).
122. See Yoder, *Preface*, 136. Put differently, such communities are marked by "a combination of fluidity (or better, complexity) of structure together with the awareness that Messiah [has] come"; McClendon, *Ethics*, 231.
123. See Yoder, *Priestly Kingdom*, 105–47. The river analogy may also address Gregory's concerns by suggesting a baptist approach to catholicity, not through an imposed unity, but a "catholicity from below" through shared argument and in anticipation of eschatological harmony; cf. James

is to say that communal discernment is checked against the logic inherent to the theopolitical confession "Jesus is Lord," particularly in its original setting to which churches continually return in every new situation.[124] Figuring out implications of this confession is not automatic, but takes practice, particularly as Christians today are called to address questions informed by but not directly addressed by scripture, and unimagined by discerners of ages past. Indeed, the kind of practice that is called for is not that of the bloodless bureaucrat, but a group of people debating the quality of a jazz solo: some notes can be off, others right on key; but learning to tell the difference between skillful and unskillful performance requires a familiarity with the intention of the music being played, the nature of the instrument, and a recollection of past performances that were particularly skillful. This is not relativistic—a song *can* be played poorly. Nor is it rigidly absolutist, as the playing of a good jazz song has seemingly endless room for variation, and is always open to surprising interpretations. Rather, as Sam Wells writes, ethical "performance" is the creative, organic reaction of the entire community "schooled in a tradition so thoroughly that they learn to act from habit in ways appropriate to the circumstance."[125] It is improvisational, a mode of discernment learned from doing ethics "on the run"—as fugitives—similar to what Wolin called for in democracy: a politics of improvisation, of bricolage.[126] In short, it leads to a competence that comes from participating in a practice well, thus creating *and* enabling participation in the sorts of local politics we so desperately need. Perhaps the question to pose to each newly discerned conviction is: Does this interpretation lead to behavior that conforms to Jesus Christ? If not, "Scripture has not been understood."[127]

The upshot of all this is that communal discernment does not

Wm. McClendon Jr. and John Howard Yoder, "Christian Identity in Ecumenical Perspective," in *Collected Works, Volume 1*, §21.

124. Yoder, *Preface*, 134–35.
125. Samuel Wells, *Improvisation: The Drama of Christian Ethics* (Grand Rapids: Brazos, 2004), 65–66.
126. Sheldon S. Wolin, *Politics and Vision: Continuity and Innovation in Western Political Thought*, exp. ed. (Princeton: Princeton University Press, [1960] 2004), 522.
127. McClendon, *Doctrine*, 473. Similarly, Yoder wrote that discerning communities are not awash within "a markerless morass of inconclusive inclusiveness," because for the "radical Protestant

provide certain moral knowledge—and *we shouldn't want the latter*. The desire for security, epistemological or otherwise, is not consistent with a gospel that is inherently risky in a fallen world, but is the desire born of people who want to direct the world toward less-risky endeavors, as would the manager of a mutual fund. Thus while there is a threat of communal discernment "going wrong," as we will see in the following chapter, that threat is not the threat of finitude. Sin is not the same as creaturely limitation.[128] In fact, communal discernment goes wrong precisely when it is used to deny this finitude, or seek to escape it. So the point is not, "Regrettably, communal discernment doesn't secure moral knowledge that one can be certain will hold always and forever, but it's a worthwhile practice anyway." The point is that we don't want that kind of certainty, and that forfeiting this desire is not a concession to anything, since that kind of knowledge is not available to anyone. That some long for something like it is but a manifestation of our continued indebtedness to patterns of thought and action that ironically have caused our sense of incompetence in the first place. Rather than certainty, we should want to learn a precarious faithfulness to Jesus, come what may. And anyway, as Marilynne Robinson writes, "There are worse things than uncertainty, presumption being one."[129] I will show going forward that communal discernment provides at least this: a communal, contextual, and humble competence that is just what we need—and all we have available to us.

4 Conclusion

In this chapter, I have outlined a practice of moral discernment that I believe carries unique promise for the context and challenges outlined in chapter one. This description will stand behind my work moving forward, even as it continues to be fleshed out as the argument unfolds.

---

there will always be a canon within the canon: namely, that recorded experience of practical moral reasoning in genuine human form that bears the name of Jesus." Yoder, *Priestly Kingdom*, 37.
128. Cf. McClendon, *Doctrine*, 124.
129. Marilynne Robinson, "Awakening: Whom God Loveth He Also Chastiseth," *Commonweal* (October 23, 2015): 16.

OUTLINE OF THE PROMISE OF A PRACTICE

I have introduced communal discernment as a practice that conceives of the Christian life not as set and "once and for all," but "by nature adventure, daily discovered, daily risked," in which disciples must creatively struggle to find words "in which to proclaim the revolution."[130] If this practice has been neglected, perhaps it is because churches have too easily succumbed to the spirit of individualism, squandering their "collective power potential" and assiduously avoiding discussion of controversial issues. As Lawrence Burkholder asks, "Is it too harsh to say that most Protestant congregations decide in the course of a year almost nothing of real spiritual importance? The closest they come to consensus is to adopt a budget and to dispose of other matters dictated by administrative necessity."[131]

While I have outlined communal discernment as a practice that engenders moral competence, I also argued that this must not be read as a way to avoid ambiguity or to achieve moral certainty. Rather, it is better thought of as a powerful practice that takes Jesus to be ethically normative, relevant to every sphere of existence, and that presumes the community of committed disciples has the final say in all matters of faith and practice. Such communal discernment is dynamic in that it is constantly adapting to speak within new cultural contexts. It is also risky, in that communal discernment can go wrong. And while there is no absolute safeguard against fallibility (nor should we want one!), one way of discerning when the church has erred, if only retrospectively, is by attending to the grammar of the claim that "Jesus is Lord," and by continuing to talk with one another amidst disagreement.

Moving forward, I will analyze how communal discernment aids in the creation of an alternative, faithful politics within and beyond the usual options, born of friendships inside and friendships outside the *ekklesia*. Without practices like communal discernment, gaining any sort of moral competence is but a faint hope amid the cacophonous soundscape that so marks the Western world. Indeed, while there is no question that churches can and do go wrong, we must simultaneously

---

130. McClendon, *Doctrine*, 106.
131. J. Lawrence Burkholder, "The Peace Churches as Communities of Discernment," *The Christian Century* (September 4, 1963): 1073.

avoid being "buffaloed into despair at the church's flaws or tempted into cynicism about their remedies."[132] Ultimately, such despair is avoided only through faith in the God who enables us to harmonize with a song not of our making.

---

132. McClendon, *Doctrine*, 362.

3

Power, Discernment, and the Politics of Binding and Loosing

Toward the beginning of their jointly authored book, Stanley Hauerwas and Romand Coles write that in order to foster robust political agency in the shadow of those corporate, economic forces that undermine it, what is required is the creation of spaces wherein ordinary people can relate to one another apart from these powers' immediate influence. In such spaces we may discern ways to transform these same powers "so as to make them increasingly responsive to the pressures of people cultivating knowledge, power, and hope through relationships of everyday attentive reciprocity."[1] For Hauerwas and Coles, such hope is sustained through concrete practices of "tending to one another," echoing Sheldon Wolin's politics of tending, whereby people find resources for a politics mobile enough to adapt to ever-emerging possibilities and concrete enough to resist the socio-political forces that would keep us forever on the run. This is precisely what I have

---

1. Stanley Hauerwas and Romand Coles, *Christianity, Democracy, and the Radical Ordinary: Conversations Between a Radical Democrat and a Christian* (Eugene, OR: Cascade, 2008), 8.

claimed communal discernment can provide—a claim that, to some, may represent a supreme irony. "Does not communal discern-ment as actually practiced dull receptivity toward different voices, avoid tending to difference within the church, and even isolate the church from society? Indeed, far from enabling us to tend to one another, has it not fostered a pernicious type of exclusion in the church?" From this perspective, one might grant that we need what Hauerwas and Coles say we need, but surmise that the path I have chosen is no way to achieve it.

Far from an aside, this is a central question for those articulating an account of moral discernment and political competence in the contemporary United States: How does the apparent necessity, at some point, of excluding certain voices from conversation, or making decisions as a community—when discussion must cease—fit with the communal, contextual, patient account of communal discernment defended above? This is a question both for churches of discernment and radical democratic organizations committed to analogous principles of dialogical vulnerability. Christians utilizing communal discernment have typically articulated the need for some sort of exclusion in terms of "the ban"—the process of excluding an offending member from community that is often inaccurately equated with communal discernment. Thus my goal in this chapter is to examine "the ban" as a crucial part of communal discernment, and with an eye to its import for radically democratic political engagement—as central to the process of "tending to one another" well. Such an investigation carries interest in its own right, as this practice is the most cited reason for abandoning communal discernment, particularly by Christians longing for patient receptivity in church and world alike. These concerns are sound, and addressing them requires a straightforward account of the inevitability of power and authority, which baptists have typically lacked; indeed, silence on questions of power has been a major factor in the practice's failure and abuse. The salient question, as we shall see, is not if, but *what kind* of power churches of discernment ought to exercise.

I begin by examining the givenness of power in human, political life (ecclesial or otherwise), and some important nuances in our use of the word "power." So situated, I next offer a defense of "the ban," organized through a close reading of Matthew 18, with the goal of correcting its abuse as well as maintaining the real value it carries for baptist ecclesiology and political theology. I conclude by noting ways this careful articulation of "the ban"—far from subverting the possibility of "tending to one another" in radical democratic participation—is actually integral to such endeavors, as it teaches communities to remain open to different, even "loosed" voices, while simultaneously fostering a robust, socialized conception of authority that does not deny the reality of leadership emerging from within the community. In this way, "the ban" may actually show a way of addressing political incompetence that eschews a domineering authoritarianism *and* the inverted totalitarianism that we saw Wolin associate with the end-game of political liberalism.

1 Power Happens

A pressing conundrum for advocates of communal discernment in the context of political theology, as well as adherents of radical democracy, is the place and nature of power and authority in discernment processes. While political theologians from the Northern hemisphere have traditionally held a central place for questions of authority and the legitimate use of power, others—including baptists—have tended to treat the subject with suspicion or silence, which has resulted in "a *political* incoherence at the heart of contemporary politico-theological aspirations."[2] Reasons for this silence are numerous. Some speculate that three prongs of the Anabaptist tradition—the "priesthood of all believers," emphasis on submission or *Gelassenheit*, and a pietist-influenced humility—make talk of power difficult.[3] On the surface

---

2. Oliver O'Donovan, *The Desire of the Nations: Rediscovering the Roots of Political Theology* (Cambridge: Cambridge University Press, 1996), 17.
3. Stephen C. Ainlay, "Mennonite Culture Wars: Power, Authority, and Domination," in *Power, Authority, and the Anabaptist Tradition*, ed. Benjamin W. Redekop and Calvin W. Redekop (Baltimore: Johns Hopkins University Press, 2001), 137.

there indeed seems to be a tension between the vision of the church as a fellowship of disciples equally yoked in the work of the gospel to which one yields, and the kinds of power dynamics that affect human gatherings of all kinds. Or, it may be that baptists perspicaciously recognized issues with power-as-usual and the legitimized strength of the sovereign that certain "Northern" theologians used to justify coercion against those of lower station. So attuned to the dangers of *that* kind of power, baptists may have lapsed into silence about power of any sort. Or it may simply be that baptists do not have a long history of occupying seats of power, discussing philosophy, or theorizing about natural law.[4]

Whatever the case, silence on issues of power is inadequate in the context of communal discernment, as such silence allows the practice to manifest an unresponsive, arbitrary politics. This is because power is a reality that is already present in all communities, and is especially present in communities seeking to differentiate between good and bad, faithful and unfaithful behavior. During such conversations, the question will inevitably arise as to when siblings in Christ have placed themselves outside the community of conversation, either by word or deed. When dealing with the potential of such exclusion—for whatever reason, to whatever degree, for whatever length of time, by whatever mechanisms—we must remain conscious about the reality and type of power being wielded, and to what end.

Put differently, care is required as we go about breaking this silence, especially because "power" is a tricky concept, one that tends to go on holiday. Max Weber gave classic voice to this need, distinguishing as he did between an individual or group's ability to exercise its will in spite of resistance (power), the potential exercise of such ability that is considered legitimate (authority), and that same exercise that is seen as illegitimate (coercion).[5] However, further differentiations are possible given that Weber worked with a particular view of power,

---

4. J. Lawrence Burkholder, "Power," in *Power, Authority*, 4.
5. Cf. Max Weber, *From Max Weber: Essays in Sociology*, ed. H. H. Gerth and C. Wright Mills (New York: Routledge, 1946), 180, 294–96; and Calvin Redekop, "Power in the Anabaptist Community," in *Power, Authority*, 175.

deemed "power-over," which assumed that individual wills necessarily conflict with one another, and that a certain degree of external manipulation is required in social life. Thomas Hobbes best represents this view, presuming that the natural power of human beings is not found in our abilities that enable us to achieve "some future apparent Good," but in the superiority and excess of these abilities in comparison to others.[6] The presumption of agonism is clear: "power" is power *over* another; also clear is the sense that power is zero-sum for Hobbes: "every man's power resists and hinders the effects of other men's power. This is asserted to be so universally the case that one man's power may be simply redefined as the excess of his over others'."[7]

But this is not the only type of power operative in all communities, or the only way to speak of power. Others distinguish "power-over" from "power-*to*," the latter of which specifies people's ability to use their capacities, energies, and potentiality without presuming it *always* subtracts from others' use.[8] A helpful way to differentiate these senses is through two German words. *Macht* carries the connotation of might or strength (power-over); *Kraft*, on the other hand, "means by virtue of, to be in operation, efficacy, or energy. . . . If seen as *Macht* and not as *Kraft*, power intrinsically prescribes social relationships of dominance and inequality."[9] Thus to break silence on power in communities of discernment does not necessarily mean embracing power-as-dominance; there are other sorts of power in existence, other ways to understand power.

This is important to note because as baptists have broken their silence on power, some have too quickly accepted "power-over" as inescapable or even normative in the process of impugning their ancestors for foolishly thinking anything different.[10] Others have

---

6. Thomas Hobbes, *Leviathan*, ed. C. B. Macpherson (New York: Penguin, [1651] 1968), 150.
7. C. B. Macpherson, "Introduction," in Hobbes, *Leviathan*, 35. Indeed, "Hobbes was using a mental model of society which, whether he was conscious of this or not, corresponds only to a bourgeois market society"; ibid., 38.
8. Cf. Ainlay, "Mennonite," 139.
9. Dorothy Yoder Nyce and Lynda Nyce, "Mennonite Ecclesiology: A Feminist Perspective," in *Power, Authority*, 165.
10. Cf. Burkholder, "Power," 5, 7, 8–9.

committed the opposite error—maintaining a wariness toward power-over but in the process neglecting the ubiquity of other types of power. Nancey Murphy, for instance, eloquently specifies the issues with "power" from an Anabaptist perspective, critiquing Reinhold Niebuhr and a particular interpretation of Michel Foucault. However, in this process Murphy deals almost exclusively with power-over outside the *ekklesia* in what certain theologians have called the principalities and powers. In rightly resisting the reductionist notion that the will-to-power is *all* there is to reality, baptists must not grow silent about other kinds of power in our midst.[11]

With this nuance noted, it becomes easier to affirm the reality that in all human communities—including communities of discernment—power happens. Even when we refuse to acknowledge it, the potential use of legitimate power (of whatever sort) is always there, resting with certain people. Anabaptist leaders, perhaps seeking to refuse *coercive* power, have sometimes intimated or outright stated that they do not have power in ways they clearly do. As Dorothy Yoder Nyce and Lynda Nyce report, when the CEO of a major Mennonite agency was questioned about the extent of his power, he responded, "Oh, I don't think of myself as having power." The conclusion they draw is that many Anabaptists have expressed suspicion toward bad power's exercise, but this has not made power go away; rather, it simply becomes hidden and thus more prone to subtle abuse. Reluctance to admit the presence of ecclesial power because it is "not nice" or because "power corrupts" does nothing to stop ministers from acting authoritatively; it only removes their power from needed scrutiny and consciousness.[12]

Thus it is important to attend to power's reality—in churches of discernment and grassroots organizations alike. Interestingly, the same discomfort with power may exist among certain radical democrats who try to dissolve questions of power by appealing to an

---

11. Nancey Murphy, "Missiology in the Postmodern West: A Radical Reformation Perspective," in *To Stake a Claim: Mission and the Western Crisis of Knowledge*, ed. J. Andrew Kirk and Kevin J. Vanhoozer (Maryknoll, NY: Orbis, 1999), 109–11.
12. Nyce and Nyce, "Mennonite," 157–58.

ideal of "ultra-democracy" that is so egalitarian, participatory, and decentralized that authority and leadership disappears. "Yet in practice, groups that deny the presence of authority and leadership typically become controlled by cliques, which are all the less democratically accountable for being unacknowledged."[13] That is, there is a tendency to avoid recognizing power as it occurs, or deluding oneself into thinking that if we put our chairs in a circle during meeting, the authority question goes away. It does not, and there is no need for it to do so. A proper reaction against bad power must not harden into an uncritical rejection of power-as-such. Wolin saw just this happen during the political struggles of the 1960s, which Coles summarizes as: "What began as a compelling questioning of malignant modes of authority shifted toward a rejection of the question of authority altogether."[14] And at times, Anabaptists have done the same thing. Nyce and Nyce, for instance, in rightly recognizing that appointing official leaders *can* divest church members of full participation, go on to suggest that ordination in fact *negates* the believers' church vision that all are ordained: "To re-ordain in essence discredits priesthood for all."[15] But while it is undeniable that there is a strong anticlerical strand in Anabaptist history, this did not typically lead to the rejection of leaders per se. Rather, the question was from where congregational leaders ought to emerge—the congregation itself—and to whom they were to be responsive. That Anabaptists argued for a believers' church and resisted clergy being arbitrarily assigned to them did not negate the need for or reality of leaders emerging in their midst.[16]

The real question of authoritative power is *in what does it consist?*

---

13. Romand Coles, "Of Tensions and Tricksters: Grassroots Democracy between Theory and Practice," in *Christianity*, 302.
14. Romand Coles, "Democracy and the Radical Ordinary: Wolin and the Epical Emergence of Democratic Theory," in *Christianity*, 119.
15. Nyce and Nyce, "Mennonite," 161; cf. 160–65.
16. The fifth article of the Schleitheim Confession expresses this well, casually mentioning that if a leader is killed or banished, "another should be ordained in his place immediately so that God's little people are not destroyed." Leaders exist, but are almost interchangeable. Michael Sattler, *The Schleitheim Articles*, in *The Radical Reformation*, ed. Michael G. Baylor (Cambridge: Cambridge University Press, 1991), 176.

That is, what does a community consider authoritative? What are the qualities that mark a leader? And what should a leader do with that power? For instance, Coles observes that in the early days of SNCC, there was a recognition of leadership in certain figures in the movement, notably Ella Baker. Tellingly, Baker was seen as such because she *listened best* to the needs of the group, and reinvested what she heard to further the community's stated ends.[17] My point is that the notion that there could be "no power" is illusory; power bubbles up as a practice is engaged that can be done better or worse, as judged by standards internal to the practice itself. The issue becomes not if, but what sort of authority will be recognized and operative. If left unrecognized, authoritative power will go underground, wielded unconsciously or unintentionally such that the persons in question are unaware of the authority they have, the potential damage they are doing, and unresponsive to concerns voiced by the community.

Thus even when it is avoided or wished away, power is present. Ignoring it only leaves us blind to its function. As soon as there exists a political body constituted by practices of excellence, it *emerges*. It is against this backdrop that one can affirm Weber's insistence that power is not just "out there," but constitutive of every sociality; and Foucault's claim that "power is 'always already there,' that one is never 'outside' it, that there are no 'margins' for those who break with the system to gambol in."[18] The point isn't that all power is "power-over" or that we ought to acquiesce to the panopticism of a disciplinary society, but precisely that the beginnings of resistance happen from "within" power itself, which Foucault and his interpreters eventually came to see as best embodied by smaller communities of association.[19]

---

17. Romand Coles, "'To Make This Tradition Articulate': Practiced Receptivity Matters, Or Heading West of West with Cornel West and Ella Baker," in *Christianity*, 53–67.
18. Michel Foucault, *Power/Knowledge: Selected Interviews and Other Writings, 1972-1977*, ed. Colin Gordon (New York: Pantheon, 1980), 141.
19. Cf. Jonathan Tran, *Foucault and Theology* (New York: T&T Clark, 2011), 59–63.

2 Describing the Rule of Christ

If power is present in all communities, what sort of power should be operative in communities of discernment, and how might it be consonant with the competence needed in today's world? Communal discernment is in no way devoid of power's use, and articulating a robust account of the kind of power necessary for discernment to go well is important, especially for the purposes of political theology. In the context of communal discernment, the most appropriate avenue for providing such an account is through an investigation of what is colloquially called "the ban"—an infelicitous moniker, as we will see. "The ban," also called "binding and loosing" or "the Rule of Christ," is a practice that Anabaptists reclaimed in the service of community maintenance and discipline. The practice is drawn from several scriptural texts, preeminently Matthew 18:15-20, in which Jesus states, "If your brother or sister sins, go and reprove that person when the two of you are alone. If he or she listens, you have won your brother or sister" (v 15); and "Truly I tell you, whatever you bind on earth will be bound in heaven, and whatever you loose on earth will be loosed in heaven" (v 18). John Howard Yoder observes that this process is meant to be the heartbeat of the *ekklesia*, presupposing a concrete voluntary community small enough that members can know and correct one another in love; if it were taken seriously, it would "radically restructure the life of churches."[20] Indeed, Yoder observes that only two times in the gospels do we find *ekklesia* on the lips of Jesus: in chapters sixteen and eighteen of Matthew, in connection with his bestowing authority to the gathered believers to "bind and loose." "The phrase is not a current one in our modern conversation," Yoder writes. "Yet, for Jesus and the New Testament church, it seems to have been of such importance that part of the definition of the church is that it is where this binding and loosing takes place."[21] On clear display is

---

20. John Howard Yoder, *Body Politics: Five Practices of the Christian Community Before the Watching World* (Scottdale, PA: Herald, [1992] 2001), 6–7.
21. John Howard Yoder, "The Commission to Bind and Loose," in *Revolutionary Christianity: The 1966 South American Lectures*, ed. Paul Martens et al. (Eugene, OR: Cascade, 2011), 13.

a church authorized to speak on God's behalf, "like an ambassador or an attorney empowered to sign a document in the name of someone else."[22] Yoder continues by observing that the original meaning of *ekklesia* is political, "literally a 'called meeting,' an assembly, such as a town meeting, convened to do business, to deliberate on behalf of the entire society [*polis*]."[23] Thus it is precisely in and around this practice's employment that the nature of the church as a political community is properly understood, and is central to assessing communal discernment's theopolitical potential for radical democratic engagement.

As I explore below, this practice should not be associated exclusively with punishment, nor with exclusion meted out by official leadership teams; while Anabaptists rightly retained a concern to address sin in the community, too often this concern conflated "binding and loosing" with exclusion, leaving even sympathetic theologians to remark that whatever its virtues, "it conveyed a message of exclusive rather than inclusive sociality."[24] The problem came as its focus narrowed to cases of failure, ignoring the forgiving, communal, and patient mode implicit in the practice as outlined in Matthew 18. While Catholics have kept the practice but restricted it to the confessional, and Protestants neglected it altogether, "free churches, for their part, have been tempted to transform this process of reconciliation into a tool of punishment. Instead of speaking of forgiveness, we have come to speak of church discipline."[25] Against these mistaken views, I here offer an interpretation of binding and loosing in service to my claim that in order for communal discernment to do the theopolitical work I think it can, it will require some account of what true power in the discerning community looks like, where the dangers of power's abuse actually lie, when someone ought to be "loosed" from conversation, and how to relate to such a person. I provide this by organizing my thoughts through Matthew 18, one of the central scriptural texts grounding

22. Ibid., 14.
23. Yoder, *Body Politics*, 2.
24. James Wm. McClendon Jr., *Doctrine: Systematic Theology, Volume 2* (Nashville: Abingdon, 1994), 143.
25. Yoder, "Commission," 16.

this practice. Crucially, I will consider the passage about binding and loosing (vv 15–20) in its wider narrative context, which allows for a better conception of the function, purpose, and dangers of the practice. In this process, I will address ways that the practice has been abused; indeed, I am convinced that it is only through articulating what its good practice looks like that we can judge its bad exercise. Anyone can see that communities of discernment often fail to exhibit the virtues and promise specified by their advocates; what I hope to show is that good practice of "the ban" provides the standards by which its bad practice can be judged.[26]

A final note before moving on: For some, in light of his sexually abusive conduct that has gained renewed attention in recent years, Yoder would not be a good source to follow in explicating the promise and failure of binding and loosing.[27] The issue is not simply that Yoder sinned and went through a correction process, but that the process was apparently done to such little satisfaction of all involved that it has been reopened twice over the past thirty years. Even more troubling is that this able articulator of binding and loosing reportedly blocked the discernment process from moving forward in his own case, and needed arm-twisting by Glen Stassen and James McClendon to continue with the process.[28] Finally, Yoder appeared to adjust and contradict his previous articulation of binding and loosing during the process in ways that suited his interests. There is no "getting around" these failures, nor do I wish to do so; I do claim, however, that a helpful way to examine Yoder's abusive behavior is with the theological lenses he has provided me with, "and to thereby assess the continuity between what he said and what he did."[29] Thus rather than rejecting Yoder's

---

26. I am here invoking MacIntyre's argument about judging between good and bad farming societies; cf. Alasdair MacIntyre, "Politics, Philosophy, and the Common Good," in *The MacIntyre Reader*, ed. Kelvin Knight (Notre Dame: University of Notre Dame Press, 1998), 237.
27. Cf. Rachel Waltner Goossen, "'Defanging the Beast': Mennonite Responses to John Howard Yoder's Sexual Abuse," *Mennonite Quarterly Review* 89, no. 1 (January 2015): 7–80.
28. Cf. Stanley Hauerwas, *Hannah's Child: A Theologian's Memoir* (Grand Rapids: Eerdmans, 2010), 242–47.
29. Cf. David Cramer, Jenny Howell, Jonathan Tran, and Paul Martens, "Scandalizing John Howard Yoder," *The Other Journal*, July 2014, accessed November 28, 2014, http://theotherjournal.com/2014/07/07/scandalizing-john-howard-yoder.

articulation of binding and loosing outright on the basis of his abusive behavior, I instead see a man who was not immune to his own insights concerning the reality and allure of the principalities and powers, and served as an (ironic) exemplification of the potential pitfalls of ignoring the practice—or better, of the continued presence of power in its employment, which requires constant attention by all involved.

2.1 Kenotic Power as True Authority (Matthew 18:1–5)

The speech that eventually includes Jesus's description of correction and restoration in the *ekklesia* begins when some disciples approach Jesus and ask, "Who is the greatest in the kingdom of heaven?" He replies that those who change and become humble like children are greatest in this kingdom (18:4). Thus the immediate context for the forthcoming conversation about binding and loosing is concern within Jesus's community about the nature of power and authority. This concern will arise a few chapters later as Jesus moves toward Jerusalem: he will be approached by the mother of James and John with a request for authority in his kingdom, and reply, "You know that the rulers of the gentiles lord it over them, and their great ones are tyrants over them. It will not be so among you; but whoever wishes to be great among you must be your servant" (20:25–26).[30] "Power-over" is not the rule of the way of Jesus; rather, the humility of children (not their "innocence") is the sustaining power of this political body.[31] Further, such humility is tied to the child's social location as among the weak, rather than the degree to which the child sees himself as "meek."

    A clear implication for binding and loosing is that any use of the Rule of Christ that does not manifest and sustain such humility perverts the practice itself. As Gerald Biesecker-Mast argues, only a context of patient, suffering love distinguishes the work of "reconciliation" from "the sin of judging during such a restoration process. . . . When the ban is used in a power struggle or to negotiate political space in the

---

30. In Matthew, Jesus then illustrates this upside-down political leadership through his "triumphal" entry.
31. On humility as the virtue highlighted here, cf. Stanley Hauerwas, *Matthew* (Grand Rapids: Brazos, 2006), 161–62.

church or to keep the most people happy, then the witness of biblical church discipline and separation is tarnished."[32] Put differently, the power that sustains this practice and marks leadership in the *ekklesia* is the power of self-emptying *kenosis*.

Many baptists have reflected on the theological notion of kenosis, which is relevant here not least because—as political philosopher Carl Schmitt saw—modern political concepts of the state are "secularized theological concepts," such that understanding them requires an understanding of the theology they evoke, whether consciously or not.[33] To truly understand the politics of binding and loosing, then—including ways it is perverted—one must address the theological vision of authority embedded therein. Indeed, correcting harmful notions of rule requires a better theological vision that allows one to take someone like Schmitt's insights seriously while also addressing his deepest theological assumptions at their root. *Some* metaphysic is always operative; the question is which ought be operative for the *ekklesia*, at least as envisioned in Matthew 18. It is here that certain theologians' thoughts on kenosis helpfully connect with the humility, "true greatness," and servant leadership that alone forms the context where binding and loosing can promote flourishing.

Viewing kenotic power as true authority carries different connotations for binding and loosing if it is understood as a "this-worldly" phenomenon. McClendon, for instance, persuasively argues that a close reading of "the Christ hymn" in Philippians 2:5–11—perhaps the oldest christological reflection in the New Testament—does not yield a narrative of a heavenly being who emptied himself of divinity pre-incarnation in order to become human. Rather, the Christ hymn tells the story of a Messiah who refused the temptations of pride, prestige, and a certain kind of authority (power-over), and thus speaks of Jesus's "human circumstances as he set out

---

32. Gerald Biesecker-Mast, "Recovering the Anabaptist Body (To Separate It for the World)," in *Anabaptists and Postmodernity*, ed. Susan Biesecker-Mast and Gerald Biesecker-Mast (Telford, PA: Pandora, 2000), 200.
33. Carl Schmitt, *Political Theology: Four Chapters on the Concept of Sovereignty*, trans. George Schwab (Chicago: University of Chicago Press, [1922] 2005), 36.

to make his career," and "the human Jesus's earthly temptations."[34] On this view, Jesus's kenosis is first of all a juxtaposition between the uncertainties inherent to Jesus's earthly career and the claim that this humble Messiah—precisely in his humility—is Lord of all things on earth and heaven alike. Jesus's temptation is concrete and political: if he really is the liberator of Israel, he ought to seize power. It is in his refusal of this temptation and taking the path of servanthood that Jesus is the name that is above every name; Jesus's self-emptying even to the point of death on a cross embodies true sovereignty. Gospel authority is found through service.

Thus binding and loosing will need guidance from leaders in the community of discernment, but the criteria for who is recognized as a leader, as well as the marker of whether the discernment process has been legitimate, is a capacity for patient, attentive listening to all parties.[35] While Yoder argues against any New Testament basis for a professionalized ministerial leadership or a non-engaged "laity," he also points to an orienting center around which the multifarious ministries of the church constellate: servanthood. Servanthood is the nature and marker of the Anointed One, and thus the form of all Messianic ministry: "The notion that God himself has *renounced rule* for servanthood and calls us to do the same (Phil 2:5-11) is paradoxically a powerful thought. It explodes the categories with which we think about social process."[36] In this way is a stress on kenosis as cruciform rule crucial to the right practice of binding and loosing. Conversely, an ecclesial context that emphasizes biblical images of rule without attention to Jesus's inversion of power—say, a church that sees Jesus's rule as in simple continuity with Old Testament images of kingship—will be at a disadvantage in employing the practice without it becoming a tool for power-over.[37]

---

34. McClendon, *Doctrine*, 266–67. McClendon notes that this does not negate what the New Testament teaches elsewhere about the eternal deity of God the Word (Heb 1:1-3; John 1:1-14).
35. Similarly, Coles points out that leaders in IAF are typically those who listen best and are able to reinvest their authority in the community, rather than manifesting a deaf, immutable form of power; Coles, "Tensions," 305–6.
36. John Howard Yoder, *The Fullness of Christ: Paul's Vision of Universal Ministry* (Elgin, IL: Brethren, 1987), 67.
37. This sort of political theology is represented by Oliver O'Donovan in *Desire of the Nations*. For a

2.2 Submission as Liberative (Matthew 18:6-9)

For binding and loosing, an important point following an emphasis on authority as kenotic is a healthy conception of submission or "yieldedness" *to* that authority. In Matthew 18, Jesus follows his reflections on true greatness with warnings about stumbling blocks. "If any of you put a stumbling block before one of these little ones who believe in me, it would be better for you if a great millstone were fastened around your neck and you were drowned in the depth of the sea" (18:6). Jesus continues this extreme imagery with the famous claim that if a hand or foot causes you to stumble, "cut it off and throw it away" (18:8). This text has often been interpreted individualistically, driving some in Christian history to self-mutilation in the service of personal holiness, as in the (likely apocryphal) tale of Origen's castration of himself to deal with sexual temptation. A better read of this passage, however, is as a description of the kind of community Jesus wants, a warning to those in authority not to exercise it to the detriment of the weakest among them, and the overall importance of fashioning a people who have the patience and ability to "exorcise those aspects of the body that cause the little ones to stumble.... Jesus teaches his disciples that at times they may well discover it is better for the church to 'cut off' a hand or a foot if such members make it impossible to grasp or walk."[38]

Read thusly, the implications of these verses for binding and loosing become at once obvious and more interesting: obvious, for this passage now clearly fits with the pericope's ecclesial focus on binding and loosing; more interesting, for now the focus can shift to the implied communal danger worthy of such drastic measures. The primary concern seems to be with those members of the body who not only reject Jesus's kenotic vision of true greatness, but who exercise power in such a way that the weak and vulnerable who would come to Jesus

---

critique of O'Donovan's view of "rule" as Christologically suspect, cf. Stanley Hauerwas, *Wilderness Wanderings: Probing Twentieth-Century Theology and Philosophy* (Boulder, CO: Westview, 1997), 199–224.

38. Hauerwas, *Matthew*, 163.

RADICAL FRIENDSHIP

are prevented from doing so; the danger this kind of power has for the community is great, and needs addressing in no uncertain terms. This passage becomes a text of warning to the powerful. It is not the "little ones" that are being addressed about being lopped off, but the proud who directly contradict what true greatness actually entails.

Thus is the message here quite relevant to the historic Anabaptist emphasis on submission or *Gelassenheit*, and the justified concerns about its dangers. Yieldedness to God through community is life-giving only as the *ekklesia* and its leadership manifest the kind of power Jesus has already identified as part and parcel of the kingdom of heaven. Submission is destructive when it encourages self-negation in those already low on the power-scale, or encourages deference to ecclesial procedure for its own sake. This mistake is well narrated using categories from Schmitt. One of the reasons Schmitt so despised political liberalism—albeit from a profoundly autocratic point of view—was that it produced a people who were slavishly devoted to "procedure," such that the personal, human element in politics is masked from the actors involved. For Schmitt, this is a major flaw: by appealing to law over decision makers, liberalism "says nothing about who should apply it."[39] Of course, this leads to Schmitt's deeply problematic affirmation of the overarching sovereign; but the threat, for Schmitt, does approach what Wolin says of liberalism as well: "the triumph of non-political, inhuman technologizing."[40]

In recognizing that such proceduralism suffocates human life, either in communities of discernment who bind and loose or elsewhere, Schmitt is on to something important, and provides a helpful way to know when binding and loosing becomes toxic. When yieldedness becomes not yieldedness to God through the community but deference to an ecclesial-judicial procedure in which dissenting voices are muted, this powerful practice has become suffocating, taking on a life of its own that outstrips the community it was meant to sustain. Indeed,

---

39. Schmitt, *Political Theology*, 31; cf. 29, 31–33.
40. Tracy B. Strong, "Foreword," in Schmitt, *Political Theology*, xxv. Cf. Schmitt, *Political Theology*, 65; and John P. McCormick, *Carl Schmitt's Critique of Liberalism: Against Politics as Technology* (Cambridge: Cambridge University Press, 1997).

POWER, DISCERNMENT, BINDING AND LOOSING

it is easy for binding and loosing to foster nosiness, the perversion of the virtue of presence,[41] and a concomitant acquiescence to such needling—a mistake that is not only unhelpful to any discernment process, but arguably is not in line with the original intent of subordination language in the New Testament. According to Yoder, the goal of "submission talk" in the household codes, for instance, is not to defend quietistic deference, but to encourage subtle, patient-yet-revolutionary subversion of the status quo by those of lower status, the means by which their liberation in Christ can reach into "every kind of bondage" over time.[42] Whatever caveats we need to add to Yoder's argument,[43] if he is correct it clearly undermines any use of yieldedness as a warrant for a "get in line or else" mentality. Thus the issue isn't that I should avoid bringing myself and my actions to the community, including what I wear, my sexual activity, where I work, or how much I work, offensive though this is in polite society; it's that the function of the practice ought to enable a back-and-forth about these conversations, not a "fall in line or else" mentality—thus creating a community deaf to the possibility of the majority's need to change through the witness of the prophetic voice.[44]

My point is that yieldedness to the community is not necessarily detrimental to a healthy conception of binding and loosing. Quite the opposite, it can be a means of faithfully subverting unhealthy social hierarchies without falling into impatient violence or quietism. Such is the opposite of deference to procedure, and can be liberative if housed within a community that God is pleased to allow his kenotic authority to dwell. It is to recognize, with McClendon, that community

---

41. James Wm. McClendon Jr. *Ethics: Systematic Theology, Volume 1*, rev. ed. (Nashville: Abingdon, [1986] 2002), 116.
42. John Howard Yoder, *The Politics of Jesus*, 2nd ed. (Grand Rapids: Eerdmans, [1972] 1994), 185, 190–92.
43. On reading Yoder with concerns about quietism in mind, cf. Nekeisha Alexis-Baker, "Freedom of the Cross: John Howard Yoder and Womanist Theologies in Conversation," in *Power and Practices: Engaging the Work of John Howard Yoder*, ed. Jeremy M. Bergen and Anthony G. Siegrist (Scottdale, PA: Herald, 2009).
44. Yoder observes that ideally, binding and loosing helps community standards to be challenged, refined, confirmed, "or changed as is found necessary, in the course of their being applied." Community standards, in other words, are neither arbitrary nor unchanging; John Howard Yoder, "Binding and Loosing," in *The Royal Priesthood: Essays Ecclesiastical and Ecumenical*, ed. Michael G. Cartwright (Grand Rapids: Eerdmans, 1994), 328.

and individual liberty constitute a dialectic: "Community without liberty is oppressive; liberty without community is chaos."[45] And it is to recognize with Matthew 18:6–9 that the real danger rests with those in leadership who would wield power poorly, encouraging a deference to their own authority or self-negation in their fellow disciples.

2.3 Forgiveness (Matthew 18:10–14, 21–35)

Jesus's words of warning are followed by specifying the most important point to remember for the right practice of correction and restoration in the church: the presence of stubborn, persistent forgiveness, especially toward those who are the most vulnerable in the community. Readers often ignore that Jesus's directions about binding and loosing are sandwiched between the parable of the lost sheep, his command to forgive indefinitely, and a parable about an unforgiving servant. Coupled with Jesus's reflections on true greatness, forgiveness provides the unrelenting logic of the Rule of Christ. In the same way that a shepherd leaves ninety-nine sheep "in search of the one that went astray" (18:12), so has God gone after the lowly, and so does Jesus want his followers to give preference to such as these—not settle for the stability and prosperity of the ninety-nine. No sheep is unimportant in God's economy; no cost-benefit analysis can justify an ultimate forgetting of even a single one in favor of the many. Following Jesus's directions about merciful restoration in the *ekklesia*, Peter catches the true gist of the message ("He didn't specify an end to how long we must endure repeat offenders!"), and seeks an outer limit where the community can finally be rid of even a repentant offender. No such limit is offered. Such is the nature of the community Jesus is establishing.

On my read, this affects the practice of binding and loosing in at least three ways. First, the practice's aim is forgiveness, not punishment or "discipline" per se. This is not to say that there can be restoration of

---

45. James Wm. McClendon Jr., "The Mennonite and Baptist Vision," in *The Collected Works of James Wm. McClendon, Jr., Volume 1*, ed. Ryan Andrew Newson and Andrew C. Wright (Waco, TX: Baylor University Press, 2014), 142.

an offending party without judgment (see below), but the practice's means and end is reconciliation. So related is forgiveness to discernment that Yoder links them inseparably, existing not as "two poles of a tension but two sides of a coin. Each presupposes and includes the other."[46] And, as noted above, in this context the practice is not universal and set, to be applied rigidly, but is itself the means by which standards may, over time, change—an impossibility if done without the humility that also places oneself in the class of the forgiven. Neither communal purity nor protecting reputation nor defense against moral laxity or relativism are reasons to bind and loose; each of these "put the church in a posture of maintaining its own righteousness, whereas the New Testament speaks of shared forgiveness."[47]

Second, how the church comes to decision is as important as the decision itself; it matters to whatever decisions are made. This is the inverse of Schmitt's claim that the ultimate marker of a political community is its ability (through the sovereign) to make a decision, even and especially when placed in moments of crisis. Summarizing counter-revolutionary political philosopher Joseph de Maistre, Schmitt writes that "as far as the most essential issues are concerned, making a decision is more important than how a decision is made."[48] Essential, for Schmitt through de Maistre, is that an authoritative decision has no place for appeal. The exact opposite is the case, however, regarding decisions reached through binding and loosing. A spirit of forgiveness (indeed, "appealability," contra Schmitt) and attention to the "least" in communities having a preferred voice in such discussions *validates* the practice, the absence of which serves to delegitimize decisions reached. As we will see in the next chapter, a church's decisions are authoritative and valid only insofar as the procedure of the meeting was practiced in a suitable, forgiving spirit.[49] Of course, some decisions

---

46. Yoder, "Binding and Loosing," 329.
47. Ibid., 336.
48. Schmitt, *Political Theology*, 55–56.
49. John Howard Yoder, *The Priestly Kingdom: Social Ethics as Gospel* (Notre Dame: University of Notre Dame Press, 1984), 22–23.

are made in this spirit and thus hold—the goal isn't perpetual discussion, which Schmitt detested[50]—but the emphasis now falls on holding off decision for much longer than is typically thought, particularly when that decision may result in a person being "loosed" from the *ekklesia*. The goal is not to find a way to throw a person out, but to prolong the process of loosing from fellowship as long as possible, in the hope that God's Spirit may yet move in the community's midst. Thus do the layers of confrontation Jesus mentions in Matthew 18 serve to lengthen the process at hand: first confront personally, then get two or three witnesses, then bring the whole church together, and only then consider making a binding decision.

Finally, attention to forgiveness as the form of binding and loosing changes the type of politics it manifests. As McClendon argues, forgiveness marks a politics that not only opens up a potentially closed community, but is able to bring offender and offended together, enfolding both within a new story in which the injury that separated now invites union. The "structural, political process" of Matthew 18 marks a fluid community with a law, indeed, but a "living law—law, that is, where ongoing reconciliation is a goal."[51] Hauerwas notes that one may read Peter's incredulity at Jesus's "seventy-times seven" not as priggishness, but as echoing a very important question: "What kind of community would be sustained on the presumption that forgiveness is always to be offered?"[52] Here, Schmitt's voice emerges again with a similar observation about the need for any truly political body to defend itself against enemies within and without: "It would be ludicrous to believe that a defenseless people has nothing but friends, and it would be a deranged calculation to suppose that the enemy could perhaps be touched by the absence of a resistance. . . . Only a weak people will disappear."[53]

---

50. On Schmitt's disdain for the indecision of "the discussing class," see Schmitt, *Political Theology*, 59; and Jacob Taubes, "Carl Schmitt: Apocalyptic Prophet of the Counterrevolution," in *To Carl Schmitt: Letters and Reflections* (New York: Columbia University Press, [1987] 2013), 6–7.
51. James Wm. McClendon Jr., "The Politics of Forgiveness," in *Collected Works, Volume 1*, 227–29; cf. McClendon, *Ethics*, 231.
52. Hauerwas, *Matthew*, 166.
53. Carl Schmitt, *The Concept of the Political*, trans. George Schwab (Chicago: University of Chicago Press, [1932] 1996), 53.

Against the backdrop of forgiveness, binding and loosing offers a political alternative to both liberal permissiveness and Schmitt's authoritarianism. There is power in the patience of forgiveness that Schmitt cannot see, a very real sense in which forgiveness *can* restore the equilibrium of a society marked by rupture,[54] and thus can sustain a community of a different sort, at the same time undermining the friend-enemy distinction by putting each in indefinite relation with the other. Binding and loosing in this light marks an alternative authority for a community that is neither naive nor exclusionary, and reinforces the sense in which forgiveness is not only a form of forgetting, but also of remembering "under the aspect of membership in the body of Christ: it is knowing that he who is our body and we, forgiven and forgiver, are all one. In this sense, to forgive is to learn a new and truer story about myself by discovering how fully my life is bound up even with those whose sins are sins against myself."[55] Conversely, those in power who do not exercise their authority with a constant eye to fostering radical, persistent forgiveness—both to others and between others confronting one another—will have that authority ripped away. To act like a ruler who demands retribution by choking someone in his debt (18:28) is to insult the One from whom that authority comes.

2.4 The Givenness of Judgment (Matthew 18:15-20)

Having come this far, I can now exegete the practice of binding and loosing in service to a reclamation of communal discernment and baptist political theology. First, note that what is described in Matthew 18:15-20 is a "judicial" process of the *ekklesia* (albeit an alternative process to the status quo because of its underlying structural norm

---

54. McClendon, *Ethics*, 227.
55. Ibid., 228. Michael Hollerich points out that Schmitt could not see this kind of move in part because he equated God with absolute power-over, but also because of a deficient ecclesiology in which the church is "political" only as "conservator of the world as it is, either directly as judge or as underwriter of the political form of the state. The church became a last-ditch defense against social chaos and breakdown, 'the ark of Noah in a flood of sin.'" Michael Hollerich, "Carl Schmitt," in *The Blackwell Companion to Political Theology*, ed. Peter Scott and William T. Cavanaugh (Malden, MA: Blackwell, 2004), 119.

of forgiveness rather than punishment),[56] and as such involves discriminations and judgments. There is a popular sense that the judgment called for in this text is offensive, if not vaguely unchristian; does not Jesus, after all, tell his disciples not to judge (Matt 7:1)? But while "do not judge" has become something of a cultural mantra, this simplistic view fails to differentiate between making judgments and being judgmental, between being discerning and thinking oneself better than one ought. Jesus, after all, repeatedly says to his disciples, "Judge for yourselves." As Jean Bethke Elshtain points out, we cannot possibly avoid judging, but we can see to it that our judgments are fair; judging *well* is central to humanity and sociality: "it helps us to disentangle, analyze, separate, discern and, in so doing, puts us smack dab in a world of others—not apart, not above, not below, but *among*."[57] We cannot strike judging from our midst; compassion and forgiveness are crucial, but they cannot replace discernment. What is really at stake, Elshtain writes, is not whether we make judgments or not, but "the discernment of what it means to judge well," and the ability to differentiate "between rash judging—not judging well—and the kind of judging that lies at the heart of what it means to be a self-respecting human subject in a community of other equally self-respecting subjects."[58] And anyway, as Hauerwas notes, we are always already under one another's judgment, although we typically resist voicing these judgments because we know that it would open up conversational space whereby we may also be subject to correction, either about our wrongdoing or our concerns being silly, overblown, or incorrect. Binding and loosing at least makes these judgments less arbitrary.[59]

Where does this "judge not" attitude come from, this reticence

---

56. McClendon, *Ethics*, 226–27.
57. Jean Bethke Elshtain, "Judge Not?" in *The Moral Life: An Introductory Reader in Ethics and Literature*, 3rd ed., ed. Louis P. Pojman and Lewis Vaughn (New York: Oxford University Press, 2007), 200. Cf. McClendon, *Doctrine*, 478: "Warnings of the riskiness of judgment (e.g., Matt 7:1) and against mere private judgment (Rom 14:10) must be balanced against the inevitability that in a living community someone, somehow, shall indeed judge."
58. Elshtain, "Judge Not?" 193.
59. Stanley Hauerwas, "Peacemaking: The Virtue of the Church," in *Christian Existence Today: Essays on Church, World, and Living In Between* (Durham, NC: Labyrinth, 1988), 89–97.

toward the possibility of making discriminating moral judgments? Philosopher Alasdair MacIntyre has a helpful theory. MacIntyre notes that disagreements inevitably arise in any community. Certain disagreements may signify deeper, more systematic rifts, while others may be the sort that healthy communities must *foster*, especially communities inquiring together "about how it would be best for them to act."[60] When any such disagreement arises, MacIntyre points to twin evils that can occur: One is the evil of suppression, where conflict is supposedly avoided by depriving one group of their ability to express their convictions and concerns. The other is the "evil of disruption," the kind of disagreement that destroys the possibility of arriving at the sort of consensus that is required for shared decision making. "Sometimes one of these evils is produced by those who are attempting to avoid the other. It is on occasion the prospect of disruption that leads to suppression. And it is sometimes the fear of suppression that engenders disruptive attitudes." Now, MacIntyre takes it for granted that every group is intolerant of certain views—no paper defending phlogiston will be accepted in a reputable scientific journal. So the real task is determining the difference between "justified intolerance" and "unjustified suppression," determining who gets to draw that line, and determining how it will be enforced as a conversation-governing norm.[61] For MacIntyre, the key is whether the judgment arises from within the community itself; intolerance imposed from without (as from the nation-state, as he argues later in the essay) is bound to be arbitrary, while views that frustrate a community's ability to achieve goods are less likely to be proscribed arbitrarily. The evil of suppression corresponds with the fear liberalism attempts to correct, but in our current context, an equally pervasive error is that of a bland, unthinking toleration of which "don't judge" is the slogan. So while binding and loosing must avoid harsh or arbitrary judgment, to be sure, so too must it avoid succumbing "to a conventional kind

---

60. Alasdair MacIntyre, "Toleration and the Goods of Conflict," in *Ethics and Politics: Selected Essays, Volume 2* (Cambridge: Cambridge University Press, 2006), 205.
61. Ibid., 206.

of political correctness" or replacing "biblical discipline with liberal autonomy."[62]

Second, note that in Matthew 18:15-20 the answer to the question, "Who decides?" or "Who is to make that judgment?" is the entire community. There is little embarrassment in this text about authority resting with the *ekklesia*. Ultimately, of course, all authority is God's in Jesus (Matt 28:18), and it would be easier to say the church's authority is one thing and God's another. But while all authority is God's, the scandalous assertion here is that it has been shared, and the mode of God's authority enacted in the world has been laid upon the disciples as well[63]—and more specifically, with the community as they argue about the kinds of hard decisions that are central to any community of inquiry. That is, Jesus's promise to be where "two or three are gathered" in his name is not *automatic*, but occurs when disciples partake in the kind of hard arguments requiring decision, especially in relation to restoration. Decisions reached under these conditions—where true authority is in humility, where forgiveness is the process's beginning and end—do hold, and in faith, the church affirms that Jesus empowers us during these arguments. Indeed, at certain points God may even *cause* community tension in order to stimulate church growth.[64]

At this point, it is important to see that binding and loosing is a practice that is laid before the community as a whole; indeed, one of the main ways this practice goes wrong is when it is tied to the function of an official clergy, rather than an interpersonal practice that gradually moves to include the entire community. In Matthew 18 *whoever* knows about an offense is authorized to address it.[65] The words "whoever sins *against you*" are not in the most reliable ancient manuscripts of Matthew 18:15, and no such limitation is in Luke 17:3,

---

62. Biesecker-Mast, "Recovering," 200.
63. James Wm. McClendon Jr., "The Concept of Authority: A Baptist View," in *Collected Works, Volume 1*, 120. Cf. Yoder, "Binding and Loosing," 330.
64. Takashi Yamada, "Reconciliation in the Church," in *Baptist Roots: A Reader in the Theology of a Christian People*, ed. Curtis W. Freeman, James Wm. McClendon Jr., and C. Rosalee Velloso Ewell (Valley Forge, PA: Judson, 1999), 365.
65. Yoder, *Body Politics*, 2-3. This is precisely one place where Yoder hedged his argument when it came to his own abusive actions.

Galatians 6:1–2, or James 5:19–20.⁶⁶ Therefore, limiting who can address sin to an official leader (or, for that matter, the one sinned against, which would create problems in cases of abuse of power, as in sexual abuse) is misguided. Community leaders may be included in the process, but to see such figures as "normally or exclusively the disciplinarian, to the extent that others no longer share in bearing the same burden, undermines both the reconciling process and this person's other leadership ministries."⁶⁷ Taken together, then, the question of "who decides to bind and loose" is the entire community, not an individual or leadership team.

Of course, for Schmitt this would all be nonsense, as on his view no political community can function without a singular leader who ultimately has the authority to decide on such matters. Indeed, for Schmitt this reality is constitutive of authority and sovereignty: "Sovereign is he who decides on the exception."⁶⁸ What this means, for Schmitt, is not simply that lasting polities require a sovereign who will make decisions in exceptional times; more, the person with authority is the one who decides what circumstances constitute "exceptional" times, and thus is able to suspend normal procedures such that he protects the law precisely by acting against and outside of it.⁶⁹ These exceptional moments where the community is shown to be upheld by a sovereign's actions—circumstances that may be called "abnormal"—for Schmitt reveal the norm that is always operative and justifying truly political entities (the exception *is* the norm); it is always under the surface, only occasionally becoming explicit.⁷⁰ So for Schmitt, because the "political entity is by its very nature the decisive entity,"⁷¹ the question for binding and loosing communities of

---

66. Yoder, "Binding and Loosing," 334.
67. Ibid., 335. Yoder denies the existence of "lay" Christians, meaning those with no ministry. "The bishop is a member of the laity just like everyone else. The use of the word 'lay' to mean 'non-minister' is heretical, and arises only generations later." Yoder, *Fullness*, 14.
68. Schmitt, *Political Theology*, 5.
69. Ibid., 7–8. Agamben clarifies that Schmitt does not support dictatorship; the role of the sovereign is to bolster and finally reinstate constitutional law. Schmitt wants to show that the locus of authority in nation-states finally rests with this singular decider. Giorgio Agamben, *State of Exception*, trans. Kevin Attell (Chicago: University of Chicago Press, [2003] 2005), 35, 47–50.
70. Schmitt, *Political Theology*, 15.
71. Schmitt, *Concept*, 43.

discernment is whether this vision will hold up when circumstances force the need for decision, particularly if it is to have import for radical democratic participation, where the timetable for momentous decision is set by a variety of factors outside the control of the patiently deliberating body. Indeed, Schmitt saw that questions of decision get heightened "concerning those matters for which there are no positive stipulations" and in situations "for which competence has not been anticipated"; when "the legal system fails to answer the question of competence," the question will naturally arise as to "who is competent to act."[72] Awareness of this potential incompetence leads Schmitt to affirm a political theory in which the sovereign is the ultimate arbiter between competing visions of the good, expressing (even discovering?) the authority to settle such debates—or at least to act decisively in the midst of them.[73] Thus for Schmitt and others, there will be doubt as to whether a communal, open process of decision that specifies no automatic leader is adequate.

However, I tend to think this doubt springs from the practice's neglect. To tweak an aphorism of G. K. Chesterton, "The Rule of Christ has not been tried and found wanting; it has been found difficult and left untried." To be sure, the vision of binding and loosing presented here gives no guarantees as to its form, function, or success in making decisions; what is guaranteed instead is the kind of risk inherent to maintaining the health of any community. "A vital community does not necessarily guarantee us smooth, easy and peaceful living; it is rather a challenging, exciting and adventurous way of living."[74] In any case, Schmitt's emphasis on a *singular* decider is theologically deficient insofar as he ties sovereignty to an autocratic, overwhelmingly powerful vision of God that is totally devoid of the Christological considerations I summarized above.[75]

---

72. Schmitt, *Political Theology*, 10–11.
73. Ibid., 9.
74. Yamada, "Reconciliation," 364.
75. Cf. Hollerich, "Carl Schmitt," 117–18.

2.5 Tax Collector Treatment (Matthew 18:15-20)

Finally, loosing from the community must sometimes occur, according to this text. This can sit uncomfortably with some people—although fewer have issues when the reason for exclusion is being a slave owner, as with certain nineteenth-century Baptist abolitionists,[76] or committing violent slaughter, as with Ambrose after Theodosius's massacre of Thessalonica in 390 CE. But first, notice that the call for loosing is the final recourse rather than enforcing authority "with sword and rack"; in this way it is the "visible backbone of the gentle constraint of the Spirit."[77] As the last resort, it is as much a failure of and judgment on the community doing the loosing as it is on the offending party. And second, there is no warrant here for complete exclusion, for "shunning" or banning in the way traditionally understood. Jesus says to let the offender "be to you as a gentile and a tax collector" (18:17). One must remember that in Matthew's Gospel, "being an outsider is a hopeful state,"[78] and any expulsion "puts the offender in the class of those Jesus uniquely befriended—Gentiles and tax collectors."[79] To treat someone in the same way Jesus treated a tax collector, in other words, is to be in a certain kind of relationship with them, not ignore them. While indeed constituting a form of loosing, exclusion, or MacIntyrean "intolerance," this occurs when the offense manifests at heart a rejection of God's judgment in the community,[80] and even then, the line between offender and community is permeable—"a kind of standing invitation to think again and to return."[81]

All this said, there's no denying that it is here that binding and loosing has most frequently erred, used as a tool to reinforce hard

---

76. Cf. the Baptized Licking-Locust Association, Friends of Humanity, founded by David Barrow in 1807, described in Bill J. Leonard, *Baptists in America* (New York: Columbia University Press, 2005), 186.
77. McClendon, *Doctrine*, 481–82.
78. McClendon, "Politics," 229.
79. McClendon, *Ethics*, 226. McClendon continues: "This procedure is not equivalent to the reckless excluding or shunning practiced by some modern sectarians. Its genius lies rather in the confidence it places in the church's ongoing conversation as a means of pastoral guidance."
80. O'Donovan, *Desire*, 150.
81. Ibid., 259.

group boundaries or to achieve "purity." Of course, from Schmitt's perspective, such boundary demarcation would simply manifest the distinction that holds for any truly political group: the friend-enemy distinction. Indeed, Schmitt's work is in many ways a defense of the kind of boundary-hardening exclusions that, when manifest in discerning congregations, are signs that the Rule of Christ has gone awry. For Schmitt, "the political" is fundamentally marked by the distinction between friend and enemy, those inside and outside a group—just as morality rests on the distinction between good and evil, or aesthetics between beauty and ugliness—and "denotes the utmost degree of intensity of a union or separation, of an association or dissociation."[82] Delineating a *political* enemy does not mean that one must always avoid or feel a special animosity toward him, or even necessarily regard him as evil or ugly; the category is "objective," marking a person who is of another, threatening group and thus "existentially something different and alien."[83] Crucially for Schmitt, an enemy is not one who is disliked, but a person and group that one is willing to kill; "enemy" is no metaphor, but the category reserved for just this relation,[84] and is *required* by all actually "political" groups (that is, no group is "political" without such an enemy, and lacking such enemies, "politics" properly so-called does not exist).[85] Thus does Schmitt argue that the injunction to "love your enemy" (Matt 5:44) only applies to one's private adversary, rather than a collectivity's "public enemy"; "Never in the thousand-year struggle between Christians and Moslems did it occur to a Christian to surrender rather than defend Europe out of love toward the Saracens or Turks."[86]

The point is *not* that Schmitt would see all in-group/out-group distinctions as manifestations of the friend-enemy criterion. But it is to say that such distinctions approach the creation of a properly political community, for Schmitt, for although the political "is the

82. Schmitt, *Concept*, 26.
83. Ibid., 27.
84. Ibid., 32–33, 37.
85. Ibid., 35.
86. Ibid., 29. Of course, we saw in the last chapter that this *did* occur to certain Anabaptists in relation to the Turks—and the scandal it caused.

most intense and extreme antagonism," other distinctions exist on a kind of spectrum toward the political, such that "every concrete antagonism becomes that much more political the closer it approaches the most extreme point, that of the friend-enemy grouping."[87] Thus might Schmitt say that churches are political entities only insofar as they delineate an enemy, either through ostracism, expulsion, proscription, or outlawry.[88] Giorgio Agamben takes this further, arguing that the fundamental distinction in Western politics is not friend-enemy, but between "bare life" and "political existence," human life qualified by political interactivity, as Aristotle conceived it.[89] In so arguing, Agamben keys on a central feature of Western political history: that of the *banned individual*, the person who has committed a crime such that he or she is excluded from the realm of human life and reduced to existence in a liminal, human-yet-not-human space.[90] To be "banned" in this sense, Agamben notes, is an ever-present possibility in contemporary nation-states, and is an exclusion "more intimate and primary than the extraneousness of the foreigner."[91]

One way to trace when the Rule of Christ is going wrong from a baptist perspective, then, is when it functions as a "ban" in this classic sense, reinforcing a hard friend-enemy distinction or the creation of non-persons by total exclusion from the discerning body. Whereas according to Schmitt this is simply what political entities *do,* I think those who suspect that this is not how the practice should operate for gospel communities are correct. While there is a continued place for actual separation and community distinctions, according to Matthew 18 this ought be a separation that ultimately subverts the type of differentiation that Schmitt and Agamben point out.[92] Put differently,

---

87. Ibid., 29.
88. Ibid., 46–47.
89. Giorgio Agamben, *Homo Sacer: Sovereign Power and Bare Life*, trans. Daniel Heller-Roazen (Stanford, CA: Stanford University Press, 1998), 8, 110.
90. Ibid., 104.
91. Ibid., 110–11.
92. For instance: "He who has been banned is not, in fact, simply set outside the law and made indifferent to it but rather *abandoned* by it, that is, exposed and threatened on the threshold in which life and law, outside and inside, become indistinguishable." Ibid., 28.

binding and loosing is altogether different from the classical "ban"; the latter is only understood rightly when redescribed Christologically such that an entirely different concept of "exclusion" is developed, housed by its own type of practice and guided by its own ends. The Rule of Christ must not create hard boundaries between even those treated as tax collectors, but stand as a gate through which people come in and go out (John 10:9). To loose is not to shun, nor to designate a Schmittian "enemy"; proper separation still transformatively engages even the one separated from. In short, "the ban" is a terrible term for all that's happening with binding and loosing.

2.6 Broader Ecclesiological Observations

Overall, the picture of binding and loosing I have presented presupposes and itself creates a theopolitical community of *restraint* that disallows its communal processes from landing on the weakest among us. The practice is slowed so that the purpose of restoration might be kept in view, and so that one can see the fallible human judgments within such decisions. The danger associated with binding and loosing is placed on those with authority in the community. Decisions are reached, but there is a patience here that is often unrecognized, and even after decision, the orientation of the *ekklesia* is toward the one sheep, rather than enclosed around one's friends. The personal function of binding and loosing must not be hidden behind an impersonal "process" that cavalierly and automatically barrels on, the feature of liberalism that Schmitt so detested;[93] in order for this to happen, an ecclesiology is required that does not detest, and perhaps privileges, communities of limited size. It is harder (though still possible, of course) to hide behind "procedure" or send an impersonal "letter of rebuke" in a community of seventy; conversely, it is easier for this to occur in communities housed in massive, necessarily bureaucratic institutions. Size doesn't automatically fix everything,

---

93. Cf. Yoder, "Binding and Loosing," 333, 347. The practice errs when the focus moves from one's brother or sister to the standards themselves, thus protecting the church's identity, reputation, or power structure; ibid., 343.

but it may address some things. At the least, in smaller communities one knows who to address if one feels mistreated. As MacIntyre writes, "What is important about such face-to-face encounters is that in them we cannot evade responsibility for our assertions; we show ourselves as deserving of a hearing only insofar as we have made ourselves accountable in this way."[94]

An equally important warrant for local polity—more than effectiveness, grassroots appeal, or historical precedence—is that the nature of authority itself, as McClendon points out, is incurably diverse as it arises in and impinges on the congregation, pertaining to a number of areas and manifest in many people, and which gains its justification in dependence on the Spirit-infused *ekklesia*.[95] The community is the site of God's authority, with the diversity of gifts that arise in this context dependent upon and in service to the functioning of this body.[96] Binding and loosing functions best in a structure that explicitly recognizes and honors the diverse nature of manifested divine authority, as well as recognizes the voluntary nature of the authoritative congregation in question. As Yoder points out, central to binding and loosing is an ecclesiology in which those so participating have agreed, through baptism, to participate in this process, even if they don't fully know what they're getting into when they enter such a covenant. "We can pursue reconciling confrontation," Yoder goes on, "because we trust one another and because we asked to be placed under this kind of loving guidance. To do the same things in a nonvoluntary community gives them a quite different meaning; this is where in our culture the word *Puritan* got its bad taste."[97] Put differently, there are agreements implicit to joining this community that are not arbitrary, but internal to its life and practices. If I join a pick-up basketball game, the rules are internal to the practice itself; if I want to play, I have to dribble, pass the ball (an unwritten rule), and I can't tackle an opposing player. So long as no one is forcing me to play,

---

94. MacIntyre, "Toleration," 222.
95. McClendon, *Doctrine*, 479–80.
96. Cf. Yoder, *Priestly Kingdom*, 28–34.
97. Yoder, *Body Politics*, 5.

I cannot say, "No dribbling for me! And my baskets count six points apiece."[98]

None of this is to suggest that local congregations are or should be isolated from one another. Yoder is correct that while the concrete church has centrality precisely because it is required for the right practice of binding and loosing, this does not mean that *only* the local gathering is "church"; for one thing, scripture also uses *ekklesia* for all Christians in a city, as well as the cosmic assembly of Christ's body. "The concept of local congregational autonomy has, therefore, been misunderstood when it was held to deny mutual responsibilities between congregations or between Christians of different congregations."[99] The issue is not if, but what kind of wider accountability binding and loosing congregations will be a part. Coles's image of a network of interconnected grassroots organizations that are competent to work on their own, but also accountable to other similarly-minded groups,[100] is analogous to what Yoder is pointing to here. Without denying the value of bishops when they are receptive to healthy congregational and congregant pressure, there is no requirement for bishops in the way usually meant: a singular "overseer" of discerning congregations. Mutual accountability between congregations, however, is required to keep churches from isolation and ossification. As McClendon writes,

> the strength of connectional polity lies in the extension of these very elements of trust, diversity, openness, obedience to the wider peoplehood of which each congregation is but a part. What justifies any polity is not its effectiveness, for on occasion any may crumble, nor its convenience, for any may cause trouble: it is justified by the Spirit that indwells such communities of concern.[101]

---

98. Of course, a game's rules do change over time—there was not always a three-point shot, or a shot clock, or even (*very* early on) the requirement to dribble—but this happens slowly, over much debate, and usually of necessity.
99. Yoder, "Binding and Loosing," 352.
100. Coles, "Tensions and Tricksters," 283.
101. McClendon, *Doctrine*, 479.

3 Conclusion: Beginning Implications for Radical Democratic Participation

In this chapter, I have set myself an unpopular task, arguing for a nuanced reclamation of a practice that has some baggage, to say the least. If I have been successful, binding and loosing will now appear to be integral to communal discernment as well as baptist political theology, especially one that does not seek to escape from authority or power, but manifest a different sort of power, or inhabit power differently—and in this way emulate the powerful weakness of the politics of Jesus.[102] "Fair enough," a critic may reply, "but 'baptists' have never had trouble with the significance of church practices. The question is how this impinges on the political realities of those who do not claim Jesus as Lord, or in organizations that do not invoke the Spirit in their gatherings. Even granting your specification of a radical democratic context, how is this practice *actually* relevant elsewhere?" Articulating a direct response to this challenge is coming—although the descriptions contained within each chapter so far are themselves eroding the plausibility of the question. However, the beginning of a response can be outlined here, as the question does get at an important concern: In what ways, specifically, are communal discernment and the Rule of Christ relevant to radical democratic participation?

Churches embodying this practice may effect change elsewhere in at least two ways: First, as churches go about practicing binding and loosing *well*, they may serve as a witness to other bodies who see the church gaining political "competence" even amidst serious disagreement with one another, without lapsing into harsh exclusion or impotence. This presupposes churches that are visibly, politically engaged with non-ecclesial bodies, without collapsing the difference between them or denying that the church is, in important ways, distinct. By its very nature (not only by implication), churches that bind and loose are social, practical, and public; "without any complex argumentative bridge being needed either to explain or to justify, these

---

102. Cf. Yoder, *Politics*, chs. 8, 12.

practices can be prototypes for what others can do in the wider world."[103] A grassroots political organization may see the binding and loosing *ekklesia* (as the two work together on issues of racial injustice, for instance) and be suitably impressed with the way the community handles hard moments of decision. Second, as churches and their members participate in ad hoc, on-the-ground democratic struggles, they will bring the virtues inculcated through the practice of binding and loosing to bear in this context. Virtues, after all, are "systematically extended," and are considered virtues insofar as they manifest themselves throughout a flourishing person's various activities. As Yoder writes, there is a "real common agenda" that occurs in various ways between the faith community and other social structures that is not so distant as a mental translation or conceptual bridging, "but rather the concrete historical presence, among their neighbors, of believers who for Jesus's sake do ordinary social things differently."[104] Besides eating and friendship, one could add political engagement in the context specified in chapter one. Christians may lead others to foster a political presence that is "not one of sovereignty, whereby we should increasingly bring it about that the world should be ruled by believers (or by their ideas), but by servanthood. We have been trained to give priority to lordship models of social process, whereby the Lord makes laws and the bureaucrat implements them."[105]

Hopefully I can now name some specifics about *what*, in particular, a binding and loosing *ekklesia* offers grassroots radically democratic processes. The search for competence—having at least a modicum of knowing one's way about even in extreme circumstances—is a recurring concern in political theology. Whether against the "inverted totalitarianism" of Wolin, where the processes of political organization are intentionally subverted by myriad powerful entities, the frozenness that comes when procedure and "politics as technology" overwhelm our humanity, or the sense of apathy generally recognized

---

103. Yoder, *Body Politics*, 46. Yoder repeats this point often, against the assumed necessity of "translation" into a neutral public language.
104. Ibid., 75.
105. Ibid.

as infecting the contemporary United States, the search for competence is ongoing. In noting this, one must recognize that certain responses to incompetence may rightly assess the issue, but offer a balm that is worse than the disease. As we already saw, Schmitt addresses incompetence through a strong, singular sovereign who upholds the law in extreme circumstances precisely by acting outside and even against it. This path may resist incompetence, but I am unclear as to why, faced with a choice between Schmitt's sovereign and liberal proceduralism, I ought not prefer the latter. In any case, communities of discernment offer a third choice between liberalism and authoritarianism: a competence won through friendship. Friendship is not compatible with an impersonal proceduralism that would bury political decision in process, but neither is it compatible with a sovereignty that divides and keeps forever at arm's length one's friends from one's enemies. Competence through friendship comes by way of acting and deciding *with*, rather than on another's behalf; in this way, friendship "secretes" from discernment together, something I return to in the final chapter. More specifically related to binding and loosing, the community that postpones decision as long as possible may gain the ability to see ongoing possibilities for relationship and grassroots action between "enemies" that will be missed by those who would hastily decide on who is "with us" and who is "against us." It is in such prolonging that friendships can sprout between surprising parties.

Relatedly, radical democratic movements are sometimes forced to decision before they are ready by a variety of external pressures. As Coles noted above, democratic movements sometimes tend to be suspicious not only of bad authority but authority per se, not only of decisions reached poorly and unfairly but decisions per se. In the same way that binding and loosing churches approach decisions with patient listening, and with an understanding that all members are at least potentially involved in the process, democratic groups also require decisions on a variety of issues—including contentious matters. Decision in these situations rests with the group as a whole; on the ground, a "don't judge" mantra cannot be maintained, for as soon as any practice is undertaken, standards of excellence internal to that practice are in play. Even the most ironic hipster makes judgments about the proper roasting of coffee.

Crucially, baptists can teach radical democrats a way toward judgment that is still patient and "fugitive," but not in the sense of ghostly, formless, or a manifestation of perpetual discussion. Rather, it teaches us to recognize the binding yet contingent nature of all such decisions, made as they are by people doing their best with the limited options available to them. Further, the community that binds and loosens knows that the weakest of a political group are not the ones who should bear the brunt of any such decision. Quite the opposite, such communities will be extra vigilant that those with the least power are treated with special care. Indeed, such communities will judge those in power by the effects their decisions have on the least, and what is more, will *be able to see* certain classes of people as "little ones," rather than as threats to eliminate.

Finally, when certain decisions are made where a segment of the community does not get its wish—as will happen in grassroots work given limitations of time and differences of vision—this presentation of binding and loosing teaches that the inevitable result in such a scenario is not the disowning and distancing of the two parties, splintering into rival organizations with rival names and mission statements. A bond can endure even through disagreement. Similarly, when community organizations face enmity from non-sympathetic groups, a baptist ecclesiology teaches a patience whereby one refuses to disown members of the competing group, without pretending they all get along. The forgiving love that maintains the *ekklesia* even through binding and loosing can serve as a model for other political communities, whereby even those "loosed"—even those one is working against on an issue—are not denied humanity, the potential for relationship, or a continued ear, and this *without dulling the firm stance* taken by the discerning democratic community. As Romand Coles writes, "blocking" another's voice is sometimes necessary, for there "is much that calls to be blocked"—racism, sexism, jingoism, heterosexism—"the question is how to do so without closing down the relationships. Blocking does not have to be violent. . . . Blocking can be integral to opening."[106] In this way might judgment open onto new relational possibilities, thus serving as an alternative to Schmitt's friend-enemy distinction. Put differently, a baptist political theology discovered through communal discernment reveals a more robust view of friend than what Schmitt articulated. Indeed, in contemplating why Schmitt eventually supported Nazism, Tracy Strong speculates that he was led to think that opponents of the regime were "enemies" in the sense specified by his work. What emerges from this recognition is a concern with his "overly simplistic notion of friend. There is a way in which Schmitt allowed his notion of enemy to generate his idea of friend."[107] Thus a more positive vision of friendship undetermined by Schmitt's vision of an absolute enemy is needed, one that subverts the primordial friend-enemy distinction and instead fosters a radical friendship across given political lines.

Are these paths to competence sufficient? Schmitt would say no, and that calls for a "sovereignty from below" create a power vacuum that will ironically be filled by an even worse form of dictatorship.[108] Perhaps; but the proof is in the pudding. If and when communities arise that exercise sovereignty from below without themselves devolving into chaos or ushering society at large into totalitarianism, Schmitt's suggestion will appear less plausible, or less as *destiny*. Thus work that documents people and groups who have successfully manifested an authority from below gain central importance, as such lives stand as living testimonies against the false choice Schmitt has presented. Memories of lives that were competent in extreme times yet manifested the fiercely kenotic power of patient listening, reinvesting their power back in the community—people like Ella Baker—make a baptist political theology look plausible, even if they don't "prove" anything. For this reason, such lives are the well-spring of both

---

106. Romand Coles, "Letter of July 17, 2006," in *Christianity*, 40n14.
107. Tracy B. Strong, "Foreword," in *Concept*, xxiv.
108. Schmitt, *Political Theology*, 24–26.

Christian and radical democratic authority: their memories provide clear, noncoercive yet compelling sources for what has worked, what is authoritative, and what should be emulated in the future.[109] True authority, McClendon reminds us, is found in such models of discipleship,[110] even as no authority can solve beforehand challenges that will come in the future. Such is the value of this practice, more "a style of approaching any question" than an answer to a particular moral choice, and marked by a "flexibility and readiness to approach any new challenge" that frees one to engage any and every context.[111]

Even so, there is no denying the reality of risk in this vision of church life. But there's no place of total safety in this world. In the same way that we are always already politically involved in some way—even to refuse politics is a political choice—so is the choice between faithful and unfaithful risk, rather than no risk at all. And anyway, is anything truly worthwhile ever gained without any risk whatsoever?

---

109. As Hauerwas and Coles write, "When resources like Vanier, Baker, and the IAF go unnoticed, we are condemned to cynicism and despair"; cf. *Christianity*, 9.
110. McClendon, *Doctrine*, 143–44.
111. Yoder, *Body Politics*, 46.

4

Practical Matters

> Everything ritualistic (everything that, as it were, smacks of the high priest) must be strictly avoided, because it immediately turns rotten. Of course a kiss is a ritual too and it isn't rotten, but ritual is permissible only to the extent that it is as genuine as a kiss.[1]
> —Ludwig Wittgenstein

At its heart, incompetence is an embodied problem and a social problem, naming a feature of communities whose categories and capacities for discernment have become blunted, if not broken. This means, among other things, that the therapy for incompetence cannot be simply the recommendation to adjust individual thinking, but must be at least as embodied and social as the problem itself as it seeks to address its root connections to political liberalism. Thus the path I have proposed to address political incompetence has been thoroughly "practical." If incompetence is a kind of social diminishment that is formed onto human bodies, then it stands to reason that the social, embodied formation available through the recovery of certain practices might be part of the solution.

---

1. Ludwig Wittgenstein, *Culture and Value*, 2nd ed., trans. Peter Winch (Oxford: Blackwell, [1931] 1980), 8e.

But how would this work, exactly? Proposals recommending practices must avoid a naive optimism that would act as though practices easily or automatically address any problem at hand. If they are therapeutic, it is not in a simplistic way, and a terrible consequence of any proposal would be to lull people into a false sense of competence when nothing of the sort has been gained (for as we all know, the most dangerous drivers are those who are unaware of their inabilities).

With this caveat in mind, my aim in this chapter is to show how communal discernment may do the theopolitical work I have suggested it can: by functioning as a practice that breeds competence in churches, enabling discerning participation by Christians in a complex society. By functioning in this way, communal discernment fosters one side of "radical friendship"—between Christians in the *ekklesia*—such that we are able and willing to participate in radical democratic action without losing who we are, or having to hold onto our convictions loosely, with cosmopolitan irony. On the other hand, this concept simultaneously enables one to see that the line between church and world, while real, is not impermeable, but cuts through the Christian community and each Christian heart. This prepares the way for my work in the final chapter, where I will explore analogues to this practice "out" in the world. This move is not arbitrary, but follows directly from my argument in this chapter that the dividing line between church and world is porous and internal. There, I will explore in more detail the kinds of deliberative friendship that lead to competence that communally discerning Christians should celebrate, and look at how communal discernment helps us receive and incorporate these "fugitive" movements of the Spirit into our ongoing life together.

1 Powerful Practices: Beyond a Generic Picture of Society

So, how might communal discernment enable competence given the reality of Sheldon Wolin's "inverted totalitarianism," which erodes the capacities of the populace to even know that they are being manipulated? One way communal discernment so functions is as a powerful counter-practice within a multifaceted yet interconnected society. In this section, I clarify the sense in which society is "multifaceted" by following James McClendon's description of the social realm as an entangled web of powerful practices—a description that provides the needed backdrop for understanding how communal discernment can function as a theopolitical competence-builder, if it is to function that way at all.

1.1 Practices and Complex Space

For McClendon, it is important to recognize that society is not a smooth, blended whole, but is instead a complex, interwoven bundle of practices that emerge out of embodied life together.[2] The point is not that societies and institutions therein make use of or house practices, but that societies are themselves constituted by practices of various sorts, such as medicine, family, and law. Practices make life possible: humans never exist pre- or non-practically, but are sustained—from birth to death—by participation in social practices of one kind or another.

Because practices aim at goods that are internal to the activity in question, an irreducible plurality marks this view of society, for while some goods will indeed be found across multiple practices, others remain particular to each practice; basketball has its own goods that are distinct from those in parenting or theological writing. Each aims to bring about a state of affairs (an end or goal) that is achieved by following rules that prohibit certain means to that end, and which must be followed with the proper attitude.[3] Indeed, the rules of any game are internal to its being played well; they are not arbitrary additions that can be discarded at will. "It is exactly the constitutive rules that make tennis the game it is, or bridge, and without them we would have no way to say which game we were playing."[4] To practice something is to *do* something, and thus to acquire the capacities and

---

2. James Wm. McClendon Jr., *Ethics: Systematic Theology, Volume 1*, rev. ed. (Nashville: Abingdon, [1986] 2002), ch. 6.
3. Ibid., 169–71.
4. Ibid., 170.

vision that come from performing that activity in the face of the barriers and challenges that naturally arise as one aims for excellence. "So in the professional world there is the practice of law, which means doing what lawyers do, and the practice of architecture, which is doing what architects do, and in each case there are various lesser practices (such as the architectural practice of providing suitable drainage for building sites in a wet climate) that contribute to the master practice itself."[5] Clearly, McClendon's view of human life is complex and dynamic, since different practices constitute different strands of society; and although these strands interrelate at a certain level (see below), this interrelation nonetheless maintains their distinct—not isolated, but distinct—rules, virtues, and ends. Thus while many continue to speak of "participation in" or "transformation of" society as an all-or-nothing affair—influenced by speech-patterns inherited from H. Richard Niebuhr—if McClendon is right, then "there can be no generic answer to the question, 'What is the relation of the Christian to society?' for the excellent reason that society is not a generic whole. The relation of the Christian to the police cannot be the same as to the garden club, because the police are no garden club."[6]

An ally on this point is political theologian William Cavanaugh. Cavanaugh affirms the multifaceted picture of society defended by McClendon but goes further, analyzing the theological, philosophical, and political inheritances that led to the erosion of this multiplicity in our own time. For Cavanaugh, it is a subversive thing to attempt to reclaim a picture of society as an overlapping web of multiple communal loyalties and practices, because this picture is antithetical to the goal of nation-states as they have predominantly functioned in history. That is, similar to Wolin's analysis of modern power in terms of a desire to "intend" one's ends on others irrespective of the diversity or local culture constitutive of a people,[7] Cavanaugh sees that

---

5. James Wm. McClendon Jr., "A Practical Theory of Religion," in *The Collected Works of James Wm. McClendon, Jr., Volume 2*, ed. Ryan Andrew Newson and Andrew C. Wright (Waco, TX: Baylor University Press, 2014), 277.
6. James Wm. McClendon Jr., "Social Ethics for Radical Christians," in *The Collected Works of James Wm. McClendon, Jr., Volume 1*, ed. Ryan Andrew Newson and Andrew C. Wright (Waco, TX: Baylor University Press, 2014), 178. Cf. McClendon, *Ethics*, 181–82.

neutralizing this multiplicity was the desired result of a constellation of philosophical, theological arguments. Conversely, Cavanaugh sees that to recognize the multifaceted nature of society is to begin to foster a different sort of politics entirely—in Wolin's terms, a politics of tending. The phrase Cavanaugh uses in these matters is society as "complex space," which is opposed to the typical nation-state goal of *simplifying* political space in order that direct interaction (and thus manipulation) can occur between the individual and the state.[8]

By invoking the concept of complex space, Cavanaugh wants to remind us that the emergence of nation-states as ways of organizing bodies (both human and social) is contingent—they are "imagined communities" that have not existed from time immemorial.[9] Because it is easy to operate as though the nation-state always existed or *must* exist, at least if we are to avoid the "wars of religion," this recognition is important, as it helps rob the nation-state of its "must be" power. McClendon agrees, arguing that once one notes the characteristically modern nature of generic, simplified visions of society, one will more easily recognize the fact that humans have not always thought this way—we certainly did not in the Middle Ages, nor in antiquity—and thus one "need not think this way today."[10] Further, one will then be able to see this "flattened" picture of society as logically dependent on the modern theories of knowledge, language, and ontology from which it emerged. Indeed, McClendon rightly connects this mode of political organization with the philosophical resources that created an entire way of structuring the world, including Cavanaugh's "unified simple space" and a "modern generic individualist" anthropology, wherein individuals were pictured as identical for all relevant purposes.[11] This connection is evident in Hobbes's *Leviathan*, the paradigmatic

---

7. Sheldon S. Wolin, *The Presence of the Past: Essays on the State and the Constitution* (Baltimore: Johns Hopkins University Press, 1989), esp. 82–92.
8. William T. Cavanaugh, "'Killing for the Telephone Company': Why the Nation-State Is Not the Keeper of the Common Good," in *Migrations of the Holy* (Grand Rapids: Eerdmans, 2011), 19.
9. Ibid., 9–18, 33–36. Cf. Benedict Anderson, *Imagined Communities: Reflections on the Origin and Spread of Nationalism*, rev. ed. (New York: Verso, [1983] 2006).
10. McClendon, "Social Ethics," 177.
11. Nancey Murphy and James Wm. McClendon Jr., "Distinguishing Modern and Postmodern Theologies," in *Collected Works, Volume 2*, 46–48.

articulation of these moves. While many readers isolate the "strictly" political aspects of Hobbes's argument from the rest, in point of fact his theories of political life and sovereignty are unintelligible apart from the linguistic and anthropological moves that he spends the entire first quarter of the book defending. It is as though some "choose to leave out the stuff about speech and human nature (appetite, aversion, and all the rest), as if this is dross or icing on the cake and you can hive off the piece of Hobbes that you want.... He wasn't two people when he wrote *Leviathan*—God forfend, given his stress on oneness and unity!"[12] The trick, then, is to go beyond the categories that gave rise to the simplification of complex space in the first place, without yearning for premodernity.

Additionally, Cavanaugh reminds us that this contingent historical phenomenon has been *detrimental* to the health of complex space properly so called. For Cavanaugh, the atrophying of "intermediate associations," to use John Courtney Murray's terminology, is connected to the rise of the nation-state. As we saw in chapter one, a wide variety of scholars now recognize that such atrophying is occurring; fewer recognize that the existence of multiple social practices has been inversely related to the proliferation of the nation-state in actual practice. While theologians following in the worthy footsteps of Murray paint an "attractively balanced picture" of the relationship between civil society and the state as a neutral creator and sustainer of the latter—which on this view does not pursue a vision of the good but creates the space wherein more robust conceptions of the common good can be articulated and debated—such a picture was never a reality.[13] In the same way that Jeffrey Stout accuses certain theologians of not paying attention to what has occurred in on-the-ground democratic practice, Cavanaugh argues that one must not allow an ideal theory of state-association balance to obscure what has actually transpired as nation-states have grown. And what has actually transpired has been the reimagining and simplification of space in

---

12. Jean Bethke Elshtain, *Sovereignty: God, State, and Self* (New York: Basic, 2008), 114.
13. Cavanaugh, "Killing," 24–26; William T. Cavanaugh, "The Church as Political," in *Migrations of the Holy*, 133–34.

order to relativize associational connections, guilds, and other "non-voluntary" alliances that were not chosen by the individual. In this way, society's complex, multilayered fabric was flattened, as much as possible, such that intermediate associations became accidental to political life. What may have started as an important corrective to the ecclesial imposition of its vision on others, or out of a desire to protect religious liberty, led to the erosion of intermediate associations such that the main political "entities" became the individual and the state, and perhaps an atomized conception of family.

My point is that any account of communal discernment that would seek to counteract these shifts must attend to and itself foster the plurality of practices that constitute healthy social life, thus helping us begin to move beyond entrapment in ways of being dominated by the nation-state. To specify this as the context within which communal discernment may do work is to begin to get at the root of contemporary incompetence.

1.2 Powerful Practices

Of course, noticing this plurality is but the first step, as the practices that constitute society are not just "external," but indelibly shape the lives of human beings. My character, my affective sensibility, my aesthetic, are all colored by this complex of practices such that moving differently or transformatively within this milieu is complicated. McClendon is especially clear on this point. Adopting the Pauline language of "principalities and powers" (cf. Col 1:15-17; Eph 6:12; Gal 4:1-11), McClendon argues that the practices that constitute ourselves and society alike are not benign, but "powerful." That is, while practices are intended to enable human flourishing, they regularly overstep their intended scope, tempting people to serve them alone, or confuse them with the end all and be all of life.[14] While everyone recognizes that certain practices carry this danger, in reality any

---

14. McClendon, *Ethics*, 181.

practice may be turned to harm the practitioner, it could also help flourish.

McClendon follows those scholars who remark that the biblical concept of "principalities and powers" originated with the ancient Near Eastern association of alien gods and spiritual forces with both power and the successes and failures of society. While the precise origin of this understanding is complex, by the time of the New Testament such powers have been presented as creations of God, subordinate to yet rebellious against God's rule, and typically identified with empire and its rulers.[15] The New Testament's interest in the powers, however, is not with their origins or even much with their precise nature; the point consistently made of them is that through "the whole course of his obedient life, with its successive moments of proclamation, healing, instruction, the gathering of a redemptive community, and his costly submission to the way of the cross with its death and resurrection" (i.e., his kenosis), Jesus confronted and disarmed these powers, making "a public spectacle of them, leading them as captives in his triumphal procession" (Col 2:15, REB).[16] McClendon pays special attention to the sense in the New Testament that the powers' reign has been challenged, and yet remains influential. They are not destroyed, but something objective *has* occurred: they have been dethroned. In the time between the resurrection and the final coming of Christ, the powers are in an ambiguous state, and in that state "delimit and define the moral task of Jesus' followers, who encounter in the form of these powers crosses of their own. To them, the disciple must witness concerning the reversal of power achieved in Christ's resurrection; that is, must make plain that these civil, military, economic, traditional, cultural, social, yes *religious* and other structures are not themselves the end and meaning of life." The hope of the New Testament—hinted at more than

---

15. Ibid., 179.
16. Ibid., 180. Cf. Nancey Murphy, "Traditions, Practices, and the Powers," in *Transforming the Powers: Peace, Justice, and the Domination System*, ed. Ray Gingerich and Ted Grimsrud (Minneapolis: Fortress Press, 2006), 89–91.

proclaimed—is that "the final destiny of all the powers conquered by the cross will be not their abolition but their full restoration."[17]

Combining society's multifaceted, practical nature with this understanding of the powers, what comes into focus is that the multiple practices that constitute social life are inherently neither good nor bad. Certainly this analysis corrects what McClendon perceives to be an overly positive assessment of practices in the highly influential account provided by Alasdair MacIntyre, in which practices are pitted against an overly negative account of the institutions that house them and manufacture external goods from practices' internal value.[18] Instead, McClendon speaks of practices as ubiquitous and powerfully double-edged, conduits of the highest human excellences as well as our most destructive tendencies. By their very nature they can send us soaring, but precisely because of this potentiality, are also open to profound abuse. No matter how life-giving in one moment, they can become toxic in the next; there is no guarantee that a practice cannot turn to thwart flourishing.[19]

But more importantly, the value of this analysis is that it provides a way to conceptualize the political incompetence that has been my focus, and which Cavanaugh and Wolin alike connected with the rise and ramification of political liberalism. While there is indeed a sense in which the principalities and powers metaphysically underlie the created order, my interest is in the sense that the powerful practices of our contemporary political landscape are manifestations of those principalities with a specifiable origin and history, and lead to the particular form of incompetence that perdures in the United States today. Indeed, there is a connection between analyzing social realities that shape (and in some cases undermine) our capacity to think about the world on the one hand, and Wolin's "inverted totalitarianism" on the other, which refers to the sapping of political, moral capacities by

---

17. McClendon, *Ethics*, 181.
18. Ibid., 179. McClendon's response is that institutions do not house practices, but are themselves constituted by sets of practices, such that "institutions," like the bundles of practices that make them up, can be good or bad.
19. James Wm. McClendon Jr., *Doctrine: Systematic Theology, Volume 2* (Nashville: Abingdon, 1994), 33. This clearly applies to churches as well.

the populace of the United States by social forces that were intended for our good but have now outstripped the capacity to be questioned.[20] For instance, in describing inverted totalitarianism as it exists today, Wolin points to structural, created social realities that were meant to aid human flourishing (to "stop the wars of religion," to aid in the "pursuit of happiness"), but over time have had the opposite effect, undermining the very agency they sought to bolster. Contemporary life seems *unimaginable* without political liberalism, Wolin writes—unwittingly providing as apt a description of moral incompetency as one will find in terms that echo the best descriptions of powerful practices: "The demos has been hammered into resignation, into fearful acceptance of the economy as the basic reality of its existence, so huge, so sensitive, so ramifying in its consequences that no group, party, or political actors dare alter its fundamental structure."[21] The first trick of powerful practices is making people believe they are unquestionable and perennial, such that one cannot imagine life without them. Insofar as the coalescence of practices specified in chapter one has made this the case for "politics as usual"; insofar as these practices are created realities intended for humanity's flourishing but have now become confused with the unquestionable condition of life or its ultimate end; insofar as this context "slips" such that it is notoriously hard to nail down; and insofar as there is no "escape" from this context, one could reasonably say that contemporary political incompetence is the natural consequence of a particular set of powerful practices running amok. Or perhaps better, incompetence is the principal "virtue" of these powerful practices, breeding not just a sense of overpowered subjugation, but moral frozenness. In short, powerful practices provide a helpful and typically baptist framework for understanding the form of incompetence wrought by political liberalism.

---

20. Sheldon S. Wolin, *Politics and Vision: Continuity and Innovation in Western Political Thought*, exp. ed. (Princeton: Princeton University Press, [1960] 2004), 591–92. For a readable account of many Founding Fathers' aversion to democracy, see David Graeber, *The Democracy Project: A History, A Crisis, A Movement* (New York: Spiegel & Grau, 2013), ch. 3.
21. Wolin, *Politics and Vision*, 578.

1.3 There Is No Outside, but Better Ways to Be Inside

Finding a redemptive way to move within a complex society of powerful practices is critical, and I have claimed that communal discernment must find its place within this milieu if it is to function as a competence-building practice in today's world. However, a clarification is immediately required if the forthcoming analysis is not to be misunderstood as providing a simplistic avenue of *escaping* our inherited incompetence.

I mentioned above that "engagement" becomes much more complex given society's multiplicity, for the different practices that constitute society require different things of its participants. The answer to "How should Christians engage society?" is "It depends"—both on the particular powerful practice one is dealing with, and on the particular cultural and historical moment one occupies.[22] Christians should seek to be separatists in some regards ("from deliberate participation in modern warfare"), and engaged in others ("paying taxes to support social benefits").[23] In reality, it is impossible not to exercise some degree of practical selectivity. Certain practices simply cannot work in tandem: war making and peacemaking, for instance, or evangelical poverty and large-scale property ownership.[24] And anyway, that the multiple practices in which we do participate partially constitute both self and society is of course true; that they should have such a say, or should continue to have a say in the same way and to the same degree, is another point entirely.

This point holds about selectivity. Yet it must be made carefully, as society is not only multifaceted, but interconnected. Recognizing this interconnectivity is important if one is to avoid appearing to argue as though there is an escape from society in general, or contemporary incompetence in particular. Theological ethicist Philip Wogaman, for instance, points out that although society is composed of "distinct

---

22. McClendon, *Ethics*, 181.
23. McClendon, "Social Ethics," 178.
24. James Wm. McClendon Jr., "How Can a Christian Be a Law Librarian?" in *Collected Works, Volume 2*, 336.

practices," it does not follow that Christians can therefore sharply distinguish between them, or avoid implication (at least) in each and every one. Is it possible for a pluralistic social model such as the one I have articulated to "do justice to the systemic interrelationships of the social world? Granted, of course, that the world presents us with a bewildering diversity of cultures, subgroups, power centers, and narrative histories, is it not also the case that social wholes do exist and that our behavior is to a substantial and increasing extent tied to the behavior of others?"[25] The question, for Wogaman, is whether "it is even *possible* to avoid doing what the state is doing.... [I]s it not the case that even the normal activities of social life—which do not involve us directly in violence or other sin—are ultimately supportive of those very things?"[26]

Wogaman is certainly right that there is no "outside" to the complex web within which the variety of social practices that constitute human life interconnect at some level—no practice is autonomous, existing in isolation. What I question is that these connections take the form that Wogaman seems to assume they must, *and* that this recognition carries the implications he thinks it does. Regarding society's interconnectedness, I believe that this takes dialectical form such that one "can give a connected account of society only by attending to its plurality and diversity."[27] That is, adequately accounting for powerful practices' interrelation paradoxically requires recognizing their distinctiveness—the sense that they are not interchangeable, that their differences are a mark of their relation. Retaining a view of practices' irreducible distinctiveness is necessary to the sort of social engagement I am advocating, as is clear from my indebtedness to Wolin's political philosophy. As we saw above, Wolin recognizes that to adequately appreciate the interconnectivity of a given place, one must see the distinctive variety that is present therein. To work toward a place's flourishing requires that one tend to inchoate possibilities

---

25. J. Philip Wogaman, *Christian Perspectives on Politics*, rev. and exp. (Louisville: Westminster John Knox, [1988] 2000), 77.
26. Ibid.
27. McClendon, "Social Ethics," 178.

present in certain aspects of a place, rather than monolithically assume that the whole is of one kind—the sort of flaw Wolin associates with intending a vision of the good on a place. Indeed, the inability or unwillingness to attend to such distinctives is a particular inheritance, the result of which is that the terms, conditions, and possibilities of "the political" are limited, trapped within the imaginative horizon of political liberalism.

McClendon himself describes this dual commitment to the distinctiveness and interrelation of powerful practices in narrative terms: "What *is* indispensable for making any society (or culture or community) *one* society is that it shall have a narrative tradition whose function is to provide a setting for the several practices of that society, one that unites them in a single web of meaning."[28] And again, "The human social life that is formed by such practices requires interconnections best described as narrative continuity and coherence. In other words, practices imply stories, and making sense of social life requires eliciting the stories it embodies."[29] Thus the accurate point about society's interconnectivity ought not negate attention to the practical distinctions that exist therein; in fact, an adequate conception of this interconnectivity is only possible by attending to these distinctions, even while recognizing that these distinctions do not get one outside the whole. Interrelation is not interchangeability; the nature of these relations is narratival rather than neatly correlative.

More troubling are the implications Wogaman draws from interconnectivity, well represented in the quote above: it is not possible to "avoid what the state is doing." From this lack of avoidance, Wogaman seems to suggest that we are each equally implicated in everything a nation-state does. But surely this isn't right. The notion that we are all implicated in the practice of torture performed by the US government, for instance, is in a certain sense true. Society's interconnectedness comes by way of shared narratives and a certain

---

28. McClendon, *Ethics*, 177.
29. McClendon, *Doctrine*, 132.

economic collaboration, and thus one could say that all are implicated in the actions performed at Guantanamo Bay insofar as we are formed by a story (about protecting the good guys from the bad by any means necessary: about the United States being a light to all nations and the hope of the earth) that makes those actions intelligible. But to suggest that this sort of implication is the same as a one-to-one correspondence is nonsense; connectivity at a narrative level cannot be used to suggest that we are all equally, intimately involved in or responsible for the practice of torture as such. To suggest that we are is not only imprecise, but serves to subdue a populace that may otherwise be repulsed by such activities, and moved to work against their acceptability. Wogaman comes across as administering this sort of opiate when he writes that his concern with McClendon's multifaceted picture of society is that it "significantly weakens the theological legitimation of the political order."[30] Such is the perennial concern of Constantinianism, which can only see the variety of powerful practices "as 'orders of society' or 'mandates,' often making the state paradigmatic for all the rest," even though the New Testament never presents society in this way.[31] Nor do radical democrats. And nor do I. Indeed, that this sentiment even arises in the first place is likely a manifestation of inverted totalitarianism doing its work, tricking me into a form of acquiescent hopelessness in the face of problems that I (apparently) am as implicated in as anyone else. Retaining the distinctiveness of interrelated practices implies that torture is not the same or of equal weight as careerism, that they function with different kinds of relation to one another, and thus that Christian communities engage each differently without being guilty of escapism or incoherence.

Instead, while there is no "outside" to the web within which we all operate, there are better, transformative ways to be "inside," as I am sure Wogaman would agree; ways to push back on practices like torture, for instance, without purporting to any kind of false purity.

---

30. Wogaman, *Christian*, 77–78.
31. McClendon, *Ethics*, 182.

Interconnectivity should not lead to immobility—to the view that no competence for partial change is there to be had—even despite feeling, at times, overwhelmed by the interconnectivity or false totality of it all. To repeat Foucault's line from the previous chapter, it does not follow from the fact that there is no "outside" (to society's interconnectivity or to power) that distinctions between powerful practices are therefore meaningless; indeed, it is from these very practices that resistance to the kind of power associated with more dominant forces in society may be fostered. Another way to put this is that on this side of the eschaton there are not really two Augustinian cities (or three or four), but one. The distinct practices we engage in *do* interconnect, and yet this must not be used to oust "selectivity" for and with Christians, but to describe it differently: there are some parts of the city where we do not go; others into which we only go with caution and with the aim of transforming; and everywhere, with an ear to learning from others with whom we ultimately share the same place.[32]

All of this is but a way of saying that there is no "non-practiced" place to go, no escape from powerful practices. They are dangerous and they are *ubiquitous*. That is, the point about practices being "powerful" includes within it their indispensability in human formation. That they are powerful is tied up with how some such practice is always and inevitably forming us toward some end, whether we realize it or not. In recognizing the riskiness and deeply formative power of practices, it may be tempting to seek refuge from practices altogether; but this is a nonstarter: "Where would you go? Family life is itself a powerful practice, and so is the PTA. So, in fact, is every valuable human endeavor."[33] Life as we know it is impossible without powerful practices. The real question is not *if* we'll encounter powerful practices, or *if* our lives will be profoundly shaped by and put in service to some practice, but *which* practices will so function; not if, but *how* we will encounter and inhabit these practices. And anyway, while it is

---

32. Cf. Cavanaugh's use of Michel de Certeau in *Theopolitical Imagination* (London: T&T Clark, 2002), 92–93.
33. James Wm. McClendon Jr., "Ethics for a Career," in *Collected Works, Volume 2*, 323.

indeed true that we may sometimes need to avoid a practice out of faithfulness, McClendon is right that "in general the risk-free life is not worth living. Isn't the live question rather this: To what risks of practice am I to expose my life, and what precautions must I take when I do so?"[34]

Counter-Practices and the Church-World Divide

Thus far, I have argued that in order to understand how communal discernment can take its place in the constellation of practices forming Christian competence in the world such as it is, it is important to note the interconnected, "practical" nature of society, as well as the patterns that work against it or prevent it from being seen. Having clarified this starting point, I can now consider what I mean by communal discernment as a powerful *counter-practice* that is situated within this milieu. This will require a bit more attention to the identity-constituting nature of powerful practices—the sense in which practices are "made flesh" within us before we ever venture into more conscious engagement with the world. That practices shape multifaceted identities toward certain ends I take to be a given; the more interesting question is *how* this formation happens, a question that is not incidental to figuring out how to enter the world without pretending the world doesn't also enter us.

2.1 Human Nature and Ordered Inhabitation

McClendon's previous statement about the inescapability of powerful practices comes from recognizing the extent to which such practices make us who we are, anthropologically speaking. I am who I am because of the various practices in which I have taken part—family, bible study, academia, basketball, music, friendship. From this there is no escape; to practice something well is to become someone different than I otherwise would have been. Far from a mildly interesting observation and nothing more, this point is relevant to understanding

---

34. Ibid., 320–21.

how a powerful practice, and communal discernment in particular, functions regarding social engagement today, in at least two ways.

First, it means that to a very real extent we are all children of liberalism—an observation drawn from practices' identity-constituting quality. Human bodies are always already embedded in a wide array of social practices from birth to death, and one cannot talk about identity or social engagement solely with reference to things going on "in one's head." Rather, who I am in the world is a result of my previous and ongoing formation, as I have developed and continue to develop only in relation to some particular social scaffolding and the practices constitutive thereof.[35] For those of us living in the contemporary United States, this means that we are inescapably implicated in and formed by the powerful practices of political liberalism.

Political philosopher Romand Coles makes this point by invoking the concept of mirror neurons, a neurological phenomenon whereby the same neurons that would "fire" if I were to perform a certain action actually do fire as I watch another person do that action, to a weaker degree.[36] Even just watching someone perform an activity primes me to perform that same action. Playing on this concept, Coles argues that in our contemporary context, we together unconsciously participate in a regenerating, formative, self-reinforcing social reality in which we prime one another to take liberal patterns of thought and action for granted. Numerous factors—religious, economic, governmental, educational, scientific—coalesce into a political context in which a "spiritual ethos" is formed in its inhabitants, marked by a diminished capacity to recognize the reality of difference in others, let alone see such differences as gifts to be welcomed. That is, for Coles, the skills necessary to be receptive toward one another "are weakened in ways that greatly impede our social perception, understanding, imagination—our political vision. These deficits are deleteriously

---

35. Cf. Warren Brown and Brad Strawn, "Beyond the Isolated Self: Extended Mind and Spirituality," in *Practicing to Aim at Truth: Theological Engagements in Honor of Nancey Murphy*, ed. Ryan Andrew Newson and Brad J. Kallenberg (Eugene, OR: Cascade, 2015), 66–67.
36. Nancey Murphy and Warren Brown, *Did My Neurons Make Me Do It? Philosophical and Neurobiological Perspectives on Moral Responsibility and Free Will* (New York: Oxford University Press, 2007), 119.

entangled with erosions of democratic capacities for empathy, dialogue, judgement, and hope born of both cooperative action and respectful agonistic struggles across difference."[37] This context and its concomitant incompetence is our birthright, and not avoided as easily as some radical democrats have assumed. That is, the phenomenon of mirroring points to a primal intersubjectivity in which our mutual perception of the world is shaped by and solidified through interactions with others.[38] While this indeed opens the possibility of sustaining empathetic "mirrorings" toward each other, this possibility just as often is manipulated by corporate superpowers to reinforce "practices that tend to shut down, deflect, or diminish resonant relationships among us that enable people to open towards the plurality and complexity of the world."[39] So first of all, whatever faithful theopolitical engagement looks like in our current context, it cannot ignore the descriptive point that each of us carries this incompetence within us. There's no getting outside of the context of "intending" that many of the American forefathers hoped would spread through time, as well as from sea to shining sea. We come to perception within this context, and it thus becomes one of the innermost rings of our identities.

Second, that powerful practices form us in this way means that no one, Christians included, engage a socio-political context that is totally exterior to oneself, nor do so merely as "one thing." Rather, we engage a reality that forms our very identities, participating in multiple powerful practices that bolster one another in ways both explicit and subtle, such that we act in the world as complex, variously formed agents. This recognition need not lead to the overdrawn conclusion that anthropological multiplicity negates the conviction that one "aspect" of our identity ought to order the rest. Instead, its value comes in enabling one to see how powerful practices constitute

---

37. Romand Coles, "The Neuropolitical *Habitus* of Resonant Receptive Democracy," *Ethics & Global Politics* 4, no. 4 (2011): 275, 283.
38. Ibid., 278–79. Cf. Romand Coles, *Visionary Pragmatism: Radical and Ecological Democracy in Neoliberal Times* (Durham, NC: Duke University Press, 2016), 40–49.
39. Coles, "Neuropolitical *Habitus*," 281.

human lives in ways that are never eliminable; a complex society creates complex people, and it is here that the superiority of speaking of powerful *practices* rather than "the powers" in general is evident. Humans are passionate beings that desire multiple things—we act "from the gut," and that gut is very much formed as we interact with the world; it does not fall from the sky, or constitute a *tabula rasa*. To be sure, these passions are not morally neutral; it is possible to will the wrong thing. But to neglect this as a *starting point* for political engagement is a mistake indeed.[40] The question becomes whether recognition of our multiplicity or the inevitability of our liberal inheritance means we are determined to act in this or that way. If not, what might an alternative look like that takes these observations seriously?

A hopeful path forward is through what McClendon calls "counter-practices." As we saw above, McClendon views society as a complex web of powerful practices that in turn shapes individual identities. McClendon is crystal clear that there is no getting away from this milieu—that would be to get away from human life altogether. Instead, he emphasizes the importance of *alternative* communal practices in enabling one to reform or transformatively engage this plethora of powerful practices.

By counter-practices, McClendon means equally embodied, equally powerful practices that equip adherents to participate in other practices (such as career, marriage, or academia) without being tossed about by their formative power. Counter-practices, in other words, are differentiated by their functionality. The path this move opens up is the recognition that there is no way to get away from powerful practices' formative pull, but that this does not mean that one's only recourse is acquiescence. Rather, the question becomes not *whether* to engage this world, but *how* to engage it. Counter-practices provide the

---

40. On recognizing the multiple stories that constitute who we are as a moral starting point, cf. Stanley Hauerwas, "A Tale of Two Stories: On Being a Christian and a Texan," in *Christian Existence Today: Essays on Church, World, and Living In Between* (Durham, NC: Labyrinth, 1988), 25–45; and "Habit Matters: The Bodily Character of the Virtues," in *Approaching the End: Eschatological Reflections on Church, Politics, and Life* (Grand Rapids: Eerdmans, 2013), 173–75.

energy and skills required for Christians to sustain faithful inhabitation in such a world, energy that cannot come from standing outside practices altogether, or from one's "bare" subjectivity.

While examples of counter-practices are varied in principle, McClendon provides some clues about their nature in an essay where he traces the transformative effect law school has on its students, as exemplified in Scott Turow's novel *One L*. Turow outlines the ways first-year law students are formed into a particular mode of acting, speaking, and thinking, such that a great many are completely changed by the experience. However, McClendon points to friendship and marriage as practices that allowed one student to "counter" some of the molds that law school was trying to force him into. Of course, friendship and marriage are powerful practices in their own right, making their own claims upon one's allegiances; and in Turow's story, both were ultimately ineffective. But McClendon's point is that without *something* like friendship or marriage, practices such as law school remain as powerful and unchecked as ever.[41] And while there is nowhere to go that is not already "practiced," counter-practices at least enable the degree of engaged selectivity that is required for faithful movement within a world of powerful practices, without being swallowed by them whole. To put it another way, they inculcate the virtues required for a radical political engagement that is sustainable.

It is this combination—recognition of powerful practices' intensely formative power *and* a desire to resist the pernicious effect state discipline has on our competence and imagination—that necessitates attending to counter-practices in this way. Put differently, if the first task of powerful practices run amok is to constrict the range of live possibilities until its own ends are seen as all-encompassing and unquestionable (to paraphrase Pierre Bourdieu, going without saying because they come without saying[42]), counter-practices form the virtues in people that are necessary to reopen the horizon of imaginative possibilities for alternative ways of inhabiting the world.

---

41. McClendon, "Ethics for a Career," 321–23.
42. Pierre Bourdieu, *Outline of a Theory of Practice* (Cambridge: Cambridge University Press, 1977), 167.

A parallel way of understanding this notion of counter-practices that corroborates McClendon's analysis is provided by Romand Coles. Coles agrees that it is quixotic to think one could get outside the pull of certain powerful practices and the habits they manifest, even by focusing on our potential for being receptive to others; this is because "our receptive capacities are themselves profoundly directed, shaped and limited—variously amplified and diminished—by the very topographies of inequality and subjugation that radical democrats seek to change."[43] But this does not lead Coles to despair; rather, he argues that a "counter-machine" is needed, a "complex dynamical system" that would counteract the incompetence wrought by state and hyperstate power.[44] For Coles, the very capacities that can be used to undermine competence can also be turned to respond to that threat, like with venom and antivenom. The issue is not if, but to whose discipline, or whose discipleship, one will be subject. And whereas "the discipline of the state seeks to create disciples of Leviathan, the discipline of the Church seeks to form disciples of Jesus Christ, the Prince of Peace."[45]

Of course, one may remain skeptical that counter-practices could do much in the face of whatever attitudes they happen to be ensconced within—what Bourdieu called *habitus*. Habitus, after all, is the generative principle delimiting the possibilities available to us, *regulating* improvisations, and *producing* the very practices that allegedly form possible resistance. It functions by definition subconsciously, and is very hard to notice.[46] It is constantly, subtly inscribed on our bodies,[47] and thus has a regulative—Foucault would say disciplinary—effect on counter-practices. And yet, "mimetic intercorporeal practices" that inculcate the dispositions and capacities needed for more generous, radically democratic politics also provide

---

43. Coles, "Neuropolitical *Habitus*," 273.
44. Ibid., 274–78.
45. Cavanaugh, *Theopolitical*, 85, 88.
46. Bourdieu, *Outline*, 72, 94.
47. Bourdieu, *Outline*, 94. Bourdieu elsewhere calls this process the "somatization of the cultural arbitrary"; Pierre Bourdieu and Loïc J. D. Wacquant, *An Invitation to Reflexive Sociology* (Chicago: University of Chicago Press, 1992), 172.

a means for sustaining an alternative vision, a possibility that Coles thinks Bourdieu undersells. This is not to say that any counter-practice falls outside the influence of habitus that Bourdieu ably describes, or is immune from being reincorporated into the habitus it was trying to resist; it only means that they *can* be the site of resistance, and on my view, must be if there is to be any hope for transformative inhabitation that can be sustained over time and across generations.[48]

Put differently—and to temper Wolin's stress on the "fugitivity" of any such alternative—there is a certain durability of function that is required for "flourishing improvisational practices" to carry on. While they will remain fugitive in the sense of "on the run" from forces set against them, counter-practices must not be and are not always so fugitive as to be ghostly. Durable counter-practices are a paradoxical means to a form of inhabitation that is also improvisational: as Coles writes, capacities for fugitive democracy are "indebted to the discernment and invention of significantly stable practices that tend to engender intensities and enthusiasms for democratic innovations."[49]

2.2 Counter-Practices and Receptivity

All this said, because a constantly shifting panoply of powerful practices come together to form the ongoing dance that is identity, there is one thing that I *cannot* mean when I speak of counter-practices enabling faithful inhabitation of the world: it cannot be the case that this inhabitation happens unidirectionally, or as a bit of formational prolegomena. Rather, counter-practices by their very nature assume that such inhabitation is always a two-way street, involving giving to *and receiving* from others.

Among theologians who emphasize the importance of durable practices for inhabiting the world differently, there is a tendency to endorse a subtle prioritization whereby a focus on church practices means one needs to get everything settled within one's ecclesial borders *first*, and only then move to engagement with others. The

---

48. Coles, "Neuropolitical *Habitus*," 289–90.
49. Ibid., 291.

problem, as Coles argues, is that this reinforces the belief that it is even possible to get one's practices in order prior to any engagement with others; and more, that doing so would automatically move Christians to service to the world. Lost in this picture is any inherent place for receiving from those one encounters along the way. Coles argues that a better conception of practices is to imagine them issuing from a center that is "partly constituted by the borders themselves"; such a vision of the church is not of a community that is called and gathered "prior to encountering others," but "a people equiprimordially gathered and formed precisely at the borders of the encounter."[50] This view does not neglect the cruciality of practices, but nor does it view encounter with those outside the church as secondary, or even view church practices as totally intrinsic to the church. Coles isn't against the existence of boundaries, such as between church and world; his argument is that boundaries, vital though they are, must be of a certain kind if they are to be healthy—permeable rather than rigid.[51] The danger for those who focus on practices is that this boundary can become rigid, or prioritized to the exclusion of engaging those outside one's community, despite our best intentions. Coles is even reticent about metaphors like "harmonization" and "improvisation" (both of which I employ), precisely because he worries that they presume we already fully know, prior to encountering others, the entire tune to be played or script to be acted out.[52]

Counter-practices as I have described them, following McClendon, avoid this "unidirectional" failing precisely because they imply that identity is constituted by both practices and counter-practices. To be sure, McClendon emphasizes the line between those called to follow Jesus and those who have yet to heed that call; but this line between church and world, for McClendon, constitutes not a firm boundary but a *struggle* that runs "right through each Christian heart."[53] This is no

---

50. Romand Coles, "Gentled into Being," in *Christianity, Democracy, and the Radical Ordinary: Conversation between a Radical Democrat and a Christian* (Eugene, OR: Cascade, 2008), 212.
51. Romand Coles, "The Pregnant Reticence of Rowan Williams," in *Christianity*, 190–91.
52. Ibid., 188; and Romand Coles, "Letter of July 17, 2006," in *Christianity*, 42–43.
53. McClendon, *Ethics*, 17.

mere rhetorical flourish, but follows from McClendon's conception of the church and the world as collections of powerful practices. Given this starting point, the sorts of practices that constitute church and those that constitute "world" end up quite literally constituting my very identity. For McClendon, the church is not a bounded community that "contains" powerful practices; it *is* a set of social practices that consequently constitutes Christian identity, such that the line between church and world is real but porous, ever formed in interaction with a world that is both within and without. It is for similar reasons that Cavanaugh, expanding the same thought to the social realm, writes that "the church is full of the world," precisely because the church is a relational body rather than a closed system; it is not a *polis*, but an *ekklesia*—a public meeting that "names something closer to a universal 'culture' that is assembled out of the particular cultures of the world."[54] Thus the church as a set of counter-practices forms us for service to the world, yes, but not as only one thing, or as divorced from the world itself. Counter-practices name a way of inhabiting a world that enters us, learning just how deeply our identities are the product of a *habitus* shaped by the world without denying that at least some aspects of that identity need ordering and even denying, at least if we are to begin to be oriented to gospel ends.

This then forms the beginning of a response to a fairly common concern about appropriations of practices in political theology: that they tend to be conducive to insular, inward-looking accounts of the Christian life. For instance, Timothy Beach-Verhey (following H. Richard Niebuhr) argues that a focus on the importance of the church threatens to "slip into idolatry of itself," replacing "faith in God" with "faith in that which points to God."[55] Ecclesial practices are important, but only as they help create an *open* rather than a "closed circle" view of the church.[56] Similarly, William Schweiker claims that scholars like

---

54. Cavanaugh, "Church as Political," 139–40. The inverse is also true: not only is the church full of the world, but the world is grace-soaked, haunted by a Spirit blowing at will.
55. Timothy A. Beach-Verhey, *Robust Liberalism: H. Richard Niebuhr and the Ethics of American Public Life* (Waco, TX: Baylor University Press, 2011), 134.
56. Ibid., 52–59. Beach-Verhey's main target is Hauerwas, whom Beach-Verhey thinks has good things to say to Christians—but *only* to Christians. For Beach-Verhey, in rightly rejecting Rawlsian

Hauerwas and MacIntyre, "traditionalist postmoderns," unduly focus on practices to the exclusion of ontology, "satisfied with explicating the beliefs about human existence and moral virtue found in their specific moral community."[57] And Wogaman critiques McClendon for exactly this reason, tying the critique to McClendon's believers' church ecclesiology, which emphasizes congregations being constituted by gathered, consciously confessing disciples of Jesus who "stand in sharp contrast to those who identify with other communities." Wogaman believes that given this ecclesiology, "There would seem to be little to share, little basis for mutuality between confessing Christians and those whose identity is formed by other communities." McClendon "clearly [does] not attach great importance to the participation by Christians in the civil society on the basis of the shared story, meanings, and values of that society," and is "preoccupied by the internal life of the church and by the character and identity of Christians as individuals formed in that communal context."[58]

Hopefully, the preceding account of McClendon's view of counter-practices makes it clear that this critique does not stick. To be sure, Wogaman is correct that McClendon deems it important to acknowledge the unique resources present to and with the gathered church, particularly as gleaned from the Great Story that forms and invigorates its life together. McClendon never denies the confessed truth that the gospel is the story that completes each of our incomplete stories.[59] But McClendon is also crystal clear about church practices' proclivity for creating a Christian echo chamber, which he narrates as being the inverted form of a mistake many make pre-conversion. McClendon writes that it was hard for him to hear the truth of the Christian story when he was outside the church; "but when I became an insider and fellow citizen of the saints, self-interest presented a

---

liberalism, Hauerwas too-heavily relies on MacIntyre, which leads to a "closed-circle" ecclesiology. I do not think Beach-Verhey reads Hauerwas accurately on this point.

57. William Schweiker, *Power, Value, and Conviction: Theological Ethics in the Postmodern Age* (Cleveland: Pilgrim, 1998), 93.
58. Wogaman, *Christian*, 182–83.
59. James Wm. McClendon Jr., "Story Sainthood, and Truth: *Biography as Theology* Revisited," in *Collected Works, Volume 2*, 217.

new set of temptations. The convert perceives the world in near-Manichaean terms—the good people are the convert's fellow Christians; the bad, those outsiders one has left behind."[60] McClendon as much as anyone is concerned to avoid that sort of unreceptive dualism. His recommendation is not to deny the truth of the gospel story, but to see that rightly understood, this story opens to generous participation in others' practices and stories.

Such participation and mutuality requires neither the forfeiture of Christian convictions nor a grand theory of "how to participate with others," for the church itself and the people within it are constituted by practices, many of which are shared with others outside the church. In this way we are already "engaged" with others, bound by a plethora of shared social activities; the question becomes *not if*, but *what nature* this engagement will take. Thus McClendon does not casually claim that no sharp line separates the disciple's role in the congregation from her role in society, or that such engagement with one's neighbors is not an "added extra" to Christian duty but is always already occurring "by the very nature of what church and world mean in gospel perspective."[61] Disciples simultaneously "share life with other neighbors, and in both those contexts Christian ways can distill into the wider society."[62] Contra Wogaman, McClendon writes that Christians must not withdraw into "pietist enclaves that disregarded God's magnificent creature, the powerful practice, and God's intentions for it," or "abandon hope in the costly work of witness to the structures of society"; but nor, he goes on, should we "indulge in a nonselective antipathy to whatever any government anywhere proposes."[63]

Finally, as McClendon argues, if the community in question takes on the true character of forgiveness so central to the gospel story, in part through the practice of correction and restoration as seen in Matthew 18, this will go a long way toward forestalling the temptation to foster

---

60. Ibid., 216.
61. McClendon, *Ethics*, 241.
62. James Wm. McClendon Jr., "The Politics of Forgiveness," in *Collected Works, Volume 1*, 229–30.
63. McClendon, *Ethics*, 181.

an in-group, out-group mentality. This is because such forgiveness will begin to set the character of the community as a whole as a fundamentally forgiven, and therefore forgiving, community: "Without forgiveness, the social power of a closed circle may crush its members, ruin itself, and sour its world. Examples of such soured communitarianism stain the pages of church history. But with forgiveness controlling everything, the closed circle is opened; the practice of community is redeemed and becomes redemptive."[64]

To summarize, counter-practices provide a nuanced means of inhabiting the world, shaping multifaceted identities for receptive service to others. In participating in the variety of counter-practices that enable Christians to inhabit the world transformatively—*and* in lobbying, educating, working for social reform—Christians must be careful not to "erode the distinctive Christian social witness conveyed by example more than precept."[65] Instead, we must continually and selectively engage the world of powerful practices, working within them *while* participating in a variety of Christian counter-practices that enable this engagement, thus making "the intersection of these two the basis of a challenge to the standing order."[66]

3 Communal Discernment as Counter-Practice

Thus far, I have provided an assessment of our contemporary sociopolitical context, and a description of counter-practices that may function within it. And yet, as McClendon writes, while the clues provided by this kind of analysis are helpful, "in its philosophical generality it provides too little concrete discussion of the community we are looking for."[67] As such, the above is but the needed context for a more important task: considering how communal discernment in particular may function as a competence-building counter-practice for radical democratic engagement. Put differently, if McClendon is correct that religion is "a set of practices that cohere to create a holy

---

64. McClendon, "Politics," 229.
65. McClendon, *Ethics*, 238.
66. McClendon, "Law Librarian," 337.
67. McClendon, *Ethics*, 182.

culture,"⁶⁸ then what sort of "culture" can communal discernment help foster? Does its culture have the potential to create something conducive to a counter-movement in a contemporary political life marked by ramified incompetence? What capacities does it engender? Answering this question is my task in this concluding section. As in chapter three, it is important to note the *way* in which the politics of this ecclesial practice relates to the politics of radical democratic engagement: it is not through one-to-one correspondence. Some aspects of communal discernment practiced within the church cannot carry over to a world that does not acknowledge Jesus's kenotic Lordship, as we will see. Nonetheless, it does exist as an example for others to emulate—a social, practical, public "prototype" for moving in the world—observable as Christians work with others (rather than through conceptual or theoretical "translation") whereby we "do ordinary social things differently."⁶⁹ As discerning Christians participate in the powerful practice of radical democratic engagement, we may point it in directions that it would not have gone without us, "even if that means challenging some of the standing rules [of engagement]."⁷⁰ To this end, I focus on three ways communal discernment "works" as a counter-practice in the context of radical democracy: it forms people to be *patiently receptive*, it forges a path toward *valuing structural change through local attention*, and it enables a capacity for *gospel confrontation*.

3.1 Patient Receptivity

First, Wolin's arguments in chapter one reveal a strong warrant for keeping one's focus at the local level, on challenges one can actually get one's hands around. His desire is for a democratic politics that is born of and attentive to the local idiosyncrasies that might coalesce into a wider network of cooperation and solutions that may be implemented at a larger level.⁷¹ This contrasts with liberalism, which

---

68. McClendon, "Practical Theory," 279.
69. John Howard Yoder, *Body Politics: Five Practices of the Christian Community Before the Watching World* (Scottdale, PA: Herald, [1992] 2001), 46, 75.
70. McClendon, "Law Librarian," 336.

is marked by a desire for speed and a desire to efficiently manage from afar. While Wolin's is a consistently chastened, fugitive recommendation given the success of liberalism, he nonetheless hopes for a democratic politics that is built upon caring for ("tending to") one's locality, "tempered by the feeling of concern for objects whose nature requires that they be treated as historical and biographical beings. . . . [It] requires attentiveness to differences between beings within the same general class, whether students, patients, plants, or animals. Tendance implies respect that is discriminating but not discriminatory."[72] Such attention, if fostered, necessarily combats the incompetence that is liberalism's offspring.

This proclivity toward a caring, attentive politics requires counter-practices that instill *patience* in a citizenry that is moving incredibly fast, teaching us to slow down enough to see (let alone care for) what is going on around us. Liberalism is antithetical to a politics predicated on practices that take this kind of time. This was made clear to me during a personal conversation with David Myers, a former Mennonite pastor working with the Department of Homeland Security as the Director of the Center for Faith-based and Neighborhood Partnerships.[73] As Myers discussed negotiating the inevitable tensions that exist between Anabaptist convictions and some activities of the federal government, I asked if the practice of communal discernment aided in these negotiations. Myers lamented that he had attempted this when he first moved to Washington, but soon found he had little time to give to such a process, and sought other, more individual modes of discernment. Myers said that in his line of work, everyone is going extremely fast, and that it is disorienting at first; but then you get going the same speed, and it comes to feel normal. This is not a personal criticism of Myers; rather, this conversation served to

---

71. Thus the point is not to be "against government"; it is that the *engine* for the former, if viewed properly, is fueled by and beholden to competencies gained at the grassroots level. On "networking," cf. Romand Coles, "Of Tensions and Tricksters: Grassroots Democracy between Theory and Practice," in *Christianity*, 283.
72. Wolin, *Presence*, 89.
73. Cf. Everett J. Thomas, "Myers is Mennonite presence at U.S. Homeland Security," *The Mennonite* 13, no. 12 (December 2010): 39.

highlight that the patience learned in (and required by) communal discernment and the speed of nation-state politics were, per his testimony, virtually incompatible.[74]

To this end, communal discernment as a counter-practice fosters the virtue of patience in communities and individuals, thus putting its adherents in tension with the speediness of liberalism and the drive to efficiency at all costs, and which, as a by-product, tends to create embarrassment of those who stall this efficiency.[75] Practiced well, communal discernment seeks to tend and discover an end rather than manufacture it via an Aristotelian *techne*, grounded in the belief that "the Spirit speaks to and through everyone"; it teaches patience in its adherents, since communal discernment requires being receptive to others when there is disagreement. And that necessarily makes for a slower process. "A monarchical decree is quicker than careful listening, but is usually wrong. A quick majority vote may reach a decision more rapidly but without resolving the problem or convincing the overpowered minority, so that conflict remains."[76] Discernment goes both ways—it is not issued from on high—and because of this, it both fosters a willingness to be patiently receptive to others, and will lead MacIntyre's bureaucratic manager to either chafe at this process altogether, or impatiently resolve it before consensus has been reached—precisely what happened with the Anabaptists in sixteenth-century Zürich. And while the patience required to value the practice's slowness may be lacking at first, "Trust in the value of a process can grow through its employment."[77] "Practiced well" includes prioritization of the weakest in the fellowship, as we saw in chapter three, through which one learns the patience required to be in relationship even with those who have no "point," or who, in order to be included in discernment processes, will necessarily slow it down.

---

74. Of course, contemporary corporations and universities are similarly inimical to communal discernment.
75. Cf. Stanley Hauerwas, "The Politics of Gentleness," in *Christianity*, 206-7. Recall Alexander Hamilton's revulsion toward impediments to efficiency.
76. Yoder, *Body Politics*, 70.
77. Gayle Gerber Koontz, "Meeting in the Power of the Spirit: Ecclesiology, Ethics, and the Practice of Discernment," in *The Wisdom of the Cross: Essays in Honor of John Howard Yoder*, ed. Stanley Hauerwas et al. (Grand Rapids: Eerdmans, 1999), 346.

Indeed, the conclusions reached by a congregation are valid only to the extent that its discernment has allowed all voices to be heard, and that the procedure of the meeting was conducted in a sufficiently vulnerable manner.[78]

Unsurprisingly, as a radical democrat, Coles is taken by Yoder's emphasis on patience. Throughout Yoder's theoretical work, Coles sees a "wild patience" that avers, for instance, that "the way to affirm our respect for others is to respect their particularity and learn their languages, not to project in their absence a claim that we see the truth of things with an authority unvitiated by our particularity."[79] For Yoder, Christians ought not seek liberalism's view from nowhere, but instead "must converse at every border."[80] Indeed, Yoder's prescribed method in moral reasoning *is* patience: "meeting the interlocutor on his own terms" is not simply in order to resist the chimera of a privileged point of departure, but is an entire "spirituality" and "lifestyle."[81] Thus patience deeply marks Yoder's work when it is at its best—including "political" patience that willingly works with others even as a minority voice[82]—and colors his recommendations for resistance and witness by a patient church witnessing to a patient God. Yoder dissolves "contestations to and fro between Christians who offer a bland ecumenicism and tolerance according to a liberalism that is often complicitous with—or very weak in its resistance to—odious forms of power and suffering on the one hand, and Christians who offer fundamentalisms that are violent and eschew all dialogue, on the other."[83] Yoder's vision of a patient ecclesiology, which is not so confident as to block receptivity to outsiders, is precisely what Coles thinks is needed in radical democratic organization. The lordship of Christ, for Yoder, serves to open "dialogical relations between the

---

78. John Howard Yoder, *The Priestly Kingdom: Social Ethics as Gospel* (Notre Dame: University of Notre Dame Press, 1984), 22-23.
79. Ibid., 42.
80. Ibid., 41.
81. John Howard Yoder, "'Patience' as Method in Moral Reasoning: Is an Ethic of Discipleship 'Absolute'?" in *Wisdom of the Cross*, 28.
82. Ibid., 34.
83. Romand Coles, *Beyond Gated Politics: Reflections for the Possibility of Democracy* (Minneapolis: University of Minnesota Press, 2005), 110.

church and the world in which giving and receiving is possible."[84] In this light, communal discernment stands as a practice enabling the church to hear and digest comments and criticism brought to it by those "outside" the church.

Of course, this patience grows from a center—a "jealousy" for Jesus—which worries Coles. Even though it leads Yoder to officially value theological generosity, for Coles all "jealousies" carry a danger of closing off a community's stories, habits, and practices to receptivity.[85] Despite Coles's fears, the patience learned via communal discernment very much depends on the cruciform *telos* that undergirds most articulations of the practice. As Lawrence Burkholder wrote, "If Christ does not become a living reality within the congregation, then it would appear misleading to discuss problems that presume that he has."[86] Even more than "misleading," the practice would hardly seem worth undertaking. Patient discernment together grew from a commitment to Jesus as Lord, and intended "to reopen the space for a style of practical moral reasoning genuinely free for this confessional, messianic, pneumatic empowerment."[87] In other words, the patience suited to a baptist political theology comes in response to the Truly Vulnerable One, who models the posture churches are to take toward each other and society.

Thus at its best communal discernment fosters patient receptivity in its adherents; churches who engage the practice well, and individuals formed by its exercise, can bring this learned patience to radical democratic engagement. Such patience can help protect against the drive to speed that undermines the ability to tend to a local place, instead working to support "lordship models of social process," even while "Lords" go on making laws and "bureaucrats" implementing them.[88] That said, such patient receptivity will not be wholly applicable

---

84. Ibid., 112. On Yoder's conception of patience as vital to "post-secular politics," see Troy Dostert, *Beyond Political Liberalism: Toward a Post-Secular Ethics of Public Life* (Notre Dame: University of Notre Dame Press, 2006), 182–85.
85. Coles, *Beyond*, 129, 135–36.
86. J. Lawrence Burkholder, "The Peace Churches as Communities of Discernment," *The Christian Century* (September 4, 1963): 1075.
87. Yoder, *Priestly Kingdom*, 45.
88. Yoder, *Body Politics*, 75.

outside the church—in an IAF meeting, for instance—particularly regarding the need for consensus. Yoder is right that among Christian friends discerning together, the goal is for consensus of mind to arise uncoerced through open conversation together; if no consensus is yet reached, the call is to continue patiently discerning rather than preempt the process through a majority vote or individual's decision.[89] But Yoder recognizes that one cannot simplistically transpose this conviction—built as it is on trust in the Spirit's movement—onto other kinds of processes.[90] Indeed, democratic political philosophers have pointed out the flaw in thinking consensus could work for radical engagement. Economic anthropologist and activist David Graeber, for instance, points out that consensus has been the ideal among US grassroots organizations, including SNCC; influenced by politically active Quakers (including George Lakey), the drive to consensus had as much to do with forming a culture of democracy as a set of techniques for reaching decision. However, after the antinuclear movement of the late 1970s in which the ideal of "consensus" was striven for, many came out seeing that *modified* consensus was required for larger, interconvictional groups.[91] Nonetheless, as Graeber puts it, the example set by communal discernment remains relevant, as the qualities learned from this counter-practice remain precisely of the sort needed to create anything resembling a "culture of democracy." Christians who engage communal discernment would, and should, be equipped to serve the world precisely by fostering such a culture, learning the patience that can approximate, to whatever degree, the consensus reached in the discerning *ekklesia*.

3.2 Structural Change through Local Attention

Wolin's proclivity toward local attention leads to a second feature of communal discernment as counter-practice: as we saw above, for Wolin to foster authentically democratic politics requires tending to

---

89. Ibid., 67.
90. Ibid., 74.
91. Graeber, *Democracy Project*, 194–96.

one's local place, learning and loving its idiosyncrasies and staying there long enough to plant long-term seeds of structural transformation. This requires patience, yes, but it also requires what Wolin calls "discrimination," *phronesis*, or discernment.

As a counter-practice, communal discernment is specifically bent toward the making of competent decisions, particularly when the community is facing an issue that seems to carry larger implications than are immediately evident. As we saw in chapter two, communal discernment evokes an entire culture that is much deeper than what is often relegated to "decision making," and yet it surely aids in this as well. The value of communal discernment is that it gives much more than any unchangeable set of rules is able to provide; "Just as a wisely written constitution for an institution or a government provides procedures for amendment and for decision making rather than immutable prescriptions, so the Christian community is equipped not with a code but with decision-making potential."[92] As Luke Bretherton writes, the Christian task is to forge, through the variety of resources at our disposal, "discernment of what constitutes faithful witness within the contingent flux of prevailing political conditions." "Discernment," Bretherton goes on, is similar to *phronesis*, and one could treat them interchangeably, but the benefit of "discernment" is that it "better emphasizes how faithful political judgments are responses to the prior and ongoing creative action of God in the midst of the world."[93]

As we saw in chapter two, some have worried that in seeking to foster moral competence one may fall into the opposite error of being overconfident in one's ability to see the whole of reality, such that one closes in on oneself, no longer feels the need to listen to others, and thus loses the ability to do so well. This concern is legitimate, and it seems to me that communal discernment is a counter-practice that enables competence without overconfidence precisely in the way it steadies one's gaze to problems of local attention that blossom into structural issues. Overconfidence and incompetence are the twin

---

92. Yoder, *Body Politics*, 8.
93. Luke Bretherton, *Christianity and Contemporary Politics: The Conditions and Possibilities of Faithful Witness* (Chichester, UK: Wiley-Blackwell, 2010), 20, 30n75.

errors that come when the parameters of one's gaze have outstripped one's ability to address whatever problems one may catch sight of. Against both, communal discernment focuses attention on the particularities and challenges that arise in a particular place in time, and through that kind of attention one learns not simply tweaks that need to be made within one's ongoing way of life, but also broader changes to the rules governing the discerning community as a whole. It provides the means to know where to go, what to do, what to change next, and the competence to see particular moments of issue as affecting the wider life of the church and society at large; neglecting local attention paradoxically prevents one from seeing some of the structural issues at stake.

In short, communal discernment teaches the importance of abiding in a place, with a particular community of people and a particular ongoing conversation—even when it is painful. This point is difficult to understand in a culture that is increasingly transient, and just for that is precisely what we need. Cavanaugh, for instance, notes that in a context marked by hyper-mobility—in which mobility is used as a tool by which corporations can "hold towns hostage"—resistance will be born not by fleeing but by abiding.[94] Cavanaugh focuses on the Eucharist as a counter-practice that represents the truly catholic universal (God) located inextricably in a particular location, a particular community, a particular story, a particular bread and cup. For Cavanaugh, the Eucharist overcomes the dichotomy of universal and local by "collapsing spatial divisions not by sheer mobility [globalization] but by gathering in the local assembly. . . . [Such] is not a place, but a 'spatial story' about the origin and destiny of the whole world, a story enacted in the Eucharist."[95] This is not sectarianism, but a story that allows one to find one's way in the world. Against the constant movement that tears down the possibility of mutual

---

94. Cf. Cavanaugh, *Theopolitical*, 117; and William T. Cavanaugh, "Migrant, Tourist, Pilgrim, Monk: Mobility and Identity in a Global Age," in *Migrations of the Holy*, 72–73. Cavanaugh mentions NAFTA as a harbinger of this phenomenon; Obama's Trans-Pacific Partnership (TPP) continues in this line.
95. Cavanaugh, *Theopolitical*, 113.

reciprocal relationships with the neighbor and the other, what we need is "a story of cosmic proportions within the particular face-to-face encounter of neighbors and strangers in the local eucharistic gathering."[96] By inhabiting such a story, Christians are able to foster genuine attachments, through which we can then engage the world in an ad hoc manner—neither fleeing nor baptizing the world but inhabiting it in an alternative, cruciform way. Communal discernment works similarly, allowing a truly catholic story to be recognized as always locally unfolding. "In each 'local' church (the expression is a redundancy) the wonder of community formation in Christ has occurred."[97] Communal discernment protects against the temptation to "go big," away from and past local attention, but through such local attention allows one to find the path to structural change.[98] Bretherton puts it this way: liberalism as a form of politics "represents the attempt to eliminate frailty, historical contingency, and creatureliness from political life."[99] If this is true, then the goal of communal discernment should be to clear a path to competence that does not eschew contingency, nor claim to reveal more than is given humans to know, but expand our imaginative horizon such that we begin to see *on the ground* alternatives to liberalism that are not its equal and opposite, but plant seeds for moving humanly and faithfully within and through it. Put differently, it contrasts with the family of associated political projects gathered under the heading "liberal political theory," which is typically "impatient with problems that are not yet clearly defined, much less ones that have no clear route to a solution, and hence it severely limits its ability to see, let alone address, the deepest problems we face today."[100]

---

96. Ibid., 117.
97. McClendon, *Doctrine*, 366. This is similar to an insight from Cavanaugh: "not *part* but the *whole* Body of Christ is present in each local Eucharistic assembly"; Cavanaugh, *Theopolitical*, 114–15.
98. As Stephen Toulmin writes: "The task is not to build new, larger, and yet more powerful powers, let alone a 'world state' having absolute, worldwide sovereignty. Rather, it is to fight the inequalities that were entrenched during the ascendancy of the nation-state, and to limit the absolute sovereignty of even the best-run nation-states," which he claims is done through a postmodern system based on the "the ideas of ecosystems and adaptability"; cf. *Cosmopolis: The Hidden Agenda of Modernity* (Chicago: University of Chicago Press, 1990), 192–93.
99. Bretherton, *Christianity*, 49.
100. Charles T. Mathewes, *A Theology of Public Life* (Cambridge: Cambridge University Press, 2007), 153.

This counterintuitive move—that sustainable or healthy structural change comes through local attention—is connected with the aforementioned ability to patiently listen to others. Listening is not enough, of course; we also need frequent reminders of the goals we have agreed to be working toward. As Graeber writes, people need to be continually reminded why they have gathered,[101] and without this, movements like Occupy Wall Street devolve into endless chatter with no clear direction. My argument here is that communal discernment infuses the correct desire for structural change with the recognition that the necessary capacities to bring about such change will not come through "top down" enforcement, but through participatory work in neighborhoods whereby the focus moves from charity to structural change, but in ways that arise organically from the people directly affected by these tectonic shifts.

3.3 Confrontation

Finally, communal discernment as a counter-practice instills the importance of confrontation in fostering political competence and social transformation. As we saw regarding "binding and loosing," central to communal discernment is the willingness and ability to speak openly and honestly with one's fellow Christian when he or she is perceived to be in error. This sort of confrontation, as we saw, must be done lovingly, and is itself a mark of love; to quote a 1533 Anabaptist tract preserved in the polemical response by Heinrich Bullinger, one is "bound by Christian love (if something to edification is given or revealed to him) that he should and may speak of it also in the congregation."[102] This requires both the virtue of presence among the discerning community—wherein one is truly present with people in their faults, even as one is present to oneself about one's own faults—and the virtue of *courage*, since it is difficult to broach such subjects. One risks offending a friend, being wrong in one's perceptions, and receiving a list of confrontations back about oneself.

---

101. Graeber, *Democracy Project*, 217.
102. Quoted in Yoder, *Body Politics*, 66.

Nonetheless, when exercised well communal discernment walks the line between harsh, exclusionary nosiness and a "live and let live" attitude, thus enabling a fluid, dynamic means by which people, individually and communally, grow in faithfulness.

This sort of confrontation is valuable to radical democratic engagement for at least two reasons. First, as is readily apparent, people tend to gravitate toward those with whom they agree, and who reinforce their proclivities. For instance, as social psychologist Jonathan Haidt has shown, "liberals" (to use the term conventionally) and "conservatives" generally gather in isolated groups in which one only hears those with whom one already agrees, discounting out-of-hand anything said by one's perceived adversaries. People are very good at tricking themselves into thinking they arrive at their conclusions by "bare" reason, though this is never the case.[103] However, this does not mean we are therefore trapped in whatever group-think we happen to find ourselves. By definition we cannot see our blind-spots, but we can begin to notice the edges of our vision—to notice that we are in fact looking with certain frames—by taking the time to engage in conversations with those with whom we disagree long enough and charitably enough to get a sense of them. In this process, it is indeed possible to hear challenges, even corrections, from those with whom one profoundly disagrees. Of course, the challenge is to find people willing to engage in these sorts of painful conversations in a volatile political climate, and it is hard to say precisely what motivates people to engage in such work. But we know that it can and will do that work, if engaged. My claim here is that Christians who engage in communal discernment as a counter-practice, at least, have intrinsic motivation to engage in such conversations, as they have learned that they are not self-sufficient, and are in continual need of correction. And, as a service of Christian love, they should be willing to offer their correction to those with whom they interact—not

---

103. Jonathan Haidt, *The Righteous Mind: Why Good People Are Divided by Politics and Religion* (New York: Pantheon, 2012), ch. 2.

out of self-righteousness, but as fellow-strugglers for the good of the neighborhood, the city, and even the world.

Second, this aspect of communal discernment instills in Christians the importance of not being quietistic in the face of injustice. This claim may come as a surprise to those who continue to see Anabaptist-influenced theological politics in terms of a quietism more characteristic of their character around the turn of the twentieth century than the twenty-first.[104] And while I am unconvinced that this is an adequate reading of how Anabaptists conceived of their calling, my concern is prescriptive rather than historical. That is: my claim is that Christians engaged in communal discernment are being prepared—whether they realize it or not—to see that authentic and lasting change in the world comes not by quietistic inaction, but by boldly and lovingly confronting what needs confronting with gospel means. One does not quietly and silently hope that one's brother or sister in Christ recognize and overcome a failing without speaking a word about it—at least not always or characteristically; nor ought Christians trained by communal discernment think quietistically about structures that need shifting "out" in the world. What is more, as those engaged in radical democratic organizations have gathered in small groups, drawing on feminist and Quaker models of engagement, there has been increased recognition that conflict is not only inevitable, but good and necessary to healthy grassroots politics. As Graeber writes, democratic activists in the United States have tended to be influenced by a drive to consensus influenced by Quakerism, "which has meant that for most activists, their first experience of consensus is rooted in gentle and, frankly, bourgeois sensibilities. Everyone is expected to be, at least superficially, *extremely* nice."[105] To the extent that this shaded into "upper-middle-class cocktail-party-style" emphases on politeness and euphemism, and "avoiding any open display of uncomfortable emotions at all," this blocked important conversations that needed to happen for these groups to achieve their stated goals—or even to

---

104. For a narration of this shift, see Ervin R. Stutzman, *From Nonresistance to Justice: The Transformation of Mennonite Church Peace Rhetoric 1908-2008* (Scottdale, PA: Herald, 2011).
105. Graeber, *Democracy Project*, 218.

recognize what those goals should be.[106] Against that model, communal discernment as I have described it instills in its adherents a capacity for confrontation that they can then bring to discerning conversations in democratic organizational meetings, knowing as they will that clearly, charitably, and forcefully presenting one's views on a matter—even telling a fellow member that he or she is wrong—is the only path to competence. Given the sense in which contemporary folks are tempted to a semi-quiestistic stance in the face of incompetence-producing forces, this kind of hopeful confrontation is important in renewing what Wolin calls a "civic conscience": "The central challenge at this moment is not about reconciliation but about dissonance, not about democracy's supplying legitimacy to totality but about nurturing a discordant democracy—discordant . . . because, in being rooted in the ordinary, it affirms the value of limits."[107]

4 Conclusion: The Powers Unmasked

In this chapter, I have named one way to understand how communal discernment is relevant to contemporary radically democratic engagement—as a counter-practice fostering competence amidst an interconnected web of powerful practices. Christians are not condemned to acquiescence in this context, but can faithfully and creatively work to foster a politics of tending through capacities uniquely gained through discerning the will of God together. Of course, I have presumed throughout that communal discernment is one of many practices that can do this sort of work—it cannot function alone. And yet, communal discernment has its own role to play. The community of friends who gather to discern the dynamic will of God, as well as to discern how to engage or resist the various powerful practices that make up this world, constitute an objective sign of the powers' unmasking and proleptic defeat by the cross of Jesus. Such communities recognize, celebrate, and live into the fact that the

---

106. This sort of confrontational-yet-discerning mode returns below in my discussion of the "charrette" model used in Durham during the civil rights era.
107. Wolin, *Politics and Vision*, 605–6.

powerful practices that so dominate the created order do not have the final say, but are even now being bent back to their redemptive intention. This is good news indeed. As theologian Nate Kerr has argued, such messianic communities stand as ongoing witnesses to the apocalyptic reality in which the powers no longer have domineering sway over human life, and in which the divisions of race, gender, and the like *begin* to lose their bite.[108]

Of course, the question that is invited by this conclusion—and which Kerr forcefully asks—is whether the new in Christ witnessed to by the practices of the *ekklesia* is subtly or not-so-subtly confined to this community, restricted within ecclesial borders. Does the friendship borne of discerning together expand beyond the gathered church, beyond the direct witness provided by discerning communities engaged in the world as well as the agents it so equips? The answer to this has to be "Yes," given the wildness of the God who always moves ahead of the discerning community, surprising us at every turn. The real question is how to understand this affirmation, and how the gathered church might recognize and incorporate awareness of this movement into its life together. It is this that I move to address in the final chapter: the form of politics that communal discernment not only creates but can recognize, which I describe in terms of "radical friendship" between discerning, active parties even from variant convictional communities.

And yet I conclude here by emphasizing the ground gained thus far: Communal discernment as a counter-practice carries tremendous promise for equipping both those who discern in gathered churches, and communities of discernment as a whole, for contributing to grassroots political action. To be sure, the contribution outlined here is not much help with political engagement if one means by "political" merely running for national office. As a counter-practice, communal discernment is not enough to prevent the powerful practices involved in *that* sort of politics from overwhelming us. But when it comes to the sort of politics advocated by Wolin, Coles, and others, communal

---

108. Nathan R. Kerr, *Christ, History, and Apocalyptic* (Eugene, OR: Cascade, 2009).

discernment is immensely relevant to faithful political engagement, and Christians should not hesitate to bring these gifts to bear on such work. Thus should one aspect of the politics of communal discernment now be clear: it can form people who are able and willing to engage in radical democratic work, and who thus can provide a standing witness to the patient, peaceful, truthful Reign of God through this engagement. It does not get one outside the multiple practices that mark contemporary life in the United States, but it does give one a means of going on within this milieu that is marked by hope. To be sure, given the threats we all face in the years ahead, there will be times when communal discernment seems a feeble defense indeed, hopelessly slow in the face of forces that continue their inexorable spread over and beyond our agency. What we need reminding of in those moments is that communal discernment, like any counter-practice, is not a "solution" that would forever protect its adherents from all incompetencies, but a sign pointing to a victory already won. "The church's job," as Cavanaugh writes, "is to try to discern in each concrete circumstance how best to embody the politics of the cross in a suffering world."[109] And these politics are ongoing.

---

109. Cavanaugh, "Church as Political," 140.

5

Radical Friendship

> ... community cannot feed for long on itself; it can only flourish where always the boundaries are giving way to the coming of others from beyond them—unknown and undiscovered brothers.[1]
>
> —Howard Thurman

At the end of Matthew's Gospel, in what must have been an incredible scene, a group of disciples gather one last time to receive a message from Jesus. Interestingly, we are told that while some listened to and worshipped this recently crucified Messiah, others doubted (Matt 28:17). While possible reasons for this doubt are legion, it is at least fair to say that the disciples, worshippers and doubters alike, are in an extreme state of flux, with little idea of what's going on. In any case, in the midst of this doubting-worshipping community, Jesus gives *everyone* present a commission, telling them that all authority has been given to this teacher of Matthew 5–7. What is more, Jesus does not hoard this authority, but immediately bestows it on his listeners: "Go therefore and disciple all peoples [*ethnoi*], baptizing them in the name of the Father and of the Son and of the Holy Spirit, and teaching them

---

1. Howard Thurman, *The Search for Common Ground* (Richmond, IN: Friends United, [1971] 1986), 104.

to obey everything that I have commanded you" (28:19–20a). Jesus does not dismiss their doubts, but sends them out to make disciples among all the peoples of the earth. It is as though Jesus is saying that competence, recognizing Jesus's movements in this world, will only be possible *as they go*. It is there that the disciples' doubts will be addressed; it is for the undertaking of this task that Jesus will orient a community; and it is in this capacity that we will have the eyes to see a Jesus who is with us as we go, "to the end of the age" (28:20b).

This passage illustrates the question to which I have built: What is the relationship between the sort of competencies gained through practices like communal discernment in the *ekklesia*, on the one hand, and the movement of God beyond the church's practical borders, on the other? If Jesus promises he will be with discerning disciples as they move with and among the various people-groups of the world, does this not imply that Jesus—who has already moved ahead of the disciples back to Galilee—will continue to move ahead of them as they go about their given task of receptive witness? Whatever fleeting competence is theirs to gain as they together "disciple peoples" into the ways Jesus has taught would seem contingent on their keeping a discerning eye out for Jesus's movements in ever-new, surprising ways. This is precisely what I am exploring in this chapter: the way that communal discernment enables Christians to look for and welcome certain activities among radical democratic activists as analogues to the sort of competence won in discerning congregations and which Christians trained by communal discernment should be able to recognize, celebrate, and incorporate.

Indeed, the concern that has run like a fault line through these pages has been to understand the particular sense of political, moral incompetence that is prevalent in the United States today. My thesis has been that distinguishing liberalism from the on-the-ground organizing that marks truly democratic practices opens up space to appreciate anew baptist contributions to political theology. In this space, I have argued that communal discernment as a counter-practice engenders in churches a type of competence (not overconfidence) marked by comfort with contingency, patience, loving confrontation, and attention to one's local place, and thus parallels the kind of politics typically advocated by radical democrats. Put differently, I have argued that communal discernment constitutes a response to political liberalism not through grand theorizing but by fostering friendships with others without thereby collapsing the narrative distinction between church and world.

Having come thus far, I can now explore how communal discernment relates to the sustenance of a robust, pluralistic approach to radical democratic action that is not relegated to the church. While other practices are important to this task, my concern is how communal discernment in particular connects to democratic action done in reciprocal relation with people from other convictional communities. To that end, in this chapter I argue that communal discernment enables Christians to see the Spirit of God moving in the course of grassroots activities in which we should participate. In particular, I argue that communal discernment trains our eyes to see certain instances of political participation together as "secular parables" of the Kingdom of God, to use Karl Barth's phrase, approximations of (and even correctives to) the practice of communal discernment that Christians who have engaged in the latter will be well prepared to recognize and make a part of their ongoing life together. An apt and ancient metaphor for the sort of politics that communal discernment prepares one to see is *friendship*, particularly since many philosophers have seen in friendship both the kind of bond necessary for any political order to flourish, and a helpful way to describe discerning action with one another.

Narrating this shift in terms of friendship is a move that is artfully defended by Peter Dula in the course of an appreciative assessment of political theologians William Cavanaugh and Daniel Bell. For Dula, Cavanaugh and Bell provide a healthy view of political action done at the level of "civil society"—grassroots social movements and the like—and rightly point out that such movements are always interwoven with and absorbable by the nation-state's "politics of intending." Any affirmation of "civil society," they argue, remains within a nation-state imaginary that is comfortable with the rules of the game as currently constituted. Dula is sympathetic with this assessment, but wonders if recommendations of churches of practice—which at least *resemble* the modes of resistance proffered in civic associations—do any better at carving out a space beyond the reach of "the system." Crucially, Dula is not disagreeing with the vision of churches as disciplined bodies formed by practices constituting their own politics distinct from politics-as-statecraft; but he is wondering how this vision "gains a privilege over or outside the society of control."[2] If the church manages to escape from this control and subsequent incompetence, this must be accounted for.

I have been clear that I do not think there is a way to get outside this context; liberalism is our inheritance, whether we like it or not. Consequently, I do not have a stake in trying to specify an outside to the "society of control." However, I have claimed that communal discernment suggests a "low church" model for living within society as presently constituted, enabling communities to discover ways of living that are not *determined* by the system as such. Understanding the church as a bundle of resisting and enabling counter-practices is an important piece of this puzzle; equally important is understanding what happens as communally discerning churches and people formed within them work with those outside its borders, against the forces that threaten authentically democratic spaces of competence. As we do this, other modes of discerning together will be discovered and created, which we may see as analogous to friendships formed within communities that discern the will of God together. To this end, I am taken with Dula's suggestion that a fruitful path to pursue in light of these observations is a renewed attention to friendship.[3] My focus in this vein will be friendship as both the fruit of and prerequisite to

---

2. Peter Dula, *Cavell, Companionship, and Christian Theology* (New York: Oxford University Press, 2011), 105.
3. Peter Dula, "Fugitive Ecclesia," in *The Gift of Difference: Radical Orthodoxy, Radical Reformation*, ed. Chris K. Huebner and Tripp York (Winnipeg, MB: Canadian Mennonite University Press, 2010), 127–28.

discernment together in the world; through both, friendship provides a unique path to competence. That is, the kind of friendship that comes from and leads to discernment "out" in the world provides another space for competent resistance and transformation of politics as normally conducted that is *enough*, and that can recur between unlikely groups of people. It is this that I call "radical friendship."

The path I take to accomplish these goals begins with an examination of how discerning what to do and how best to work for the good of society with strangers can spring from friendships established by other means. In the first section I explore friendship as a forerunner to political discernment with others in democratic participation —including those not of one's convictional community. In the second section I explore the inverse of the first: that friendship can blossom from or "secrete" from communal, political discernment done between people who, at first, have no affection for one another whatsoever. Whereas in the first section friendship leads to a discerned political competence, in the second friendship springs from discernment together. In both sections I explore the notion of friendship as classically understood, with special reference to Aristotle, and note how such friendship is valuable even as it stands in need of conversion from the perspective of a baptist theological politics. Additionally, in each section I provide an example of how the sort of friendship-discernment I am recommending has worked in actual, particular struggles for political competency. This follows the lead of Stanley Hauerwas and Romand Coles, who rightly claim that the last thing the world needs is "another theory of the state," but rather "examples, drawn from actual democratic practices that might enkindle imaginations dulled by the attractions of the state."[4] The argument that emerges is twofold: both that such discerning relationships are analogous to communal discernment, and that communal discernment enables Christians to see these as possibilities worth pursuing —themselves signs of competence that should be celebrated rather

---

4. Stanley Hauerwas and Romand Coles, *Christianity, Democracy, and the Radical Ordinary: Conversation between a Radical Democrat and a Christian* (Eugene, OR: Cascade, 2008), 9.

than reluctantly acknowledged. In the final section, I tie up this analysis by showing how communal discernment is helpful in incorporating such discerned kingdom seeds into the life of the church. I narrate this primarily in terms of Wolin's concept of fugitivity, transformation, and preparation. The basic idea is that at its best, *ekklesia* serves to anticipate and welcome the beloved community or the Reign of God which bursts forth ever past ecclesial limits. Communal discernment is especially suited for this preparatory, incorporating task, I will argue, and does not, as Dula puts it, preclude finding joy outside the church's borders.[5]

1 Radical Friendship as Prerequisite to Discernment

Let us begin by considering the proposal that friendship can lead to instances of competence-building discernment out in the world that baptists, trained by communal discernment, can recognize and appreciate as we go about working with others. The claim that friendships can serve as forerunners to the competence we need in the current milieu is perhaps counterintuitive, and it is precisely because of this potential confusion that some context is needed about the recurring significance of "friendship" in theological, philosophical, political history. It is through this background that one can best see the significance of affirming the possibility of discerning friendships *between people of differing convictional communities, abilities, and economic means*—one side of radical friendship.

1.1 Converting Aristotelian Friendship

One way to narrate the socio-political significance of communal discernment is as the harbinger of competence brought about through friendships with one's fellow discerning disciples, as we saw in chapter four. Without undermining the ground gained there, it is important to acknowledge that this sort of competence is not imprisoned in the church, or confined within its borders; analogues, or what McClendon

---

5. Dula, *Cavell*, 111–12.

calls seeds of the kingdom (cf. Mark 4:2b–9), are spread throughout creation.[6] This is especially important to acknowledge given that theological appropriations of friendship can sometimes neglect the presence of such seeds, as Dula so eloquently makes clear. In the course of introducing "companionship" as a theological option in the climate of politics as statecraft, Dula gives a compact summary of the importance friendship plays in Aristotle's project, noting in particular how for Aristotle, friendship is central to the proper functioning of any polity, as evidenced by the famous passage where Aristotle praises Sparta for just this reason.[7] Dula notes approvingly Stanley Hauerwas and Charles Pinches's summation of this passage: "Thus friendship becomes for Aristotle the ground of a true polity. Further, if a state fails to achieve this polity, the only available resource of virtue is, again, the association among friends"; and, "The failure of the political represents a failure in political friendship, the only recourse after the failure being a narrower friendship that begins the pursuit of virtue over again at a much reduced level."[8] Dula agrees that in light of the ills of political liberalism, "friendship" must take on renewed political weight—particularly given that liberal political theorists have had little time for the notion except as an afterthought. But Dula also wonders if highlighting the friendship called "church," while important, might prevent Hauerwas and Pinches from attending to the importance of friendships occurring outside the church, which are surely *also* of importance in a context in need of competence wherever it can be learned.[9] While we ought not downplay the importance of church as friendship, or even that such friendships take a kind of priority over others, nor ought we deny that friendships occur elsewhere and that these also are important for discerning, moral competence. In my view, this is but a way of saying that Aristotle's vision of friendship needs converting.

---

6. James Wm. McClendon Jr., *Witness: Systematic Theology, Volume 3* (Nashville: Abingdon, 2000), 59–63.
7. *Nicomachean Ethics*, 1180a25.
8. Stanley Hauerwas and Charles Pinches, *Christians among the Virtues: Theological Conversations with Ancient and Modern Ethics* (Notre Dame: University of Notre Dame Press, 1997), 37–38.
9. Ibid., 186n4; Dula, *Cavell*, 112–13.

Of course, in order to understand this claim one must begin with a firm grasp of Aristotle's account, which sets the context for recent retrievals of friendship. Aristotle's understanding of friendship is built upon his analysis of virtue, arguing that friendship is either a virtue or involves virtue.[10] For Aristotle, flourishing is not possible without a group of friends who move one toward the good; he means it when he writes that "without friends no one would choose to live, though he had all other goods."[11] Further, Aristotle claims that healthy friendships are the lifeblood of a well-functioning city-state, a claim that is intelligible only in light of his particular nuance of "friend." Aristotle distinguishes between three types of friendship: friendships of pleasure, friendships of usefulness, and friendships of character. For Aristotle, some friendships arise from the mutual benefit that the relationship provides to each party—certain business relationships in which persons work together for a time, perhaps in order to accomplish a common task, but in which the relationship dissolves once the common task is complete. A second type of friendship arises out of the mutual pleasure enjoyed by two parties, but the relationship is unsustainable; once the pleasure fades, the relationship does as well.[12] In both cases, Aristotle uses the term "friendship" as a placeholder, but neither is *true* friendship, at least of the deepest sort. True friendship, for Aristotle, is reserved for what he calls friendships of virtue, relationships based on and leading its adherents to flourishing. In Aristotle's terms, perfect friendship leads the parties involved to "wish well alike to each other *qua* good, and they are good in themselves. Now those who wish well to their friends for their sake are most truly friends; for they do this by reason of their own nature and not incidentally; therefore their friendship lasts as long as they are good—and goodness is an enduring thing."[13]

Thus a key facet of Aristotelian friendship is the degree of permanence that marks its occurrence. Whereas friendships of

---

10. *Nicomachean Ethics*, 1155a1–5.
11. *Nicomachean Ethics*, 1155a6.
12. *Nicomachean Ethics*, 1156a6–20.
13. *Nicomachean Ethics*, 1156b5–12.

pleasure and benefit dissolve as soon as the external factor holding the two parties together is gone, true friendships, for Aristotle, have a lasting quality amidst life's contingency.[14] They provide an oasis from the whims of tragedy and fate, as it were, and it is this latter aspect of Aristotle's account that needs converting. For Aristotle, true friendships are necessarily rare, reserved for the exceptional group of magnanimous men who, despite circumstance and through growth in virtue, achieve maturity in, through, and with one another.[15] Further, given Aristotle's convictions concerning the unity and constancy of virtue, true friendships are marked by *similarity*, existing as they do for the sake of and in light of the virtue each sees in the other. Friends grow more and more alike with respect to virtue, and this remains the case given that if a member of a group of true friends is ripped from virtue by the vicissitudes of time, entropy, or misfortune, their sustaining group of friends must release this person to their misery, insulating themselves from what would ruin their own flourishing. Crucially, the virtuous person will willingly bear this burden alone rather than inflict their misfortune on friends.[16]

That true friendship is marked by sameness and a kind of insularity, even toward a friend in pain, causes Aristotle to deny that friendship can occur between people who are unequally yoked, or not of the same set of friends. On a strictly Aristotelian view, talk of friendship occurring across lines of polity and status is incoherent. What is more, for Aristotle true friends celebrate not the other person in their difference, but one's own virtue that one sees reflected back in the other. This means that Aristotle's views on friendship, while retaining much of value, cannot be appropriated by Christians wholesale, a point made by basically every Christian interpreter of Aristotle starting with Aquinas. Hauerwas and Pinches, for instance, criticize Aristotle's sense that virtuous friendship requires that friends grow more and more identical over time. Indeed, they identify a deep connection between Aristotle's view that perfect friendship leads to likeness and his praise

14. Cf. Hauerwas and Pinches, *Christians*, 35.
15. *Nicomachean Ethics*, 1158a10–16.
16. *Nicomachean Ethics*, 1171b1–10; Hauerwas and Pinches, *Christians*, 41–43, 47.

of insulation from one another's suffering, arguing instead that "Christians cannot accept a vision of friendship which excludes (or overcomes) otherness in the friend, or which shelters her from sharing our sufferings and defeats."[17] This is all the more true when viewed from the perspective of God's friendship with humanity, which Christians affirm as a reality and as the ultimately "unequal" relationship out of which all of our lives emerge. Friendship with God comes "extrinsically," rather than through any inherent capacity in humans.[18] More, God's friendship with humanity is kenotic, beginning and ending with God's love in Jesus as the ultimately condescending, humbling action such that we might share in his life, and he in ours. Christians need not deny that friendship "encourages similarity in crucial respects"[19]—in particular, growth in the kind of virtues modeled by Jesus's kenotic life, death, and resurrection—but such growth must not lead to an insular community of friends that negates difference, or denies the possibility of friendships occurring between Christians and other people.

Hauerwas and Pinches narrate the possibility of friendship between people of different communities through Aristotle's suggestion that friendships of pleasure and usefulness may always grow into friendships of character, over time.[20] Given that no one is born "fully formed" but grows into agency through dependence on others (which, for the first years of life, constitute relationships of extreme inequality), it seems likely that all friendships of character necessarily spring from such soil. Whether or not Hauerwas and Pinches have therefore adequately addressed the possibility of friendships occurring outside the community of character without immediately assimilating "friendship" to "church" is not my concern.[21] My concern is whether or not the practice of communal discernment, perhaps accidentally, implies an Aristotelian type of friendship, or views the possibility of

---

17. Hauerwas and Pinches, *Christians*, 44.
18. Cf. Hans S. Reinders, *Receiving the Gift of Friendship: Profound Disability, Theological Anthropology, and Ethics* (Grand Rapids: Eerdmans, 2008), ch. 10.
19. Hauerwas and Pinches, *Christians*, 50.
20. Ibid., 37–38.
21. Cf. Dula, *Cavell*, 113, 249n60.

friendships occurring *extra ekklesia* as at best unimportant, and at worst impossible. Does communal discernment lead to, or in this case require, an insular community of friends that is at odds with the call to suffer with one another and befriend those of all walks of life in the same manner as the kenotic Lord? Put differently, does communal discernment blind those who practice it from seeing friendships between others as *also* of moral import—or only acknowledging this begrudgingly?

If this were the case, communal discernment would be antithetical to radical democratic action between people with differences of any kind; and to be sure, communal discernment *can* rely upon and feed a "closed circle" mentality, encouraging communities of friends that circle the wagons against an imposing and threatening world. Of course, this tendency is hardly unique to communal discernment as such, but is to a degree basic to friendship, relying as it does on some level of preference for one person or group over another. Friendship carries the inherent danger of reinforcing an in-group, out-group mentality: what Miroslav Volf calls an embrace predicated on a more basic exclusion, or what Carl Schmitt delineated as "friend" in contradistinction to his understanding of enemy.[22] In McClendon's terms, friendship is first of all a social phenomenon, having to do with our communities' forms of life and helping to direct our embodied desires toward some *telos*. Left to its own devices, or viewed in light of particular metaphysical convictions (Aristotle's "unmoved mover," for instance), friendship indeed closes in on itself. But friendship born of and ordered by Jesus's kenosis can be different, "opening" Aristotle's friendship of like-to-like such that it is transformed into "present participation in the power of the future; here the image of God is—the risen Christ."[23]

---

22. Cf. Miroslav Volf, *Exclusion and Embrace: A Theological Exploration of Identity, Otherness, and Reconciliation* (Nashville: Abingdon, 1996); Tracy B. Strong, "Foreword," in Carl Schmitt, *The Concept of the Political*, trans. George Schwab (Chicago: University of Chicago Press, [1932] 1996), xxiv.

23. James Wm. McClendon Jr., "Three Strands of Christian Ethics," *Collected Works, Volume 2*, 23. This is not to say, with Gilbert Meilaender, that there are two kinds of loves—one universal and existing *beyond* friendship (*agape*), another social and in the tradition of Aristotle (*philia*)—which are separable, even antithetical. While Meilaender is on to something regarding the tension between

The question thus becomes whether communal discernment encourages a closed sort of friendship, or prevents one from seeing the possibility or import of friendships elsewhere—and I do not think it does. At its best, communal discernment as described here—with its emphasis on patience, structural change through local attention, gospel confrontation, and the like—prepares its practitioners to see certain instances of friendship between people of different convictional backgrounds as the ripest of soils for faithful political competence. Indeed, it allows its adherents to intuitively sense the power of discerning together with strangers; after all, even our brother or sister in Christ can be a stranger to us at times, gathered as we are by the ultimate stranger who pitched his tent among us. Thus situated, communally discerning Christians can look and see counter-examples of vulnerable, cross-convictional friendships that breed competence and belie Aristotle's delineations and restrictions. None of this is to deny the importance, even priority, of discerning friendships forged in the *ekklesia*; nor is it to deny the fact of our divisions in the world. However, it is to say that such divisions need not rest as they sit, but can be changed from relationships of "enmities and misunderstandings into understandings and friendships."[24] After all, communally discerning Christians have seen such happen through the alchemy of grace in their own midst; why should we not also expect something similar to occur as we look for Jesus's movements throughout creation, including between people gathering who have little in common, either in terms of character or background? Rather than continue to speak abstractly on this point, I turn now to an example of the kind of friendship communal discernment enables us to see and celebrate, which can stand behind discernment as a powerful practice for contemporary political engagement—or better, portend a different kind of politics.

---

these two forms, in my view they remain interwoven; the real issue is how *agape* can order and open *philia*, rather than viewing them as at odds. Cf. *Friendship: A Study in Theological Ethics* (Notre Dame: University of Notre Dame Press, 1981).

24. James Wm. McClendon Jr., "'Convictions' After Twenty Years," in *The Collected Works of James Wm. McClendon, Jr., Volume 2*, ed. Ryan Andrew Newson and Andrew C. Wright (Waco, TX: Baylor University Press, 2014), 149.

1.2 Open Friendship in Mississippi

In his book *Open Friendship in a Closed Society*, Peter Slade traces the work and lived theology of "Mission Mississippi," a group founded in the early 1990s whose task remains setting up networks of cooperation between black and white folks, particularly evangelical Christians. Embedded in the practices of Mission Mississippi, Slade sees a central commitment to the power of Christian friendship to bring about reconciliation and change to racially divided Mississippi.[25]

Slade frames his discussion of the work of Mission Mississippi with the concept of "open friendship" as advocated by Jürgen Moltmann. Similar to my above analysis, Moltmann analyzes the classical concept of "friendship" in terms of a "closedness" that tends to accompany such approaches, particularly in the work of Aristotle.[26] While there is much to recommend these approaches, an unavoidable tension remains between Aristotelian friendship and the friendship of Jesus as witnessed to in the New Testament. As Moltmann helpfully points out, Jesus is called "friend" in only two places in the New Testament: John 15, in the context of a conversation with his disciples wherein they are elevated above the status of slaves and called upon to lay down their lives for their friends as the expression of the greatest love (the parallels to kenosis yet again ring loud); and Luke 7:34, where Jesus contrasts himself with John the Baptist. "The Son of Man has come eating and drinking; and you say, 'Behold, a glutton and a drunkard, a friend of tax collectors and sinners!'"[27] Thus and significantly, Jesus as friend is associated with sacrifice for others (through which one is connected to the "true vine"), and being in relationship with those who are "unequal" from oneself—those of "bad character." Aristotle would have recoiled at both. It is important, for Moltmann, that friendship

---

25. Peter Slade, *Open Friendship in a Closed Society: Mission Mississippi and a Theology of Friendship* (New York: Oxford University Press, 2009), 4, 74.
26. Jürgen Moltmann, "Open Friendship: Aristotelian and Christian Concepts of Friendship," in *The Changing Face of Friendship*, ed. Leroy S. Rouner (Notre Dame: University of Notre Dame Press, 1994), 29–42. Cf. Jürgen Moltmann, *The Church in the Power of the Spirit: A Contribution of Messianic Ecclesiology* (London: SCM, 1977), 114–21.
27. Moltmann, "Open Friendship," 34–35.

be reclaimed as a central *political* category, as it was in classic Greek thought, so long as it does not reinforce the Greek model of exclusivity in political friendship. Even the possibility of such reclamation likely rings strangely in contemporary ears trained to hear only modern notes; we have retained the importance of "enemy" as a political, "public" category (recall Schmitt), but have relegated "friend" to some private sphere. What is needed instead is a friendship that is as publicly relevant as classical notions, but broken open by Christ. If this were to happen, Christians would "have to break through their unconscious and sometimes, unfortunately, also very deliberate exclusivity with respect to the 'evil world' and 'unbelievers'—and be ready for friendship with the friendless. Then they would have to assemble in grass roots communities that would live close to the people and with the people in the friendship of Jesus."[28]

Slade sees this kind of friendship embedded in the work of Mission Mississippi, striving as it does to forge open friendships that can lead to discernment between and amongst people who have deep differences. The regular meetings of Mission Mississippi—in which participants gather for conversation, shared struggle, bible study, and prayer—are the lifeblood of the organization, the *engine* that makes the whole thing go. In these meetings, friendships are formed across lines of race and class, bound by an implicit conviction that God shows up in the process. Over time, these friendships enable those involved to discern changes that are needed in their context, as well as concerns that the participants share in common, such as rising crime rates in the city.[29] Key to Mission Mississippi's success is the sense in which the relationships they forge, in the words of former Executive Director Dolphus Weary, are constituted by "a conversation of understanding, not a conversation of convincing."[30] According to Slade, the open friendship embedded in Mission Mississippi grows into a long-term, sustainable drive against racism in the state, into community development work of various kinds, and into networks of economic

28. Ibid., 40.
29. Slade, *Open Friendship*, 45–46.
30. Ibid., 130.

opportunity.³¹ In short, the simple practice of praying and eating breakfast together creates a path to political transformation, which contains a power of which even its participants may not be fully aware.³²

What this friendship across difference does, in part, is to prevent small groups that form out of such relationships from becoming echo chambers, as the creative tensions implicit in such gatherings prevent people from getting too comfortable. As Slade points out, this is especially important given the tendency of many "small groups" in the United States to devolve into emotional support groups, reinforcing one's inherited convictions and functioning to encourage each other, with little to no room for criticism or guidance. "Rather than finding comfort in a homogenous closed prayer circle, the participant [of Mission Mississippi's prayer meetings] engages in the often uncomfortable task of meeting people with whom they have little in common and who challenge their preconceptions."³³ One learns in this process the skill of listening to one another, and finds a loose, gospel unity in the act of prayer—a unity that remains open to surprises of the Spirit.³⁴

My reason for evoking Slade's theological ethnography of Mission Mississippi is that it serves as a fitting example of the first way friendship can relate to discernment in radical democratic action: as its prerequisite and harbinger. Mission Mississippi shows how friendships forged in regular meeting with one another, even with those with whom one has significant differences, can create bonds that hold through one's disagreements (as is required, as we saw, of communal discernment done well). By their very nature, such friendships threaten a closed, racist society that necessarily "bans" dissenters, since such societies shy away "from the openness to the ambiguities and possibilities of an unknown future."³⁵ Of course, Mission

---

31. Ibid., 134, 140.
32. Ibid., 149.
33. Ibid., 160.
34. Ibid., 165, 170, 178–79.
35. Ibid., 35. As an example, Slade discusses the way Will Campbell, who worked at Ole Miss, was "banned" from that society for his views on racial reconciliation; cf. ibid., 28–32. For Campbell's

Mississippi is far from flawless. As Slade points out, its adherents, working largely within a traditionally evangelical framework, tend to sharply distinguish "personal" from "interpersonal" reconciliation, prioritizing individual salvation over reconciliation with neighbor, which Slade rightly sees as both sociologically and theologically problematic.[36] Further and relatedly, missing from Mission Mississippi is an *explicit* acknowledgment of the reality of systemic, structural racism as a part of the problem, and thus working for racial justice on a more structural level is likewise absent.[37] I could not agree more; the challenge, in light of Wolin's critique of liberalism, is to avoid letting "structural change" go proxy for instantiating change on the nation-state's terms, which ironically will not get *enough* at the roots of the issues that breed incompetence in citizens today. The structural change needed must go through the sort of friendship that Mission Mississippi exemplifies, building into the kinds of networks for which Coles advocates.[38]

Other critiques of Mission Mississippi, especially for my purposes here, are easy to imagine. For one, while the men and women who gather together in Mission Mississippi are from different racial communities, they are quite similar in other respects; those gathered are Christians, mostly of the evangelical variety, they are from the South, and they come ready to be amicable. An important question is whether a similar sort of discernment could grow from relationships

---

reflections on this time, including the mixed motives for his actions, cf. *Brother to a Dragonfly* (New York: Bloomsbury, [1977] 2000), 112–39.

36. Slade, *Open Friendship*, 68, 84. While critiquing this tendency, Slade also shows that in Mission Mississippi's actual practice, this distinction is tenuous.
37. Ibid., 75, 77, 83.
38. Romand Coles, "Of Tensions and Tricksters: Grassroots Democracy between Theory and Practice," in *Christianity*, 283. This is one possible response to Wogaman, who argues that pacifism has no way to account for the goods secured for black people in the 1960s through state coercive violence. If not for these laws and their enforcement by the FBI, police, National Guard, and US Army, justice would not have been served. (J. Philip Wogaman, *Christian Perspectives on Politics*, rev. and exp. [Louisville: Westminster John Knox, (1988) 2000], 76–77). I hear Wogaman's point, but wonder if this also forestalled the grassroots work that, in the long term, might have enabled the law to be received by a racist people. This was the genius of SNCC, it seems to me: its patient commitment to structural change. Once this was replaced with working by *strictly* legal means, racism went underground—but as should be abundantly clear, it did not go away. Thus it is unsurprising that gains made by these means—voter ID laws, Affirmative Action, etc.—are now being overturned.

where even more and deeper differences are present, or between people of different faiths. I believe it can, which I explore in the next section.

Another critique, which gets to the heart of the matter, is whether or not people have time for this sort of approach to social change. That is, can friendship really hold up as the engine for liberative political action and moral competence in the face of forces that demand some kind of action be taken *now* to ensure at least a modicum of justice? Is there really time for this slower approach to social change, that, as we saw in the previous chapter, values patience and relationships over speed and "effectiveness"? I do not take this as a question of crass expedience, but a concern voiced by those who both recognize the urgency of the problems facing people in real, on-the-ground situations, and who have seen how cries of "patience" have as often been used to thwart radical political movements as they have fostered their renewal.[39] Indeed, this sort of concern was recognized as early as 1524 by Andreas Karlstadt—writing toward the beginning of the German Peasants' War—who rejected Martin Luther's insistence that for the sake of "the weak," gospel reform ought to be done slowly.[40] For Karlstadt, whether intentional or not, Luther's argument only doused the fires that led to gospel reform, particularly as applied to the sociopolitical hierarchy, which Luther wanted to avoid. More recently, Willis Jenkins identifies this as a concern voiced by advocates of "the strategy of moral cosmology," who worry that the kind of path to competence I am advocating here will simply "proceed too softly and too slowly" to do much actual good in the world.[41] And indeed, the construction of theoretical frameworks that would deal with problems

---

39. Consider, for example, how cries for "patience" were meant to dissuade Martin Luther King Jr. from agitating for social change, which King dismantled in his "Letter from Birmingham Jail." This letter is reprinted in King's response to such cries in *Why We Can't Wait* (Boston: Beacon, [1963] 2010).
40. Andreas Karlstadt, *Whether One Should Proceed Slowly*, in Michael G. Baylor, ed., *The Radical Reformation* (Cambridge: Cambridge University Press, 1991), 49–73.
41. Willis Jenkins, "Atmospheric Powers, Global Injustice, and Moral Incompetence: Challenges to Doing Social Ethics from Below," *Journal of the Society of Christian Ethics* 34, no. 1 (2013): 79; Willis Jenkins, *The Future of Ethics: Sustainability, Social Justice, and Religious Creativity* (Washington, DC: Georgetown University Press, 2013), 75–81.

that demand responsible action remains a temptation, for such threats are real and demand drastic attention.

But it is a temptation properly so called, and a temptation Jenkins resists: not because it is somehow "too effective," but because he worries it diminishes the importance of what projects working for reform (in his case, on climate change) are actually doing to foster meaningful action, which comes not by new theories of conceptualization, but "by cultivating pluralist exchanges that empower communities to confront their problems."[42] In my words, it moves too quickly, and does not lay down the roots that make for lasting change. Indeed, communal discernment primes one to see friendships like the ones fostered in Mission Mississippi as important for precisely these reasons: they disallow one from moving too swiftly to structural changes—a move that indeed needs to be made!—or in such a way as to leave untouched the sense of disempowerment and incompetence in people who are looking for ways to make a difference in their own lives.[43] For all the ways Mission Mississippi can be critiqued, communal discernment helps Christians to *see* these very important aspects of this grassroots organization, as well as to *cultivate* and *expand* the friendships found therein toward the liberative potential they contain. They certainly will not view the organization as suspicious for being too slow, but will see in Mission Mississippi's commitment to sustainable, patient, amicable relations between strangers and enemies an analogue to communal discernment "proper," and a parable of God's Kingdom.

Nonetheless, this concern about the slowness of this mode of addressing incompetence is important, and will become even more acute in the next section. My point here and moving forward is that communal discernment enables one to see in such friendships an engine for lasting social change, moral discernment, and political competence that is capable of transforming contemporary politics. Put

---

42. Jenkins, "Atmospheric Powers," 67.
43. Rebecca Todd Peters expresses a similar concern that sidestepping this incompetence ironically leaves the systems that create unjust situations in the first place unchallenged. Cf. *Solidarity Ethics: Transformation in a Globalized World* (Minneapolis: Fortress Press, 2014), 88.

differently, open friendship is a prerequisite to moral, communal discernment "out" in the world, in radical democratic perspective.

2 Radical Friendship Secreting from Communal Discernment

Having examined one side of my proposed dialectic concerning discernment and friendship, consider now its inverse: that friendship can blossom out of moral discernment done with others, including discernment done between those from different convictional backgrounds from oneself. This too serves as a sign of God's wild movement in the world that the counter-practice of communal discernment enables one to see and celebrate. Whereas above I claimed that friendship can lead to a discerned competence together, here I am saying that struggling toward discernment can lead to friendship, even between folks who have little in common, or strongly dislike one another. How might this work?

2.1 Common Judgment as Unifying Bond

The claim that moral discernment is linked to friendship, and that both constitute an approach to "politics" that has been neglected, is unremarkably Aristotelian. For Aristotle, no political community can flourish without friendships among its people that form the bonds able to sustain it. Friendship is the "bond of the *polis*," as it were; but even more deeply, a degree of "concord" is needed for relationships of all sorts to function in the city.[44] The upshot for Aristotle, as Guido de Graaff argues, is that friendship is politically significant "not because it cements the city's socio-political order, but rather on account of the process of *interaction* underlying it."[45] For Aristotle, the concord that marks "political friendship" is needed between all members of a *polis*, not just its ruling elites.[46] If this interpretation of Aristotle is correct, however, then it seems patently unworkable. Given Aristotle's

---

44. *Nicomachean Ethics*, 1155a23–25.
45. Guido de Graaff, *Politics in Friendship: A Theological Account* (New York: Bloomsbury T&T Clark, 2014), 64.
46. Ibid., 67.

view of the kind of virtuous bond implicit in his third, "true" type of friendship, it seems impossible for that kind of bond to be widespread. As de Graaff writes, "To consider city-wide harmony as similar to concord in Aristotle's 'perfect' friendship is absurd as long as concord is considered a *quality*, something you can *possess* and *share*." However, de Graaff rescues this potential contradiction in a way that is directly relevant to my work here regarding discernment and friendship: namely, "concord and virtue can also be understood as manifesting themselves primarily in *action*. On this view, virtuous friends enjoy concord not simply because they match each other in their level of virtuousness, but insofar as they show virtue in how they *act together*."[47] De Graaff recognizes a tension in Aristotle on this point: sometimes Aristotle speaks of virtues as dispositions; but at other times he stresses *praxis* as the actualization of such dispositions.[48] Virtue remains dispositional in both cases; but to neglect that it is also active is to fail to grasp virtue's full reality. As Danielle Allen writes, for Aristotle "it is not the emotions of friendship that are relevant to politics but rather its core practices."[49]

The point for de Graaff, and the source of my interest in his analysis, is that understanding Aristotle's conception of political friendship can come only by understanding the practice of *deliberative* action together through which the former is born. De Graaff argues that "concord" between citizens turns on the existence of participants who are truly active, meaning involved in the process of deliberation itself; "common action involves not only cooperation and common purposes but interdependence between the agents involved: each must incorporate the agency of the other(s) into his own actions, a process that makes the common activity more than the sum of the individual contributions."[50] This process of deliberation can be burdensome, but it highlights an important element of friendship: the recognition,

---

47. Ibid., 68.
48. Ibid., 68–69.
49. Danielle S. Allen, *Talking to Strangers: Anxieties of Citizenship Since Brown v. Board of Education* (Chicago: University of Chicago Press, 2004), 120.
50. De Graaff, *Politics in Friendship*, 70.

practice, and experience of mutual dependence. Seeing this element is the key to recognizing that political friendship "is not primarily about 'getting things done,' but about doing and experiencing things *together*, and shared understanding and enjoying as part of that process."[51] The concord that marks friendship, as de Graaff helpfully puts it, "is a unity of minds that manifests itself in action. Concord, whether among friends or citizens, is realized in common action."[52]

Interestingly, at this point de Graaff moves to consider judgment as "the heart of all specifically political practice,"[53] including the politics of friendship. De Graaff thinks "common action" is too wide a category to be helpful in understanding friendship, because it fails to specify the "political" in a sufficiently precise sense, as distinct from the "social," "civic," or "public."[54] Judgment together, however, narrows the scope in a way that brings needed precision. Following Hannah Arendt, de Graaff rightly notes that judgment belongs to the life of action (rather than existing separate from or "prior" to it): "it involves reflection on human affairs taking place in the world. Indeed, as Arendt emphasizes, judgement cannot be exercised in isolation—in the privacy of thought—but only in the company of others."[55] Elsewhere, Arendt speaks of the absurdity and banality of evil, and while she recognizes the power of forgiveness in many circumstances, she thinks it reaches its limit in the face of "radical evil." Arendt comes to argue that judgment is the political remedy to wrongdoing, rather than silence (which is not enough) or forgiveness (which is inappropriate for evil that is at its root unforgivable).[56]

In making this kind of move, de Graaff is on to something important, especially when put in relation to communal discernment as I have described it, and the political friendship that parallels it. De Graaff is right to see that judgment done jointly, in the context of friendship,

51. Ibid.
52. Ibid., 72.
53. Ibid., 91.
54. Ibid., 6.
55. Ibid., 93.
56. Ibid., 97–99. Cf. Hannah Arendt, *Eichmann in Jerusalem: A Report on the Banality of Evil* (New York: Penguin, 1963); Hannah Arendt, *The Human Condition* (Chicago: Chicago University Press, [1959] 1998), 241. Arendt calls this the "predicament of irreversibility"; ibid., 237.

constitutes the form of the "politics of friendship." I worry, however, that de Graaff's argument fails at the point where he works with a carefully circumscribed understanding of what is properly "political," versus public or civic. Interpreting Oliver O'Donovan and others, de Graaff sees the task of government as constituting the core of political activity, and that its fundamental task is to protect the integrity of public life.[57] All governing authorities are "secular"—meaning contingent, temporal, and limited in comparison to the Kingdom of God—and entities falling outside of this task, while important, are not strictly speaking "political." But once this move is made, de Graaff is left with an understanding of judgment that is constricted to the realm of rule. Both de Graaff and O'Donovan see that judgment and forgiveness ought not be divorced as in Arendt, but rather are two sides of the same coin in theological understanding,[58] as I argued in chapter three. But O'Donovan mostly pushes the relevance of forgiveness and reconciliation resulting from Christ's death and resurrection to the eschaton, leaving a tendency to "dismiss any ongoing human judicial practice as failing to recognize the cosmic and comprehensive scope of God's judgment in Christ—particularly in the light of Jesus' injunction *not* to judge."[59] In this time between the times and following Martin Luther, judgment is retained only as a possibility for the public, ruling authorities—carefully directed to the goal of public order, setting limits to private vengeance, and achieving a modicum of justice through punishment.[60]

Here I simply depart from de Graaff and O'Donovan and the restriction of judgment to "the political," with "political" meaning

---

57. De Graaff, *Politics in Friendship*, 89–90, 99; de Graaff relies heavily on Oliver O'Donovan, *The Ways of Judgment* (Grand Rapids: Eerdmans, 2005).
58. De Graaff, *Politics in Friendship*, 100. De Graaff shows that Arendt sees forgiveness only as a response to harm done as a result of our fallibility; judgment is the opposite of forgiveness, for Arendt, and is the proper response to intentional harm done; Ibid., 98–99. De Graaff and O'Donovan rightly see that judgment and forgiveness are not so easily distinguishable, and that forgiveness through judgment of even radical evil is possible—as a *divine* possibility.
59. Ibid., 100. De Graaff argues that this is the thrust of O'Donovan's argument in part III of *Ways of Judgment*.
60. O'Donovan, *Ways of Judgment*, 99. De Graaff cites Luther's *Temporal Authority* (1523) as O'Donovan's historical parallel, a view clearly distinct from the defenses of the German Peasants' War and Anabaptist responses to its failure.

governmental rule. Even if I agreed that "judgment" as a category should be restricted to an act of "moral discrimination that pronounces [only] upon a preceding act or existing state of affairs to establish a new public context,"[61] I would remain unconvinced that such discrimination needed to be restricted to the category of rule as typically understood, or necessarily carried the degree of coercion O'Donovan thinks it must. While de Graaff looks to argue that the political significance of friendship via judgment can emerge in odd, extreme, or emergency situations (in the same way a citizen is granted authority in a moment of crisis to stop a mugging), and that the source of an office-holder's authority is actually in this practice of judgment that explodes outside the office's borders, in the normal run of events judgment is mediated by political office.[62] In any case, I am looking for a way to understand friendship blossoming out of moral discernment done together in the world that includes judgment without restricting its scope to governmental rule. Especially given the context outlined in chapter one in which I sought a path to faithful, "baptist" participation in radical, local democratic movements that are distinguished (though never totally separable) from political liberalism, how might I affirm much of what de Graaff identifies as the political significance of friendship without the parts I reject? In particular, I wish to retain the insight present in claims like: "common objectives are not the outcome of negotiations of private interests, but emerge between [friends]; . . . it is around such common objectives that they find each other as friends in the first place. In any case, their common objectives first take shape in the context of their *acting* together."[63]

In fact, de Graaff begins to approach what I am after when, following Arendt, he emphasizes the aesthetic and communal character of political judgment, which can lead to a particular type of friendship born of common action and the process of seeking agreement from our companions.[64] "In matters of judgement we seek agreement from

---

61. O'Donovan, *Ways of Judgment*, 7.
62. De Graaff, *Politics in Friendship*, 104.
63. Ibid., 71.
64. Ibid., 111–22; see esp. 114–16.

our companions: they make us see things from their point of view, challenging us to reconsider our judgements when they turn out to be different from theirs, and vice versa."[65] This is possible *even among people of differing convictions* because even though it remains true that there is no getting "outside" our convictions in order to deliberate with others, everyone in fact has multiple convictions that move in a kind of constellatory dance around certain central convictions that make us who we are.[66] While one cannot circumvent these in the process of forming discerning relationships of action with others, this does not mean that therefore *no* relationship is possible between different people. Certain of our other convictions may connect, "interlock," and give me a shared point of interaction with someone with whom I still do not share other convictions, even "core" convictions. At these points of connection—connections that must be *cultivated* rather than taken as "given"—something *like* communal discernment is indeed possible. There is no need to attempt to get above the fray, so to speak, or search in vain for a way to translate our differences into a neutral, "public" language of moral action—a process that "seems to wish convictional conflicts away rather than resolve them."[67] Indeed, I am convinced that the temptation to impose an "ontological" view of the good onto others is an epistemological correlate to the colonialism of old—a rose by another name that smells about the same.[68] We are both irreducibly different from one another, *and* can deliberate charitably and clearly (enough) with our neighbors; the two are not mutually exclusive. Only this allows for discerning action between *actually* differing parties. Communication is possible, but it takes work. And it is desirable because in my view, McClendon's "fallibility principle" holds, in which "even one's most cherished and tenaciously held convictions might be false and are in principle always subject

---

65. Ibid., 116.
66. I am here invoking the work of James Wm. McClendon Jr. and James M. Smith, *Convictions: Defusing Religious Relativism*, rev. ed. (Valley Forge, PA: Trinity Press International, [1975] 1994).
67. McClendon, "'Convictions' After Twenty," 144.
68. Romand Coles makes a similar accusation about both liberalism and cosmopolitanism in *Beyond Gated Politics: Reflections for the Possibility of Democracy* (Minneapolis: University of Minnesota Press, 2005), 72.

to rejection, reformulation, improvement, or reformation."[69] If this is true, then there is always motivation for communally discerning Christians to deliberate with others—we never have all the answers, and are always by definition unable to see our blindspots.

Perhaps a different way to put what I am driving at is a desire for communal deliberative action—discernment—that avoids both relativism and universalism. This is precisely what Charles Mathewes sees Augustine's theology providing to the challenge of pluralism: a response that avoids collapsing into either "anything goes" or epistemological colonialism. Instead, Christians can and do deliberate with others, in public, and the process is the same whether working with folks of other religious convictions or non-religious (or irreligious) convictions: "confront interlocutors with as much common ground as you can, and use that common ground to work towards a common understanding of both worldviews. The greater the extent to which the worldviews conflict—as long as the conflict leaves space for intelligible comparison—the better, the more clearly, you can delineate and understand each."[70] What communal discernment enables is a people capable of seeing and celebrating this possibility of deliberative action with others without downplaying all orienting convictions. The picture being offered here is friendship as a *practice* emerging from common judgment together, rather than something that is emotional or even dispositional, as in other forms of friendship. Indeed, if this analogous practice to communal discernment leads to radical democratic competence, it is certainly not a friendship that is warm or fuzzy; it is "not mainly (or not only) a sentiment of fellow-feeling for other citizens. It is more importantly a way of acting in respect to them: friendship, known to all, defines the normative aspirations. One doesn't even have to like one's fellow citizens in order to act toward them as a political friend."[71]

---

69. McClendon and Smith, *Convictions*, 112.
70. Charles T. Mathewes, *A Theology for Public Life* (Cambridge: Cambridge University Press, 2007), 138. A wonderful image Mathewes employs is that we speak not "neutral" intermediary languages, but "inter-traditional pidgin," "semi-languages that enable us to interact on matters of common concern without deluding ourselves that the tongue we use in those moments could ever be our home." Ibid., 139.

While this may seem obvious, it needs stating given the tendency among prominent political philosophers of requiring something approaching neutrality before cross-convictional agreement can occur. In particular, I am thinking of Richard Rorty, John Rawls, and their interpreters. Each argues for something like a suspension of our convictions, albeit for different reasons and with different phrases: For Rorty, bringing one's fully orbed convictions to bear in political conversation is pragmatically unwise, and serves as a "conversation-stopper."[72] For Rawls, both duty and civility require that the search for true justice be conducted only once one has entered the veil of ignorance; otherwise, he thinks something like the wars of religion will be hard to avoid. The result is similar in either case: one must translate one's moral concepts (or "comprehensive moral doctrines," to use Rawls's phrase) into a "common currency" of public reason, or risk irrelevance. Not only does this betray what Coles has called the "logic of currency," by which he means an entrapment in economic categories that subtly restricts the possibilities for political engagement to those approved of by neoliberals;[73] it also forces a picture of reality on people that leads them to think one must either support pluralistic engagement on these liberal grounds, or else countenance political impotence (at best) or withdrawn conservatism (at worst). As Jeffrey Stout has shown, such a suspension, for whatever reason, is both unnecessary in order to "go on" with the sort of deliberative action I am advocating here, and impossible.[74]

Rather than continue to describe this possibility in theoretical terms, I again turn to an example that shows the sort of thing communal discernment primes us to see as both possible and good, and hopefully (as I address in the concluding section) *incorporate* into our ongoing life together. I do this by way of an example of a friendship that blossomed out of deliberation across deep difference, and which

---

71. Allen, *Talking to Strangers*, 140.
72. Richard Rorty, "Religion as Conversation-stopper," in *Philosophy and Social Hope* (New York: Penguin, 1999), 168–74.
73. Coles, *Beyond*, 43–46.
74. Stout offers convincing criticisms of Rawls and Rorty in *Democracy and Tradition* (Princeton: Princeton University Press, 2004), 67–76, 85–91.

was an engine for the political in a particularly incompetence-producing time.

2.2 Ann Atwater and C. P. Ellis

If the discernment that emerges from Mission Mississippi is born in open friendship, the example of Ann Atwater and C. P. Ellis has no such initial amicability. In fact, the story of Atwater and Ellis begins in visceral animosity. Both residents of Durham, North Carolina in the 1950s and 1960s, the two found themselves involved in the civil rights struggle that was sweeping through the South at the time—on opposite sides. Ellis was a white, very poor day worker whose people were never able to escape a cycle of poverty and lack of educational resources, and thus served as one of many families who provided cheap labor to local industry, in particular the tobacco and textile companies.[75] Although Ellis's lot was very similar to that of his poor black counterparts, like most of his family and friends he was unable to see these similarities, convinced as he was of his own innate superiority. Ellis worked his way into owning a local gas station, but continued to feel disenfranchised by his inability to make ends meet, and his continued status as "poor white trash." The only solace Ellis found was in the Ku Klux Klan, the secret society bent on restoring the "old glory" of the American South, and which alone gave Ellis a sense of purpose, meaning, and worth. Ellis quickly rose to prominence in the organization, and as civil unrest grew in Durham among its black residents, he became involved in thwarting these movements any way he could—including with violence or the threat of violence. Although they stopped short of offering a public show of support, behind closed doors Ellis's efforts with the KKK were supported by certain members of the city council

---

75. My treatment of Atwater and Ellis relies on Osha Gray Davidson's *The Best of Enemies: Race and Redemption in the New South* (New York: Scribner, 1996). Davidson traces the history of Durham as a self-perceived beacon of racial harmony in the South. This perception was fostered by well-off black business owners, who despite Jim Crow had achieved a degree of success in Durham (such as C. C. Spaulding, eventual head of the North Carolina Mutual Insurance Company and heir to Booker T. Washington's accommodationist approach to racial reconciliation), and by the white establishment who saw the advancement of black fortunes as a point of pride.

and the Citizens' Council, a slightly more "respectable" organization that had as its explicit aim the resegregation of the schools.[76]

Atwater, on the other hand, was a black, poor, local activist agitating for change in Durham. Unsurprisingly, Atwater strongly supported desegregation, but her concerns also focused more specifically on the needs of her own lower-income black community. That is to say, she had no interest in maintaining Durham's reputation as a city of change and a place where the races were friendly toward one another; she cared about concrete changes with and through conflict, rather than the appearance of good relations without any real change in the community. In particular, Atwater wanted paved roads, better schools, and more tolerable conditions for black workers in the local factories. Atwater was no adherent of nonviolence, and carried herself with an aggressive air meant to intimidate her adversaries. She quickly gained a formidable reputation in open city council meetings about proposed changes in Durham's public school policies, and was especially unhappy with the calls for "patience" that came from both white and well-to-do black leaders in the community. Indeed, as many civil rights workers experienced, the reminder to "be patient" with reform, in the mouths of black leaders who lived in comfort and white "moderates," was either a luxury they could afford, or else a deliberate delaying tactic meant to forestall all calls for concrete change until "tomorrow" (and tomorrow and tomorrow).[77]

Throughout a turbulent decade, Atwater and Ellis knew one another from afar with no love lost between them. However, their respective stories took a surprising turn beginning in the early 1970s, which is the source of my interest in them here. Racial strife in Durham was

---

76. Davidson does a good job mapping the interconnected levels of mobilization against desegregation. The KKK served as the "muscle," consisting of poorer folks doing the "dirty work" that others were unwilling to undertake. Citizens' Councils were for the middle class. At the top tier were politicians, government officials, and others who virulently opposed desegregation, but in public opposed it by more "respectable" means. Ibid., 202–6, 235–39, 242–43. On these issues in the context of North Carolina, which had the highest Klan membership in the nation, cf. David Cunningham's *Klansville, U.S.A.: The Rise and Fall of the Civil Rights-Era Ku Klux Klan* (New York: Oxford University Press, 2013).
77. Davidson, *Best of Enemies*, 54, 80, 84–86, 219–20. In this sense there is a difference between "patience as opiate" (which Karlstadt and King, above, name) and "patience as liberative" in the sense advocated by SNCC.

running high, and a battle was being waged about the quality of public schools in the area as it related to desegregation, particularly regarding disparities between poor white and black educational facilities. As happened throughout the South, although *Brown v. Board of Education* was already the law of the land, compliance by uncooperative counties was slowly and haphazardly enforced. As desegregation slowly happened, more and more white students went to private schools (created to avoid integrated education),[78] leaving those in public schools to cope. In Durham, federal funds dedicated to enticing local communities to comply with *Brown v. Board* and smooth the road to desegregation were used to fund "charrettes." "Charrette" is a French word referring to extended forums that were meant to "open lines of communication in order that all people might understand each other's role as it relates to desegregation problems."[79] Bill Riddick, a young black community organizer and Director of Development at Shaw University in Raleigh, was tasked to lead the group. The experimental method's goal was "to bring a diverse group of people together to work out differences. Designed to produce an intense reaction . . . , the charrette involved a number of hours-long face-to-face meetings, held over successive nights."[80] Leading a charrette took creativity, patience with and through the arguments that would inevitably erupt, carefully trained listening abilities, and devotion to "what was, at heart, a technique for spiritual redemption and renewal."[81]

Riddick gathered key figures and leaders from the various, divergent communities affected in May of 1971, including Atwater and Ellis. Ellis especially was there only to make sure *"they"* didn't make the meeting all about *"their"* own interests, ignoring those of his own white community. He was there reluctantly, with plans to thwart all efforts toward reconciliation.[82] Riddick began the meeting by asking the

---

78. Ibid., 246–47.
79. Ibid., 247.
80. Ibid., 249.
81. Ibid., 250.
82. Both Ellis and Atwater knew this was the case, with Atwater putting the clash in terms of "whose God was stronger." Cf. Atwater's interview on NPR's *All Things Considered* with Melissa Block, "Civil-Rights Activist, Ex-Klansman C. P. Ellis," November 8, 2005, accessed March 18, 2015,

group—animosity palpable—to do some moral discernment together. "Are there any problems in Durham schools?" Howard Clement, leader of the Black Solidarity Committee, blamed the history of structural racism in the city; Ellis countered by blaming the problems in the schools on the mere presence of black students in the classroom. Despite a rough start, the beginning of honest communication was occurring—accompanied by the requisite anger. While some were uncomfortable with Ellis's particularly stark racist rhetoric, Clement later announced to the gathered group that Ellis was the most honest man in the room. "He hates me and he told me. The rest [of] you white liberals have hemmed and hawed about it. You don't *really* like me either; he just has the damn guts to say it."[83] From that soil grew, slowly, a committee ("Save Our Schools"), to be headed by Ellis and Atwater.[84]

The parallels with communal discernment, and my point in evoking this example here, is how friendships blossomed *out* of discernment together in Durham—from a soil of nothing other than shared interest and deliberative action, of which Atwater and Ellis serve as a poignant example. These people came together at first around nothing other than agreement on a specific, local problem—agreement that could never have occurred if they began by discussing "big," theoretical issues like race or desegregation. They began with a felt sense of incompetence about how to address this situation, but not much more; they certainly didn't begin with a shared or universal moral language. As Davidson puts it, "blacks and whites spoke two different languages, which happened to share a single vocabulary."[85] They may each have used words like "rights," "justice," or "good race relations," but they meant very different things by these utterances, tending to speak past one another in the process. But over time, committed to gather again and again, Atwater and Ellis began to understand one another. Ellis

---

http://www.npr.org/templates/story/story.php?storyId=4994854. As Atwater says, Ellis was there "to tear it apart."
83. Davidson, *Best of Enemies*, 253.
84. For Riddick, it was a basic principle of the process that local people were in control; he was there to serve as a resource; ibid., 258.
85. Ibid., 150.

RADICAL FRIENDSHIP

in particular learned that the plights of poor white and poor black children in Durham schools were similar, and that solutions to these plights were more complicated than he had once thought. Over time, Ellis heard his own concerns voiced by those he considered "enemy," and as shared concerns and calls for change were forged between him and his black conversation partners, friendships grew in that space. In particular, Ellis found himself one night in an exhausted conversation with Atwater, who was voicing nearly identical concerns with how teachers treated her children from "impoverished neighborhoods." "[Ellis] looked at [Atwater] and it was as if he was seeing her for the first time. He was stunned by what he saw. Mirrored in her face were the same deeply etched lines of work and worry that marked his own face. And suddenly he was crying. The tears came without warning, and once started, he was unable to stop them."[86] Atwater comforted him—and found herself crying too—and both left the meeting changed. The friendship that grew between them continued even when Ellis "backslid," demanding to have a KKK display put up at a session, which Atwater and others obliged.

As with Mission Mississippi, the point is not to suggest that this citizens' group was an unmitigated success; indeed, although integration of the schools did go smoothly after they turned their suggestions over to the city council, no one would say that Durham's problems with race relations and schooling were thereafter solved. The point is that this sort of moral discernment, done "out" in the world, led to a form of political friendship between a very unlikely couple that lasted, that was sustainable, as Durham continued to struggle with new, ever-evolving manifestations of racism. This friendship came at great cost, especially to Ellis, who was ostracized by his fellow Klansmen, received death threats, and suffered from depression and suicidal ideations. But something about Ellis taking part in this process changed him, despite himself—the potential for change was there in the midst of these discerning conversations, even out of initially dubious motives. What emerged was a radical friendship in the

---

86. Ibid., 276.

Aristotelian sense, born of discernment and deliberative action together across differences, of a sort that sustains a different way of moving and acting for political change in the contemporary United States, if we would only have eyes to see it. Thus the "problem" of deliberative friendship across convictional differences turns out to admit of the same solution that Diogenes the Cynic offered to the question of whether or not motion is illusory: *solvitur ambulando*—it is solved by walking.

3 Conclusion: Communal Discernment, Fugitivity, and Incorporation

My aim has been to show that communal discernment relates to radical democratic engagement by helping Christians engaged in the latter to see the political friendships that are formed as *central* to radical, sustainable politics in the current milieu. More specifically, I have argued that moral discernment relates to friendship in at least two ways: by discernment emerging from relationships between friends, as in Mission Mississippi, and by discernment preceding and enabling radical friendship, as with Atwater and Ellis. In the process of examining this thesis, I have assumed that the friendship under consideration is both consonant with Aristotle's understanding of friendship, and is "converted" and "opened" by the kenotic view of power touched on in chapter three. To close, I would like to relate these investigations back to the account of communal discernment provided in the previous chapters by way of a question: Granted that the counter-practiced friendship born of discerning together within the *ekklesia* allows one to see, recognize, and celebrate such friendships, how is this recognition *incorporated* into our ongoing life together? My claim is that some means of not only fleetingly recognizing but incorporating surprising movements of the Spirit is required if such movements are to serve as the grounds for any sustainable politics as the community moves forward in time, and that communal discernment is actually quite helpful in both recognizing these surprising movements ("discerning the spirits," as Paul writes) and incorporating them into the community's shared bank of knowledge. Communal discernment prepares Christians to welcome and incorporate into their ongoing life the recognized movements of God that are bound to occur as Christians engage the world receptively, forming new friendships out of engaged social action with others—including the two examples named above.

The tension implicit in this question has shown up in previous chapters, as well as above with concerns about Aristotle's conception of friendship. The basic concern is how a "practical" focus relates to what's going on outside the church, with the fear being that an ecclesial emphasis may dull one's ability to see and remain receptive to the latter possibility—not only with regard to other groups of people, but even more to the activity of a God who moves beyond the *ekklesia*. This is an important point, given that the church is meant to serve as a sign and pointer to the Kingdom of God rather than being preoccupied with its own internal processes. God, of course, is much greater than the church tasked to bear witness to him. Nathan Kerr in particular has argued for the importance of remembering that Christ is always going ahead of and beyond the church; it is problematic, he argues, to let narratives of "church" subsume both Jesus and world, such that church is thought to circumscribe what Jesus can mean, who Jesus can be, for each new situation.[87] Instead, it is crucial that Christians recognize the irreducibly apocalyptic nature of Christ, who is constantly breaking the expected bounds of ecclesial order. Perhaps the best way to make this point for the purposes of my argument is by applying Wolin's notion of fugitivity to the character of God and church. As Dula argues, when Wolin talks about democracy as fugitive—meaning not just "on the run" but a "recurrent possibility" that is "doomed to succeed only temporarily," inherently occasional, and an engine of the political whose gains in one generation may be lost in the next, "attenuated so as to serve other ends"[88]—the same sorts of observations could be made of *ekklesia*, marking its precarious path to competence.[89] Dula, applying

---

87. Nathan R. Kerr, *Christ, History, and Apocalyptic* (Eugene, OR: Cascade, 2009), 104–6.
88. Sheldon S. Wolin, "Fugitive Democracy," in *Democracy and Difference: Contesting the Boundaries of the Political*, ed. Seyla Benhabib (Princeton: Princeton University Press, 1996), 42–43.

this understanding to John Howard Yoder, points out that a key aspect of Yoder's ecclesiology is a conviction that the Holy Spirit continually brings forth communities that give faithful witness to Christ's Lordship; these communities often arise unpredictably, from surprising places, and can die or lose their initial transformative impetus after a generation or two.[90] The point is not just about the nature of churches as communities of character (though it is about this), but also the character of the God Christians claim to follow. God is moving beyond the borders of the church, agitating the *ekklesia* from without in surprising, unpredictable ways. What is more, the world that churches exist in relationship to is grace-soaked, as the God who calls the church into being is moving to bring about his ends there as well. While the points about fugitive *ekklesia* and God moving beyond the church are distinct, they relate in the sense that a wild God moving outside any community's borders necessitates a community that is similarly wild in its machinations and iterations, and vice versa. It would seem odd to posit a static, institutionalized God and a fugitive *ekklesia*, or a static *ekklesia* paired with a dynamic, adventuresome God.

However expressed, this point is important. God the Father of Jesus Christ, whose Spirit "blows where it chooses," is certainly as busy instantiating friendships between enemies *extra ecclesia* as he is moving between those engaged in hard discerning discussion *intra ecclesia*. How then might we relate these two points in a way that does not *negate* the truth of what folks like McClendon and Hauerwas argue concerning the importance of counter-practices and "communities of character"? What is required, in short, is a way to incorporate *both* the "fugitive" element found in the gospel notes ringing "out" in the world, and the practical element without which these notes would never be heard, or recognized as "gospel" at all. Of course, combining these elements is at the heart of the tension that is "baptist" ecclesiology, given that it is drawn from a vision that is marked by concrete practices, and can recur *whenever* a group of people gather and approach scripture and

---

89. Dula, *Cavell*, 95–113.
90. Dula, "Fugitive," 107.

world with a "shared awareness of the present Christian community as the primitive community and the eschatological community."[91] It is an ecclesiology on the move: to paraphrase Wolin, church becomes a recurrent possibility as long as the memory of the Reign of God survives.[92] And as Dula puts it, such comfort with fugitivity tends to "make some Catholics shudder."[93]

In my view, communal discernment is a particularly helpful practice for relating fugitivity to ecclesial formation (or put differently, formation to transformation) without losing either. Practiced well, communal discernment inherently involves a readiness to listen (assuming as it does that some new answer is needed for a set of unprecedented circumstances for which no easy answers are forthcoming), an openness to surprise, and a fugitivity that does not float above the ground but is manifest in and through its very practice. To borrow a phrase from Dula, it teaches congregations "to joyfully cultivate a readiness for the episodic ecclesial moment."[94] As McClendon writes, the dialectic between the surprising movements of God outside the church and the formation that happens within is perennial. Communities may discern a new action of God as good and true, formulate a new way to speak about this surprising movement of God, and pass what is learned on to the next generation, but these newly minted words may ossify over time or lose the bite they originally had when first uttered. The tension is ever this: "How can religious communities that have shaped themselves to maintain and preserve Christian life be open to the hot breath of the Spirit that creates them, open to the onset of the new that comes in Christ?"[95] McClendon's answer, and one I am taken with, is that formation is indispensable because *transformation*—the surprising acts of God *extra ecclesia*—has meaning only against a formation background; conversely, if transformation never comes, there is no good news, for

---

91. McClendon, *Ethics*, 30.
92. Democracy is "a recurrent possibility as long as the memory of the political survives"; Wolin, "Fugitive Democracy," 43.
93. Dula, *Cavell*, 98.
94. Ibid., 110.
95. James Wm. McClendon Jr., "Toward a Conversionist Spirituality," in *Collected Works, Volume 2*, 250.

then formation becomes "a lifetime of preparation for an event the community could not accommodate if it were ever to occur."[96] That is, formation provides the means by which surprising actions of God are seen, recognized, and *incorporated* into the community's life together. Indeed, God moves beyond the church, scattering seeds of the kingdom throughout the world. But being able to see certain things as kingdom seeds, and others as inimical to that kingdom, is not as straightforward as some seem to think. Both are required, but without the formation piece I am unsure how something like kenotic movements in the world will be seen as anything other than defeats—crosses without a resurrection.

McClendon himself sees communal discernment, or what he here calls "pastoral or prophetic congregational action" or "prophetic discernment," as uniquely able to live within this creative tension between transformation and formation, thus preparing its adherents for the *unpredictable*.[97] This practice, McClendon maintains, is precisely meant to recognize that there is a stretch of the Christian journey that "cannot be confined or bounded," and yet through community conversation, personal testimony, and the like, seeks to recognize, celebrate, and relate this to the common life.[98] Communal discernment can, of course, end up closing in on itself, stunting the ability to notice, care about, or incorporate new encounters with God and others that are available in the world; the advantage it has is that practiced well, it is explicitly flexible, intent on keeping practitioners open to fresh movements of the Spirit, and not least the sorts of friendships that lead to competence as well as deliberative action that lead to friendships. Both of these statements are true: nothing will go well without the movement of God outside the church, in and among discerning people (growing and leading to friendships); and nothing can avail without the perceiving community being shaped along certain lines.[99] As such, communal discernment provides training in the patience required to

---

96. Ibid., 251.
97. Ibid., 255.
98. Ibid., 257.
99. Ibid., 257–58.

be friends with those who are truly different from oneself, and not merely love the image of oneself in the other. Discerning communally is good preparation for looking for the kind of surprising gifts we find elsewhere. Without practices of this sort, we would not have the eyes to see what *sorts* of friendships are truly good; nor would we have a way of incorporating their surprising insights as a regular part of our community's life. Put differently, I require a community of discernment to help me know which relationships "out" in the world are worthy of celebration and cultivation—which ones provide the kind of competence that is faithful—and which relationships should be avoided. After all, both the Ku Klux Klan and Mission Mississippi could be described as grassroots movements leading to a kind of friendship that tells adherents how to "go on" in the world.

Thus a fitting conclusion to this chapter and the project as a whole: an affirmation of baptist fugitivity, or *ekklesia* looking for and welcoming God's Reign whenever and wherever it occurs. Communal discernment enables a readiness and ability to see the power of political friendship born of and leading to discernment, and the God who moves among these relationships, as well. What is more, communal discernment constitutes not a set, stationary practice for a lifeless church to know everything once and for all, but a means by which congregations might struggle together to figure out what to do, or who to be, in each new situation; insofar as that struggle continues, the fugitive God may continue to be recognized and welcomed by a fugitive church.[100] In this way might the church see and welcome discerning friendships out in the world as an important path to competence in contemporary society; might Christians sharpened by communal discernment more ably participate in such conversations; and thus might we more closely listen to and learn from others. So understood, political participation can be seen as "one more form of love, of seeking communion, of seeking the Beloved Community."[101]

---

100. On common struggle as the thing that enables churches now to connect to churches in the past, cf. Nancey Murphy, "Textual Relativism, Philosophy of Language, and the Baptist Vision," in *Theology without Foundations*, ed. Stanley Hauerwas, Nancey Murphy, and Mark Nation (Nashville: Abingdon, 1994), 267.

In this light, we may even come to see the disagreements that will continue between us as the "hopeful sign that more profound agreement already exists"[102]—or at least may come to exist, in expectation of the arrived and now arriving Reign of God.

---

101. Mathewes, *Theology of Public Life*, 161.
102. James Wm. McClendon Jr., "A New Way to Read the Bible," in *Collected Works, Volume 2*, 268.

Bibliography

Agamben, Giorgio. *Homo Sacer: Sovereign Power and Bare Life*. Translated by Daniel Heller-Roazen. Stanford, CA: Stanford University Press, 1998.

———. *State of Exception*. Translated by Kevin Attell. Chicago: University of Chicago Press, [2003] 2005.

Allen, Danielle S. *Talking to Strangers: Anxieties of Citizenship Since Brown v. Board of Education*. Chicago: University of Chicago Press, 2004.

Anderson, Benedict. *Imagined Communities: Reflections on the Origin and Spread of Nationalism*, revised and edited. New York: Verso, [1983] 2006.

Arendt, Hannah. *The Human Condition*. Chicago: Chicago University Press, [1959] 1998.

Aristotle. *Introduction to Aristotle*. Edited by Richard McKeon. New York: Random House, 1947.

Augustine. *The City of God against the Pagans*. Edited and translated by R. W. Dyson. Cambridge: Cambridge University Press, 1998.

Baylor, Michael G. *The German Reformation and the Peasants' War: A Brief History with Documents*. Boston: Bedford/St. Martin's, 2012.

———, *The Radical Reformation*, edited. Cambridge: Cambridge University Press, 1991.

Beach-Verhey, Timothy. A. *Robust Liberalism: H. Richard Niebuhr and the Ethics of American Public Life*. Waco, TX: Baylor University Press, 2011.

Bellah, Robert N., Richard Madsen, William M. Sullivan, Ann Swidler, and Steven M. Tipton. *Habits of the Heart: Individualism and Commitment in American Life*. Berkeley: University of California Press, [1985] 2007.

Biesecker-Mast, Gerald. "Recovering the Anabaptist Body (To Separate It for the World)." In *Anabaptists and Postmodernity*, edited by Susan Biesecker-Mast and Gerald Biesecker-Mast. Telford, PA: Pandora, 2000.

———. *Separation and the Sword in Anabaptist Persuasion: Radical Confessional Rhetoric from Schleitheim to Dordrecht*. Telford, PA: Cascadia, 2006.

Bourdieu, Pierre. *Outline of a Theory of Practice*. Cambridge: Cambridge University Press, 1977.

Bourdieu, Pierre, and Loïc J. D. Wacquant. *An Invitation to Reflexive Sociology*. Chicago: University of Chicago Press, 1992.

Bretherton, Luke. *Christianity and Contemporary Politics: The Conditions and Possibilities of Faithful Witness*. Oxford: Wiley-Blackwell, 2010.

Burkholder, Lawrence J. "The Peace Churches as Communities of Discernment." *The Christian Century* (September 4, 1963): 1072–75.

Cavanaugh, William T. *Migrations of the Holy: God, State, and the Political Meaning of the Church*. Grand Rapids: Eerdmans, 2011.

———. *The Myth of Religious Violence: Secular Ideology and the Roots of Modern Conflict*. New York: Oxford University Press, 2009.

———. *Theopolitical Imagination: Discovering the Liturgy as a Political Act in an Age of Global Consumerism*. New York: T&T Clark, 2002.

Cavanaugh, William T., Jeffrey T. Bailey, and Craig Hovey, editors. *An Eerdmans Reader in Contemporary Political Theology*. Grand Rapids: Eerdmans, 2011.

Coles, Romand. *Beyond Gated Politics: Reflections for the Possibility of Democracy*. Minneapolis: University of Minnesota Press, 2005.

———. "The Neuropolitical *Habitus* of Resonant Receptive Democracy." *Ethics & Global Politics* 4, no. 4 (2011): 273–93.

———. *Visionary Pragmatism: Radical and Ecological Democracy in Neoliberal Times*. Durham, NC: Duke University Press, 2016.

Davidson, Osha Gray. *The Best of Enemies: Race and Redemption in the New South*. New York: Scribner, 1996.

Dostert, Troy. *Beyond Political Liberalism: Toward a Post-Secular Ethics of Public Life*. Notre Dame: University of Notre Dame Press, 2006.

Dula, Peter. *Cavell, Companionship, and Christian Theology*. New York: Oxford University Press, 2011.

———. "Fugitive Ecclesia." In *The Gift of Difference: Radical Orthodoxy, Radical*

Reformation, edited by Chris K. Huebner and Tripp York. Winnipeg, MB: Canadian Mennonite University Press, 2010.

Elshtain, Jean Bethke. "Judge Not?" In *The Moral Life: An Introductory Reader in Ethics and Literature*, 3rd ed., edited by Louis P. Pojman and Lewis Vaughn. New York: Oxford University Press, 2007.

———. *Sovereignty: God, State, and Self*. New York: Basic, 2008.

Estep, William. *The Anabaptist Story: An Introduction to Sixteenth-Century Anabaptism*, 3rd edition. Grand Rapids: Eerdmans, [1975] 1996.

Foucault, Michel. *Power/Knowledge: Selected Interviews and Other Writings, 1972-1977*. Edited by Colin Gordon. New York: Pantheon, 1980.

Freeman, Curtis W., James Wm. McClendon Jr., and C. Rosalee Velloso Ewell, editors. *Baptist Roots: A Reader in the Theology of a Christian People*. Valley Forge, PA: Judson, 1999.

Givens, Tommy. *We the People: Israel and the Catholicity of Jesus*. Minneapolis: Fortress Press, 2014.

Goossen, Rachel Waltner. "'Defanging the Beast': Mennonite Responses to John Howard Yoder's Sexual Abuse." *Mennonite Quarterly Review* 89, no. 1 (January 2015): 7–80.

Graaff, Guido de. *Politics in Friendship: A Theological Account*. New York: Bloomsbury T&T Clark, 2014.

Graeber, David. *The Democracy Project: A History, A Crisis, A Movement*. New York: Spiegel & Grau, 2013.

Gregory, Brad S. *The Unintended Reformation: How a Religious Revolution Secularized Society*. Cambridge, MA: Belknap and Harvard University Press, 2012.

Gregory, Eric. *Politics and the Order of Love: An Augustinian Ethic of Democratic Citizenship*. Chicago: University of Chicago Press, 2008.

Gustafson, James M. *Moral Discernment in the Christian Life: Essays in Theological Ethics*. Edited by Theo A. Boer and Paul E. Capetz. Louisville: Westminster John Knox, 2007.

———. *Treasure in Earthen Vessels: The Church as a Human Community*. Louisville: Westminster John Knox, [1961] 2008.

Hainsworth, Deirdre King, and Scott R. Paeth, editors. *Public Theology for a Global Society: Essays in Honor of Max L. Stackhouse*. Grand Rapids: Eerdmans, 2010.

Harder, Leland, editor. *The Sources of Swiss Anabaptism*. Scottdale, PA: Herald, 1985.

Hauerwas, Stanley. *Approaching the End: Eschatological Reflections on Church, Politics, and Life*. Grand Rapids: Eerdmans, 2013.

———. *Christian Existence Today: Essays on Church, World, and Living in Between*. Durham, NC: Labyrinth, 1988.

———. *A Community of Character: Toward a Constructive Christian Social Ethic*. Notre Dame: University of Notre Dame Press, 1981.

———. *The Hauerwas Reader*. Edited by John Berkman and Michael Cartwright. Durham, NC: Duke University Press, 2001.

———. *Matthew*. Grand Rapids: Brazos, 2006.

———. *Wilderness Wanderings: Probing Twentieth-Century Theology and Philosophy*. Boulder, CO: Westview, 1997.

Hauerwas, Stanley, and Romand Coles. *Christianity, Democracy, and the Radical Ordinary: Conversations between a Radical Democrat and a Christian*. Eugene, OR: Cascade, 2008.

Hauerwas, Stanley, and Charles Pinches. *Christians among the Virtues: Theological Conversations with Ancient and Modern Ethics*. Notre Dame: University of Notre Dame Press, 1997.

Hobbes, Thomas. *Leviathan*. Edited and introduction by C. B. Macpherson. London: Penguin, [1651] 1968.

Hollerich, Michael. "Carl Schmitt." In *The Blackwell Companion to Political Theology*, edited by Peter Scott and William T. Cavanaugh. Malden, MA: Blackwell, 2004.

Huebner, Chris K. *A Precarious Peace: Yoderian Explorations of Theology, Knowledge, and Identity*. Scottdale, PA: Herald, 2006.

Jenkins, Willis. "Atmospheric Powers, Global Injustice, and Moral Incompetence: Challenges to Doing Social Ethics From Below." *Journal of the Society of Christian Ethics* 34, no. 1 (2014): 65–82.

———. *The Future of Ethics: Sustainability, Social Justice, and Religious Creativity*. Washington, DC: Georgetown University Press, 2013.

Johnson, Luke Timothy. *Scripture and Discernment: Decision Making in the Church*. Nashville: Abingdon, 1996.

BIBLIOGRAPHY

Kallenberg, Brad J. *Ethics as Grammar: Changing the Postmodern Subject.* Notre Dame: University of Notre Dame Press, 2001.

Kerr, Nathan R. *Christ, History, and Apocalyptic: The Politics of Christian Mission.* Eugene, OR: Cascade, 2009.

Klassen, William, and Walter Klassen, translators and editors. *The Writings of Pilgram Marpeck.* Scottdale, PA: Herald, 1978.

Koontz, Gayle Gerber. "Meeting in the Power of the Spirit: Ecclesiology, Ethics, and the Practice of Discernment." In *The Wisdom of the Cross: Essays in Honor of John Howard Yoder,* edited by Stanley Hauerwas, Chris K. Huebner, Harry J. Huebner, and Mark Thiessen Nation. Grand Rapids: Eerdmans, 1999.

MacIntyre, Alasdair. *After Virtue: A Study in Moral Theory,* 2nd edition. Notre Dame: University of Notre Dame Press, [1981] 1984.

_____. *Dependent Rational Animals: Why Human Beings Need the Virtues.* Chicago and La Salle, IL: Open Court, 1999.

_____. *Ethics and Politics: Selected Essays, Volume 2.* Cambridge: Cambridge University Press, 2006.

_____. *The MacIntyre Reader.* Edited by Kelvin Knight. Notre Dame: University of Notre Dame Press, 1998.

_____. *A Short History of Ethics: A History of Moral Philosophy from the Homeric Age to the Twentieth Century,* 2nd ed. Notre Dame: University of Notre Dame Press, [1966] 1998.

_____. *Whose Justice? Which Rationality?* Notre Dame: University of Notre Dame Press, 1988.

Mathewes, Charles. *The Republic of Grace: Augustinian Thoughts for Dark Times.* Grand Rapids: Eerdmans, 2010.

_____. *A Theology of Public Life.* Cambridge: Cambridge University Press, 2007.

McClendon, James Wm. Jr. *Biography as Theology: How Life Stories Can Remake Today's Theology,* revised edition. Philadelphia: Trinity Press International, 1990; original Nashville: Abingdon, 1974.

_____. *The Collected Works of James Wm. McClendon, Jr., Volume 1.* Edited by Ryan Andrew Newson and Andrew C. Wright. Waco, TX: Baylor University Press, 2014.

_____. *The Collected Works of James Wm. McClendon, Jr., Volume 2.* Edited by Ryan

Andrew Newson and Andrew C. Wright. Waco, TX: Baylor University Press, 2014.

———. *Doctrine: Systematic Theology, Volume 2*. Nashville: Abingdon, 1994.

———. *Ethics: Systematic Theology, Volume 1*, revised edition. Nashville: Abingdon, [1986] 2002.

———. *Witness: Systematic Theology, Volume 3*. Nashville: Abingdon, 2000.

McClendon, James Wm., and James M. Smith. *Convictions: Defusing Religious Relativism*. Valley Forge, PA: Trinity Press International, 1994; revised version of *Understanding Religious Convictions*. Notre Dame: University of Notre Dame Press, 1975.

McCormick, John P. *Carl Schmitt's Critique of Liberalism: Against Politics as Technology*. Cambridge: Cambridge University Press, 1997.

Meilaender, Gilbert C. *Friendship: A Study in Theological Ethics*. Notre Dame: University of Notre Dame Press, 1981.

Moltmann, Jürgen. "Open Friendship: Aristotelian and Christian Concepts of Friendship." In *The Changing Face of Friendship*, edited by Leroy S. Rouner. Notre Dame: University of Notre Dame Press, 1994.

Murphy, Nancey. *Anglo-American Postmodernity: Philosophical Perspectives on Science, Religion, and Ethics*. Boulder, CO: Westview, 1997.

———. "Missiology in the Postmodern West: A Radical Reformation Perspective." In *To Stake a Claim: Mission and the Western Crisis of Knowledge*, edited by J. Andrew Kirk and Kevin J. Vanhoozer. Maryknoll, NY: Orbis, 1999.

———. *Theology in the Age of Scientific Reasoning*. Ithaca, NY: Cornell University Press, 1990.

———. "Traditions, Practices, and the Powers." In *Transforming the Powers: Peace, Justice, and the Domination System*, edited by Ray Gingerich and Ted Grimsrud. Minneapolis: Fortress Press, 2006.

Murphy, Nancey, and George F. R. Ellis. *On the Moral Nature of the Universe: Theology, Cosmology, and Ethics*. Minneapolis: Fortress Press, 1996.

Murray, John Courtney. *We Hold These Truths: Catholic Reflections on the American Proposition*. Kansas City, MO: Sheed & Ward, 1960.

Newson, Ryan Andrew, and Brad J. Kallenberg. *Practicing to Aim at Truth:*

Theological Engagements in Honor of Nancey Murphy. Eugene, OR: Cascade, 2015.

Niebuhr, H. Richard. *The Meaning of Revelation*. Louisville: Westminster John Knox, [1941] 2006.

———. *Radical Monotheism and Western Culture*. Louisville: Westminster John Knox, [1943] 1960.

———. *The Responsible Self: An Essay in Christian Moral Philosophy*. Louisville: Westminster John Knox, 1963.

Niebuhr, Reinhold. *Moral Man and Immoral Society: A Study in Ethics and Politics*. Louisville: Westminster John Knox, [1932] 2001.

O'Donovan, Oliver. *The Desire of the Nations: Rediscovering the Roots of Political Theology*. Cambridge: Cambridge University Press, 1996.

———. *The Ways of Judgment*. Grand Rapids: Eerdmans, 2005.

Peters, Rebecca Todd. *In Search of the Good Life: The Ethics of Globalization*. New York: Continuum, 2004.

———. *Solidarity Ethics: Transformation in a Globalized World*. Minneapolis: Fortress Press, 2014.

Pipkin, H. Wayne, and John H. Yoder, editors and translators. *Balthasar Hubmaier*. Scottdale, PA: Herald, 1989.

Putnam, Robert. *Bowling Alone: The Collapse and Revival of American Community*. New York: Simon & Schuster, 2000.

Radner, Ephraim. *A Brutal Unity: The Spiritual Politics of the Christian Church*. Waco, TX: Baylor University Press, 2012.

Rasmusson, Arne. *The Church as Polis: From Political Theology to Theological Politics as Exemplified by Jürgen Moltmann and Stanley Hauerwas*. Notre Dame: University of Notre Dame Press, 1986.

Rawls, John. *A Theory of Justice*, revised edition. Cambridge, MA: Belknap and Harvard University Press, [1971] 1999.

———. *Collected Papers*. Edited by Samuel Freeman. Cambridge, MA: Harvard University Press, 1999.

———. *Justice as Fairness: A Restatement*. Edited by Erin Kelly. Cambridge, MA: Harvard University Press, 2001.

———. *Political Liberalism*. New York: Columbia University Press, [1993] 1996.

Redekop, Benjamin W., and Calvin W. Redekop. *Power, Authority, and the Anabaptist Tradition*. Baltimore: Johns Hopkins University Press, 2001.

Reinders, Hans S. *Receiving the Gift of Friendship: Profound Disability, Theological Anthropology, and Ethics*. Grand Rapids: Eerdmans, 2008.

Robbins, Jeffrey. *Radical Democracy and Political Theology*. New York: Columbia University Press, 2011.

Rorty, Richard. *Objectivity, Relativism, and Truth: Philosophical Papers, Volume 1*. Cambridge: Cambridge University Press, 1991.

———. "Religion as Conversation-stopper." In *Philosophy and Social Hope*. New York: Penguin, 1999.

Roth, John D. "Community as Conversation: A Model of Anabaptist Hermeneutics." In *Essays in Anabaptist Theology*, edited by H. Wayne Pipkin. Elkhart, IN: Institute of Mennonite Studies, 1994.

Schmitt, Carl. *The Concept of the Political*. Translated by George Schwab, foreword by Tracy B. Strong. Chicago: University of Chicago Press, [1932] 1996.

———. *Political Theology: Four Chapters on the Concept of Sovereignty*. Translated by George Schwab, foreword by Tracy B. Strong. Chicago: University of Chicago Press, [1922] 2005.

Schweiker, William. *Power, Value, and Conviction: Theological Ethics in the Postmodern Age*. Cleveland: Pilgrim, 1998.

———. *Theological Ethics and Global Dynamics: In the Time of Many Worlds*. Oxford: Blackwell, 2004.

Scott, Peter, and William T. Cavanaugh, editors. *The Blackwell Companion to Political Theology*. Malden, MA: Blackwell, 2004.

Slade, Peter. *Open Friendship in a Closed Society: Mission Mississippi and a Theology of Friendship*. New York: Oxford University Press, 2009.

Snyder, Arnold. "Beyond Polygenesis: Recovering the Unity and Diversity of Anabaptist Theology." In *Essays in Anabaptist Theology*, edited by H. Wayne Pipkin. Elkhart, IN: Institute of Mennonite Studies, 1994.

Stackhouse, Max L. *Creeds, Society, and Human Rights*. Grand Rapids: Eerdmans, 1984.

———. *God and Globalization, Volume 4: Globalization and Grace*. New York: Continuum, 2007.

Stayer, James M. *Anabaptists and the Sword*, revised and edited. Lawrence, KS: Coronado, [1972] 1976.

———. *The German Peasants' War and Anabaptist Community of Goods*. Montreal: McGill-Queen's University Press, 1991.

Stayer, James M., Werner O. Packull, and Klaus Depperman, "Monogenesis versus Polygenesis: The Historical Discussion of Anabaptist Origins." *Mennonite Quarterly Review* 49, no. 2 (April 1975): 83–121.

Stout, Jeffrey. *Democracy and Tradition*. Princeton: Princeton University Press, 2004.

———. *Ethics After Babel: The Languages of Morals and Their Discontents*. Princeton: Princeton University Press, [1988] 2001.

Stutzman, Ervin R. *From Nonresistance to Justice: The Transformation of Mennonite Church Peace Rhetoric 1908-2008*. Scottdale, PA: Herald, 2011.

Taubes, Jacob. *To Carl Schmitt: Letters and Reflections*. New York: Columbia University Press, [1987] 2013.

Taylor, Charles. *A Secular Age*. Cambridge, MA: Belknap and Harvard University Press, 2007.

Tocqueville, Alexis de. *Democracy in America*. Edited by Harvey C. Mansfield and Delba Winthrop. Chicago: University of Chicago Press, 2000.

Toulmin, Stephen. *Cosmopolis: The Hidden Agenda of Modernity*. Chicago: University of Chicago Press, 1990.

Tran, Jonathan. *Foucault and Theology*. New York: T&T Clark, 2011.

Volf, Miroslav. *Exclusion and Embrace: A Theological Exploration of Identity, Otherness, and Reconciliation*. Nashville: Abingdon, 1996.

Weber, Max. *From Max Weber: Essays in Sociology*. Edited by H. H. Gerth and C. Wright Mills. New York: Routledge, 1946.

West, Cornel. *Democracy Matters: Winning the Fight Against Imperialism*. New York: Penguin, 2004.

West, Traci C. *Disruptive Christian Ethics: When Racism and Women's Lives Matter*. Louisville: Westminster John Knox, 2006.

Wittgenstein, Ludwig. *On Certainty*. Edited by G. E. M. Anscombe and G. H. von Wright. In *Major Works: Selected Philosophical Writings*, New York: HarperCollins, [1969] 2009.

———. *Culture and Value*, 2nd edition. Translated by Peter Winch. Oxford: Blackwell, [1931] 1980.

———. *Philosophical Investigations*, 4th edition. Translated by G. E. M. Anscombe, P. M. S. Hacker, and Joachim Schulte. Chichester, UK: Wiley-Blackwell, [1953] 2009.

Wogaman, J. Philip. *Christian Perspectives on Politics*, rev. and exp. Louisville: Westminster John Knox, [1988] 2000.

Wolin, Sheldon S. *Democracy Incorporated: Managed Democracy and the Specter of Inverted Totalitarianism*. Princeton: Princeton University Press, 2008.

———. "Fugitive Democracy." In *Democracy and Difference: Contesting the Boundaries of the Political*, edited by Seyla Benhabib. Princeton: Princeton University Press, 1996.

———. *The Presence of the Past: Essays on the State and the Constitution*. Baltimore: Johns Hopkins University Press, 1989.

———. *Politics and Vision: Continuity and Innovation in Western Political Thought*, exp. ed. Princeton: Princeton University Press, [1960] 2004.

Yoder, John Howard. *Anabaptism and Reformation in Switzerland: An Historical and Theological Analysis of the Dialogues Between Anabaptists and Reformers*. Kitchener, ON: Pandora, 2004.

———. *Body Politics: Five Practices of the Christian Community Before the Watching World*. Scottdale, PA: Herald, [1992] 2001.

———. *The Fullness of Christ: Paul's Vision of Universal Ministry*. Elgin, IL: Brethren Press, 1987.

———. "Meaning after Babble: With Jeffrey Stout beyond Relativism." *Journal of Religious Ethics* 24, no. 1 (Spring 1996): 125–39.

———. *The Politics of Jesus: Vicit Agnus Noster*, 2nd edition. Grand Rapids: Eerdmans, [1972] 1994.

———. *Preface to Theology: Christology and Theological Method*. Grand Rapids: Brazos, 2002.

———. *The Priestly Kingdom: Social Ethics as Gospel*. Notre Dame: University of Notre Dame Press, 1984.

———. *Revolutionary Christianity: The 1966 South American Lectures*. Edited by Paul Martens, Mark Thiessen Nation, Matthew Porter, and Myles Werntz. Eugene, OR: Cascade, 2011.

_____. *The Royal Priesthood: Essays Ecclesiological and Ecumenical.* Edited by Michael G. Cartwright. Grand Rapids: Eerdmans, 1994.

Index

Agamben, Giorgio, 105n69, 109
Allen, Danielle, 180, 185–86
Anabaptist, xviii, xxii, 42–43, 47–51, 53, 56–67, 72–75, 83, 86–87, 90, 96, 108n86, 148, 155, 157
Arendt, Hannah, 181–83
Aristotle, xix, xx, 11–13, 43–45, 109, 148, 165–73, 179–80
Atwater, Ann and C. P. Ellis, 187–92
Augustine, 31–32, 38, 45, 133, 185
authoritarianism, xi, 83, 101, 115
authority, xv, 20, 47, 53, 55, 57–58, 59n73, 61–62, 64, 82–85, 87–89, 92–95, 97–98, 101, 104–7, 110–11, 113, 115, 117–18, 149, 161, 182–83

Baker, Ella, 88, 117, 118n109
ban. *See* binding and loosing
baptism, xviii, 56, 59, 66, 111
baptist vision, xviii, xxiii, 42, 116–17, 123n76, 194–97
basketball, 111–12, 121, 134
Baylor, Michael, 50–56

Beach-Verhey, Timothy, 10n28, 27–31, 33, 142–43
Bellah, Robert, 5, 69–70
Biesecker-Mast, Gerald, 49–51, 53–54, 56, 65n94, 92–93, 104
binding and loosing, xxii, 59, 63–64, 67, 82–83, 89–112
bishops, 105, 112
Bourdieu, Pierre, 138–40
Bretherton, Luke, xix, 6n14, 9, 38, 152, 154
Bullinger, Heinrich, 57, 155
bureaucracy, 12n35, 14, 18–20, 34, 110, 148, 150
Burkholder, J. Lawrence, 79, 84n4, 85n10, 150

Campbell, Will, 175n35
Cavanaugh, William, xv, 5, 13, 22, 35, 68, 71n105, 72, 122–25, 127, 133n32, 139, 142, 153–54, 160, 163–64
certainty, xxii, 43, 67–78
Chesterton, G. K., 106

church, xxiii, 16, 28–30, 41, 45–46, 49, 65–66, 68, 73–74, 79–80, 82, 84, 87, 89–90, 94–95, 101n55, 104, 109, 111–14, 120, 141–44, 149–50, 154, 159–60, 164, 167, 170, 193–97
civil rights, xvii, 176n38, 187–88
civil society, 5, 9, 35, 124, 143, 163–64
Coles, Romand, xvii, 2, 8–10, 13n39, 25n83, 34–36, 38–39, 42, 68n100, 70–71, 74–75, 81–82, 87–88, 94n35, 112, 115–18, 135–36, 139–41, 147n71, 149–50, 165, 176, 184n68, 186
colonialism, 35–36, 70, 184–85
communal discernment. *See* discernment
competence, xiv, 2, 15, 25, 43, 67–79, 106, 114–17, 152–54, 162, 165–67, 172, 197. *See also* incompetence
complex space, 69, 120–25, 129–30, 137
confrontation, xxii, 100–101, 111, 126, 155–58, 178, 185
Constantinianism, 34, 75–76, 132
constitution, 14–17, 24, 105n69, 152
contextualism, 47, 57, 64–67, 72
counter-practices, 137–43, 151–53, 158, 164, 194. *See also* practices

democracy, 2, 5, 8, 23–27, 34, 38–39, 68, 74, 77, 83, 86–87, 114–17, 139–40, 146–51, 156–57, 163, 193; threat of, xii, 17, 23–24, 25–26, 70, 128n20, 158. *See also* fugitive democracy
Denck, Hans, 65
decisions, xix, xxii, 44–47, 56–58, 82, 96, 99–100, 103–6, 110, 114–16, 151–52
dictatorship, xi, 105n69, 117
discernment, xiii, xix, 43–46, 60n75, 69–70, 82, 102, 119, 140, 152, 175, 180, 190; communal, xiv, xviii–xix, xxi–xxii, 2, 39, 42–43, 47–50, 56–70, 72–79, 82, 89, 115, 120–21, 145–60, 162–66, 170–72, 178, 183–86, 190, 192–97
Dostert, Troy, 18n58, 150n84
Dula, Peter, 163–64, 166–67, 170n21, 193–95

ecclesiology. *See* church
economics, xvi, 8–10, 19–20, 22–23, 25, 35–36, 49, 51, 53–54, 68, 98, 135, 186
Edwards, Jonathan, 60n75
Elshtain, Jean Bethke, 32, 102, 124
Enlightenment, 10–13, 17–18, 44
Erasmus, Desiderius, 50
Estep, William, 59, 61n78, 62
exclusion, 60, 63–64, 82, 84, 90, 101, 107–10, 113, 156, 171, 174

fact-value distinction, 10–13, 19–20
finitude, 41, 78

INDEX

forgiveness, 90, 98–102, 104, 144–45, 181–82
Foucault, Michel, 86, 88, 133, 139
friend-enemy distinction, 108–9, 117, 174
friendship, xiv, xx, xxiii, 34, 42, 79, 114–15, 117, 120, 138, 159, 163–86, 191–97; open and closed, 173–76
fugitive democracy, 8, 23–27, 77, 116, 140, 147, 193–97

German Peasants' War, 51–56, 58, 59n73, 177, 182n60
globalization, xvi, 6, 21–22, 34–36, 70–71, 153
Graaff, Guido de, 179–83
Graeber, David, 24n82, 128n20, 151, 155, 157
Grebel, Conrad, 58, 61
Gregory, Brad, 50–51, 53, 57n67, 72–75, 76n123
Gregory, Eric, 6n14, 27, 32–34
Gustafson, James, 41n2, 44–46, 75

Haidt, Jonathan, 156
Hamilton, Alexander, 14, 17, 20, 23, 26, 31, 70, 148n75
Hauerwas, Stanley, xvii, 25n83, 28–29, 33–34, 38, 41n2, 81–82, 91n28, 92n31, 95n37, 95n38, 100, 102, 118n109, 137n40, 142n56, 143, 148n75, 165, 167, 169–70, 194

hermeneutics, xviii, 48n22, 58n68
Hobbes, Thomas, 8, 13, 17, 85, 123–24
Hubmaier, Balthasar, 48n23, 56, 59n72, 62, 64
humility, 57, 60–64, 67, 69, 83, 92–94, 99, 104

IAF, 38, 94n35, 118n109, 151
Ignatius, 60n75
improvisation, xvii, 24–25, 77, 139–41
incompetence, xiii, xv–xvi, xxi, 2–7, 21, 23, 35, 37, 43, 52, 68, 69–71, 78, 106, 115, 119, 127–29, 136, 139, 152–53, 176, 178, 190
individualism, 31, 44, 46, 70, 79, 95, 97–98, 119, 123
intending, politics of, 14–18, 21–22, 70, 131, 136, 163–64. *See also* tending
inverted totalitarianism, 6, 21, 38, 43, 83, 114, 127–28, 132

Jenkins, Willis, xv–xvi, xxi, 2–5, 7, 37–38, 177–78
Johnson, Luke Timothy, 45–46
judgment, xix, 45, 47, 60, 64, 99, 101–4, 107, 110, 116–17, 152, 179–85
justice, 7, 13, 18, 28–29, 32, 35, 37, 39, 42, 54–55, 71, 176–77, 182, 186, 190

Kallenberg, Brad, 30n104, 45n11, 73n109
kenosis, 92–95, 97, 117, 126, 170–71, 173, 192, 196
Kerr, Nathan, 159, 193
King, Martin Luther, Jr., 32, 177n39, 188n77
Kingdom of God. *See* Reign of God
KKK, 187–88, 191, 197
Koontz, Gayle Gerber, 46n18, 148

leaders, leadership, xv, 83, 86–88, 90, 92–98, 105–6
liberalism, xiv, xvi, 4–6, 8–14, 17–27, 28–39, 68, 74, 83, 96, 101, 103–4, 115, 127–28, 131, 135, 142n56, 146–49, 154, 163–64, 167, 186; distinct from democracy, xvii, 2, 8, 19, 24–25, 31, 33, 34, 42, 162, 183
local, xvii, xxii, 15–17, 22, 24–26, 35–36, 54, 69, 77, 110–12, 122, 146–47, 150–55, 190
Luther, Martin, 50–51, 53–55, 57, 177, 182

Madison, James, 17, 29, 31
MacIntyre, Alasdair, 2, 11–12, 19–20, 63, 72–73, 91n26, 103, 107, 111, 127, 143, 148
Marpeck, Pilgram, 59–60, 64
Mathewes, Charles, 1, 9, 20n65, 38, 154, 185, 197–98
McClendon, James Wm., Jr., xviii, 38n126, 44, 47–48, 61–63, 66, 76n122, 77–80, 90n24, 91, 93–94, 97–98, 100–102, 104, 107, 111–12, 118, 121–23, 125–34, 137–46, 154, 166–67, 171–72, 184–85, 194–96, 198
Meilaender, Gilbert, 171n23
Mission Mississippi, 173–79
modernity, 12, 18, 35. *See also* postmodernity
Moltmann, Jürgen, 173–74
Müntzer, Thomas, 53–54, 58–59, 61–62
Murphy, Nancey, 12n34, 44n7, 60n75, 86, 123n11, 126n16, 135n36, 197n100
Murray, John Courtney, 124

narrative(s), xvi, 39, 44–45, 130–32, 163, 193
nation-state, xv, 13, 19, 21–22, 35, 105n69, 109, 122–25, 131, 147–48, 154n98, 163–64, 176
neoliberalism. *See* liberalism
Niebuhr, H. Richard, 10, 29, 31, 37n124, 122, 142
Niebuhr, Reinhold, 32, 75–76, 86
nonviolence and violence, 42, 49, 53–56, 58–59, 61–63, 65, 97, 108, 130, 149, 176n38, 187–88

O'Donovan, Oliver, 83, 94n37, 107, 182–83
overconfidence, 71, 152–53, 162

patience, 38–39, 47, 60–61, 72, 82, 92, 94–95, 97, 101, 110, 115, 146–51, 154, 176n38, 189, 196; as stalling tactic, 177, 188

Peters, Rebecca Todd, xvi, 36, 178n43

phronesis. *See* discernment

Pinches, Charles, 167, 169–70

political theology, xiv–xv, 3, 5, 28, 41–43, 55, 83, 93, 101n55, 105, 114, 117

politics, xv, 8–10, 14–20, 23–26, 32–33, 70, 83–84, 96, 99–100, 105–6, 108–9, 114, 118, 123–25, 147–48, 159–60, 163–65, 167, 172, 174, 177, 179–83, 192–93; science of, 13–14, 17, 25. *See also* intending, tending

postmodernity, 25, 35, 143, 154n98

power, xxii, 6, 14–17, 25, 81–88, 90, 92–96, 101, 105, 113, 117, 175, 192; modern, 19–21, 26, 70, 122; postmodern, 21–22, 69

practices, xxii, 4, 6, 15, 25, 27, 37–39, 42, 68, 88, 91, 111–12, 116, 121–22, 129–30, 134–36, 142–43, 145, 162, 180, 185; powerful, 79, 125–28, 132–34, 136–37, 172. *See also* counter-practices

priesthood of believers, 83, 87

principalities and powers, 7, 92, 125–27, 137, 158–59. *See also* powerful practices

Putnam, Robert, 5, 9n21, 27

radical democracy, xvii, 24–27, 38, 68, 72, 74–75, 83, 86–87, 106, 113–16, 146, 156–57. *See also* democracy

Rawls, John, 13, 18, 28–29, 32, 34, 75, 142n56, 186

relativism, 72–75, 77, 99, 185

republicanism, 15, 17, 25–26, 29, 38

risk, 78–79, 102n57, 106, 118, 133–34, 155

Robinson, Marilynne, 78

Roth, John, 48n22, 49, 58n68

Rorty, Richard, 10n30, 13, 186

Sattler, Michael, 59, 65, 87n16

Schleitheim Confession, 59, 63, 65, 67, 87n16

Schmitt, Carl, xiv, 93, 96, 99–101, 105–6, 108–10, 115, 117, 171, 174

Schweiker, William, 37n123, 142–43

scripture, xviii, 45, 47, 57–59, 61–62, 77, 194–95

sectarianism, 29, 37, 41–42, 61n76, 65, 107n79, 129, 153

SNCC, 88, 151, 176n38, 188n77

Snyder, Arnold, 50, 63n85

sociology, 8–11

speed, 68, 147–48, 177

Stackhouse, Max, 22n75, 27, 34–36, 37n123

Stayer, James, 48n20, 51n32, 54–56, 62–63, 65

Stout, Jeffrey, 5, 12, 17–18, 34, 38, 124, 186

215

Stumpf, Simon, 57–58, 60, 66
submission, 64, 66, 83, 95–98, 126
Sullivan, Andrew, xi–xii

Taylor, Charles, 52
tending, politics of, 15–17, 25, 38–39, 71, 74–75, 81, 123, 147, 158. *See also* intending
Thirty Years' War, 13, 28, 123, 128, 186
Tocqueville, Alexis, 15–16, 25
Toulmin, Stephen, 12, 17–18, 30n103, 154n98
Trump, Donald, xi–xiii

United States, xxi, 5–7, 9, 14–20, 24, 28–29, 31, 38, 127–28, 131–32, 135, 157

virtue(s), 38–39, 43–44, 68, 114, 122, 138, 143, 155, 167–70, 180
Volf, Miroslav, 171
voting, 1, 6, 18, 23, 27, 38, 176n38

Weber, Max, 84–85, 88

Wells, Sam, 77
West, Cornel, 5
West, Traci, 37–38, 42
Wittgenstein, Ludwig, 30, 45, 74, 119
Wogaman, J. Philip, 129–32, 143–44, 176n38
Wolin, Sheldon, xvii, xxi–xxii, 2, 6–10, 12, 14–27, 33–34, 36–37, 41, 69, 71, 75, 77, 81, 87, 96, 114, 120, 122–23, 127–28, 130–31, 140, 146–47, 151–52, 158, 166, 176, 193, 195

Yamada, Takashi, 104n64, 106
Yoder, John Howard, 49n24, 57n67, 61, 66n97, 73–74, 76n122, 77–78, 89–90, 94, 97, 99, 104–5, 110–14, 118, 146, 148–52, 194; sexual abuse, 91–92, 104n65
Young, Iris Marion, 48

Zwingli, Huldrych, 53–54, 57–58, 60–62, 66

www.ingramcontent.com/pod-product-compliance
Lightning Source LLC
Chambersburg PA
CBHW071156070526
44584CB00019B/2817